Exchanging Writing,
Exchanging Cultures

Exchanging Writing, Exchanging Cultures

*Lessons in School Reform
from the
United States and Great Britain*

Sarah Warshauer Freedman

National Council of Teachers of English

Harvard University Press
Cambridge, Massachusetts
London, England 1994

This book is printed on acid-free paper, and its binding materials have been chosen for strength and durability.

Library of Congress Cataloging-in-Publication Data

Freedman, Sarah Warshauer.
   Exchanging writing, exchanging cultures : lessons in school reform from the United States and Great Britain / Sarah Warshauer Freedman.
      p. cm.
   Includes bibliographical references and index.
   ISBN 0-674-27393-1 ((acid-free paper)
   1. English language—Composition and exercises—Study and teaching—United States.
2. English language—Composition and exercises—Study and teaching—Great Britain.
3. English language—Composition and exercises—United States—Ability testing.
4. English language—Composition and exercises—Great Britain—Ability testing.
5. Educational tests and measurements—United States. 6. Educational tests and measurements—Great Britain. I. Title.
LB1576.F73 1994
808'.042'071—dc20   94-14179
                                                                            CIP

NCTE Stock Number: 16442-3050

For Rachel

⟳ Contents

ᗧ A Note from the Author

This book could not have been written without the close collaboration of Alex McLeod of the University of London, Institute of Education. Alex led the entire British half of the project. As my co-researcher and principal collaborator, Alex worked with me on every phase, from the initial planning to the completion of the manuscript. Our collaboration was always joyful. Even though Alex retired from his university post when this project was in its final phases and decided not to join me as a co-author, he read every word, contributed some sections, tutored me in every aspect of the British school system, with which he has long-time experience as a teacher and teacher educator, and inserted himself and his perspectives throughout. Because of the closeness of our collaboration, I have reached a point where I have difficulty separating my thoughts from his. I am grateful for his enthusiasm, patience, intelligence, and friendship. Although not written by him, this book was in every respect written with him.

∽ Acknowledgments

My co-researcher and main collaborator in this project, Alex McLeod, joins with me in thanking those who contributed to our efforts. In London, Ellie O'Sullivan assisted Alex as a co-researcher throughout the process of the exchange, taking responsibility for much of the data collection and the interviewing. In the planning stages, her students' highly successful exchange with a Swedish class taught by Hans Sjöström was critical in getting the teams in both countries under way. Her engaging personality, creativity, critical honesty, and keen wit helped us all enjoy our work and pushed us to do our best job. Ellie read and reviewed numerous drafts of the manuscript and contributed much of herself to this effort.

We next thank the teachers and students who took the time to fill out questionnaires, and especially those who participated in the cross-national writing exchange and were also collaborators in this research, contributing their varying insider perspectives. Without them, this project would not have been possible.

During the exchange year a U.S. teacher, Nanette Koelsch, conducted an exchange with Hans Sjöström, who hoped to be of help from afar. Hans and Nanette inspired us with the possibilities of exchange work. Although their story remains untold, they have influenced much of what happened across all the exchanges.

After the exchange year, Nanette entered graduate school, and with her dual perspectives as a teacher participant and as an observer of the other exchange classes, she assumed responsibility for helping with the difficult task of synthesizing the data. She also read and commented on several drafts of the manuscript. Her contributions have enriched this study in ways that cannot be measured.

Five pairs of teachers worked with Alex, Ellie, and me on a similar exchange project the year before the one reported here: Kate Chapman, Jean Dunning, John Hickman, Alex Moore, and Sue Llewellyn in Britain and Keith Caldwell, Robin Davis, Charlene Delfino, Judy Logan, and Helen Ying in the United States. They taught us much about how to coordinate such an effort and about the kinds of activities an exchange can foster. Their stories, although not directly told, hover in the background of all the stories included in this volume.

My daughter, Rachel Freedman, in the midst of her career as a student at Brown University, volunteered to help me edit the final manuscript. It was a pleasure to switch roles and let her teach me to write. Not only was she a sensitive editor, but she was also an insightful and uncompromising critic, as she has been all her life. She quickly moved beyond her assigned editing duties to challenge my ideas, to point out sections in need of clearer explanation or development, to push me to write more forcefully. She even wrote some model paragraphs that found their way into the final manuscript.

The following individuals—then Berkeley graduate students, most now academic colleagues—assisted with data collection, organization, and synthesis: Marcia Largent Corcoran, Christian Knoeller, James Lobdell, Kay Losey, Charlotte O'Sullivan, Claire Ramsey, Dennis Shannon, and Norman Unrau. Gary Lichtenstein, a graduate student at Stanford University, also volunteered his time during the summer of 1989. Carolyn Hartsough and Mahlon Cann-Ortiz ran the statistical analyses of the questionnaires. Undergraduates Kimberly Mitchell, Regina Rodriguez, and Ruth Forman provided extra assistance during the summers of 1988 and 1989.

A number of colleagues offered helpful advice about the design and execution of the study and, in some cases, also read and commented on pieces of the manuscript. We thank James Britton, Tony Burgess, John Dixon, Anne Haas Dyson, Linda Flower, Judith Lindfors, Sandra MaKay, David Russell, Sandra Schecter, Margaret Meek Spencer, Melanie Sperling, Richard Sterling, David Tyack, and Mike Rose. We especially thank Colette Daiute, who responded to the manuscript at many stages along the way, constantly encouraging yet insightfully pushing us to consider new possibilities; Courtney Cazden, who asked the probing questions that helped us think and rethink our ideas; Bernard Gifford, who helped get the initial funding and provided the title for Chapter 1; and Eli Chiogiogi, who ably guided this project through the U.S. Office of Educational Research and Improvement and who was always supportive of our efforts. Janet White from the National Foundation for Educational Research (NFER) in England worked with us to include a computer component for the exchanges. Although that component ran into logistical difficulty, we thank Janet and her colleagues at NFER for their interest and their efforts. I am most grateful for the steady friendship and intellectual support of Rhona Weinstein and Robert Calfee. Finally, Susan Milmoe offered encouragement and wise words regarding decisions about publishing, and at Harvard University Press I thank all those involved in the production of this book but most especially Angela von der Lippe for her encouragement throughout the process and Linda Howe for her careful and sensitive editing of the manuscript.

At Berkeley Andy Bouman did a superb job of formatting and preparing the manuscript for submission. Carol Hubenthal, with her expertise in computer graphics, created the timeline figures for each exchange. Cynthia Greenleaf contributed Figure 3.7, which she created for her dissertation (Greenleaf, 1990). Trish Cascardi ably provided ongoing office assistance. In the United States, skillful transcriptionists included David Ziegler, Pat Segrestan, and Alice Guerrero; in Britain, although Alex McLeod did much of the transcription himself, he was assisted by Jean Farr, Fay Cattini, and Esmi Dobson. Also in Britain, the Institute of Education provided Alex with much needed office space and computer time. Our ability to be in immediate contact almost daily via e-mail allowed us to coordinate the U.S. and British efforts and thus made this project feasible. Also at the Institute of Education, Sharon Grattan and Christina Pulle helped us coordinate our efforts and often provided much needed and much appreciated secretarial assistance.

I also thank my family. My parents, Miriam and Samuel Warshauer, and my mother-in-law, Shirley Freedman, were always understanding of my writing schedule when they visited. My husband, Bob, and my daughter, Rachel, joined me from time to time as participants in this project. Their involvement, as well as the involvement of the family and friends of Alex McLeod and Ellie O'Sullivan, led to lasting cross-national friendships. Bob and Rachel also made many sacrifices, for which I am grateful.

Finally, I am grateful for funding provided under the Educational Research and Develpment Center Program (grant for the National Center for the Study of Writing) as administered by the Office of Eduational Research and Improvement, U.S. Department of Education. I take full responsibility, however, for the findings and opinions expressed in this book. They do not reflect the position or policies of either the Office of Educational Research and Improvement or the U.S. Department of Education.

⤳ Exchanging Writing,
Exchanging Cultures

Chapter 1

∽ Borders Are Not Boundaries

You're trying to achieve a different sort of feeling between two different sort of people with different backgrounds. And you've got to try and sort of find out. And the only way you're going to find out is, like I've said, I find out when they come back writing how you can drive at a certain age in America, and we had this really long discussion about that. And that's what we were really trying to achieve—finding out different things about each other. (Leabow, Manderley Grove Community School, London, England)

[Exchanging writing with students in England] gives us an ability to like feel what it's like in the other parts of the world. Instead of just thinking about this part of the world to think about what it's like down there or anywhere else . . . If we weren't doing this exchange, you would probably just be writing to the teacher the whole time and then you wouldn't probably try as hard to get it good. (Lisa, Costa Mesa High School, near San Francisco, California)[1]

As young adolescents on opposite sides of the Atlantic, Leabow and Lisa are living in their own culturally bound worlds, which they continually shape and reshape from their experiences with their families, friends, and wider communities. They were students in two of eight classes, four in the San Francisco Bay area and four in the greater London area, that were paired to compare what is involved in learning to write in the United States and in Great Britain. All eight classes were from urban multicultural schools that served mostly working-class students. The paired students were about the same age; their classes covered grades 6 through 9 in the United States and Forms 1 through 4 in Britain.[2] Through the experience of participating in the writing exchange, Leabow and Lisa opened up and expanded the boundaries of their worlds, as did their teachers and the university-based research teams. We all shared our thinking, our practices, our cultures, and, eventually, our beliefs and assumptions about learning to write.

In both Britain and the United States, before beginning the writing exchanges we mailed questionnaires to especially talented and reflective writing teachers representing all regions and grade levels, and to some of their students at the secondary level, which asked about the teachers' everyday practices. These questionnaires and the students' writing exchanges make up the substance of this book and provide the basis for comparing learning to write in these two major English-speaking nations, both of which have a long tradition of concern about literacy. The advantage of such a cross-national comparison is that it can stimulate us to imagine new possibilities—for familiar school organizations, classroom structures, and even ideologies—as we discover and begin to live with structures, practices, and ideologies that are unfamiliar and even strange to us. We need to envision new possibilities as we strive to re-form our urban schools into institutions able to offer a high quality education to all our students.

The Beginnings

The seeds of this cross-national comparison were planted in 1985 when I was on sabbatical in England. Alex McLeod of the Institute of Education at the University of London introduced me to several London teacher-leaders who in turn were kind enough to invite me to visit their classrooms. On these visits, I was struck by how different British English classes were from most U.S. English classes. I thought I would be able to sit in the back of the room to observe and take notes, as I often did when I visited classrooms in the United States. But that proved impossible. In the common British scenario, the teacher would introduce me to his or her pupils as "Mrs. Freedman, a teacher from America who is interested in your writing," direct them to get out their work, and then tell me to talk to them about their writing. The writing I saw impressed me as ambitious, well developed, complex, and generally above the level of that commonly produced by students of a similar age in the United States. My first forays into these British schools not only expanded my horizons but convinced me that a careful examination of the classrooms of well-respected British teacher-leaders could help U.S. educators think anew about literacy instruction. Although my interest and focus here are on what U.S. educators can learn, it would be equally possible for a British researcher to use the information from this project to study U.S. practices from which the British might learn.

One of the teachers I met was Ellie O'Sullivan at Fulham Cross School for Girls in inner London, who gave me the idea for the writing exchanges. Her twelve- and thirteen-year-old students were in the middle of an exchange with a class in Sweden. They were involved in their writing in ways I had never witnessed before. As soon as I entered the classroom, I was surrounded by groups of children eager to show me not only the elaborate books they were writing about their school but their already-completed guidebooks to London for visiting Swedish teenagers. They also shared their reactions to Swedish storybooks and to textbooks the Swedish class had sent them. Each sophisticated and elaborate project they mailed to Sweden extended over several months. The books about their school contained colorful illustrations, probing interviews with school officials, and insightful analyses of why they were learning what they were learning. They waited with excitement for each new package of writing from Sweden. Through their writing exchange they were learning about life and education in Sweden, but even more important, they were learning to be reflective about their own culture. In writing books about their school, for example, Ellie's students interviewed the head of the school and began to understand for the first time that there was a plan and order to the school curriculum. They asked the head of the school the kinds of questions that often remain unasked when one is confined within one's own tightly bounded world. At the same time, they were engaged in theoretically sound writing activities with important purposes, functions, and audiences.

I became interested in the activity of the writing exchange as a possible vehicle for permeating and studying cultural boundaries. Alex McLeod was interested in promoting writing exchanges as a part of writing in school, having worked in the late 1960s on an exchange project with students in five London schools (McLeod, 1969). Ellie O'Sullivan was interested in sharing her ideas with other teachers and working with Alex and me on the exchange project. Alex enthusiastically agreed to lead the British end of the writing exchanges with

Ellie's help and to assist with the national questionnaires in Britain. All three of us were motivated by a desire to create a vision for improving urban schools in our respective countries. And so we began five years of intense, sometimes frustrating, but more often rewarding work.

Common Theories: Teaching through Social Dialogues

In conceptualizing the exchange classrooms, the research teams on both sides of the Atlantic worked from a common theoretical base, which holds that written language is acquired through a process of social interaction. This theoretical framework was first outlined by Vygotsky (1962, 1978) and further elaborated by Wertsch (1991). The research teams also assumed that the process of social interaction consists of the complex dialogues described by Bakhtin (1986).

According to Vygotsky, social interactions occur mainly through talk and are most beneficial to the intellectual development of the student learner when they center on tasks the student cannot do alone but can do with expert assistance. This expert assistance is intended to help the student accomplish progressively more difficult tasks on his or her own. Vygotsky explains this process of learning and development through the metaphor of "buds" or "flowers" that, with assistance, will "fruit" into independent accomplishments (1978, p. 86). It is these "buds" or "flowers" that need to be nourished in the classroom. Vygotsky's (1978) theory of learning claims that these assisted interactions occur within "the zone of proximal development," which he defines as "the distance between the actual developmental level as determined by independent problem solving and the level of potential development as determined through problem solving under adult guidance or in collaboration with more capable peers" (p. 86). The implication of this theory for learning to write is that students must be engaged in social interactions that center on a writing task they cannot accomplish alone but can accomplish with assistance.

According to Wertsch (1991), Vygotsky privileges verbal social interactions. Wertsch considers nonverbal social interactions—with art, for example, or with other nonverbal graphic symbols—to be equally important. Just as Wertsch expands the repertoire of available interactions, he also expands how these interactions can be used. He explains that both verbal and nonverbal interactions are like tools in a "tool kit" (p. 93). Given the same task, individuals routinely select different tools from the tool kit to accomplish the task, and even when they select the same tool, they may each use it differently. Using different tools in different ways, different people can accomplish the same task equally well. Wertsch's amplification of Vygotsky's theory helps explain the need for classrooms that allow students to take diverse approaches to writing and learning to write.

Bakhtin (1986) elaborates on the centrality of social interactions in our language and our thought:

> Our thought itself—philosophical, scientific, and artistic—is born and shaped in the process of interaction and struggle with others' thought, and this cannot but be reflected in the forms that verbally express our thought as well . . . The utterance proves to be a very complex and multiplanar phenomenon if considered not in isolation and with respect to its author (the speaker) only, but as a link in the chain of speech communication and with respect to other, related utterances. (pp. 92–93)

This approach to social interactions forms the basis for Bakhtin's argument that all utterances are dialogic. According to Morson (1986), "Bakhtin understands discourse to be not an individual writer's or speaker's instantiating of a code but, instead, the product of a complex social situation in which real or potential audiences, earlier and possible later utterances, habits and 'genres' of speech and writing, and a variety of other complex social factors shape all utterances from the outset . . . The only way in which the individual speaker can be sole author of an utterance, according to Bakhtin, is in the purely physiological sense" (p. 83). For Bakhtin, each piece of writing will be composed of the writer's past interactions with the thoughts of others and of anticipated future interactions.

Bridges between Theory and Practice

With this theoretical base in mind, the research teams attempted to find teachers for the exchange project whose practices were consistent with the theories. From our initial observations of classrooms and discussions with the exchange teachers, we expected the classroom environments in both countries to be full of both verbal and nonverbal social interaction in which students would be able to interact in varied ways and take advantage of the rich array of social dialogues in their experience. We expected the classrooms to be places where students would discuss their ideas and ongoing writing with one another and with their teachers, where they would read or act out each other's writing, and where they might supplement their writing with artwork. We further expected the teachers to set up classrooms where students would be engaged in challenging writing activities, where they would feel comfortable asking for and receiving assistance with their writing, and where the advice they received would be valuable. Ultimately, we worked together with the teachers in designing the exchanges so that the opportunities to interact with students from abroad would complement the ongoing opportunities for social interaction in individual classrooms and thereby further stimulate writing growth. By selecting teachers whose theoretical orientation was similar, we hoped to be able to highlight how contextual differences across the two countries would affect how theory is applied in practice.

When we began to explore the dynamics of the exchange classrooms and to analyze the responses to the national questionnaires, however, we uncovered contrasts not only between the classrooms in the two countries but between classrooms within each country. We found that the application of the theory of social interaction in learning to write was subject to widely varying interpretations. Different theories seemed to underlie the practices in particular classrooms. Since these theoretical concepts provide the point of departure for most suggestions for practice in the professional literature, it became critical to understand the permutations of the theory we were observing. Our ultimate goal was to suggest a clearer definition of the theory itself.

A Preview of the Findings

The questionnaires revealed striking differences in how British and U.S. teachers and their secondary-level students viewed the teaching and learning of writing. The British teachers focused their attention mainly on understanding their students' development, while the U.S. teachers were more inclined to focus on creating innovative activities for the curriculum. Differences in the organization of British and U.S. schools appeared to account for these differing orientations. The

British schools were designed to support academic communities of teachers and learners who knew one another well. Students generally stayed together as a single class unit throughout most of the school day, and this unit stayed together for most subjects during the first five years of secondary school (the equivalent of grades 6 through 10). Like U.S. secondary teachers, British secondary teachers specialized in a discipline, but they tended to keep the same group of students from one year to the next, typically for two years and often for as long as five. U.S. schools, which did not have these academic community structures, built community in nonacademic ways, most commonly through athletic programs and school dances.

The writing exchanges highlighted additional contrasts. The British teachers, particularly those who taught younger students not preparing for national examinations, followed a common approach to teaching writing: they structured their classes by promoting an interactive exchange of responsibilities with their students. The metaphor of the writing exchange thus extended into the domain of classroom organization. Within their classrooms, teachers and students both assumed responsibility for what teachers would teach and students would learn. They jointly engaged in curricular planning and organization. They worked together to select writing activities; they shared ideas about interesting topics to write about; they decided together when it was appropriate to push forward in new directions. The British teachers, as part of this negotiation with their students, worked to motivate the entire class to participate in a literacy activity, adjusting levels according to individual needs. The teachers knew that not all students would be motivated by the same activity, but they felt that if they collaborated with the class on topic selection and did a good job of setting a motivating context for the activity, the unmotivated students would be in the minority. When students were not motivated, the British teachers took it as their responsibility to help them find an activity that would interest them. Students experienced no stigma if they chose a different activity than the rest of the group. They saw it as their responsibility to work with the teacher in finding an activity that would be both interesting and productive in terms of what they stood to learn.

In the end, after several years with the same class these British teachers expected all their students to practice writing for a variety of audiences and to master a variety of types of writing. If students did not practice and master certain types of writing, the teachers considered it their own failure to set motivating contexts. In this way, the British approach provided a frame that allowed the students flexibility and gave the teachers important responsibilities. This approach also suggests a reason why, in the questionnaires, the British teachers focused on knowing their students. In setting up their classrooms to accommodate shared responsibilities, these teachers had to know what would motivate each student, and they had to be able to track each student's progress.

By contrast, the U.S. teachers did not adhere to a consistent approach and exhibited substantial variety in their interpretations of how theory enters practice. Two of the U.S. teachers expected everyone in the class to engage in the same teacher-assigned activities (or to choose from the same set of activities), while another teacher was attempting to move toward a completely individualized classroom in which each student would have a separate curriculum and still another followed a theory, similar to the British model, that involved a sharing and an exchange of responsibilities with students. All the U.S. teachers were engaged in some kind of interchange with their students, but for some the interchange was greater than for others. In two cases, for example, when the focus was on teaching the whole class, there was little room for individual variation, but when the goal was to move to a situation in which individual variation was the expected norm and the individual rather than the group was the focus, there was more room for individual variation but less sense of the role of the community. In the case of the teacher who adhered most closely to the British model, the whole class was involved and the community was expected to serve as a motivator. Although this teacher expected that individuals might, at times, need to reshape their own activities, she did not expect such individual reshaping to be the norm.

Another striking difference between the British and U.S. classes revolved around the effects of the high-stakes national examinations in Britain, which determine who will graduate from secondary school and who will gain university entrance. The issue of national examinations is particularly important to educators in the United States because of the accelerating momentum for a national system of tests. *America 2000* (1991), for example, calls for voluntary national high-stakes achievement examinations in core subject areas, English included, for grades 4, 8, and 12. Scores would eventually be given to potential employers or used for college admission. In addition, high national standards and goals would be attached to the tests (see also Cheney, 1991; Simmons and Resnick, 1993; Tucker, 1992). Although they are not completely voluntary, national achievement tests in both English language and English literature have been given in Great Britain since the beginning of the twentieth century. Currently the British are implementing a 1987 Education Act that has set in motion a new round of extensive educational changes, including a national curriculum and mandatory testing programs for students at ages 7, 11, 14, and 16 (Department of Education and Science, 1988a, 1988b). These changes have involved setting goals and national standards for each of these age levels. As the United States embarks on its latest course of reform, information from cross-national studies becomes increasingly important, especially from nations like Great Britain, where a tradition of high-stakes national examinations attached to high standards for teaching and learning has long been in place.

In two of the four British classrooms involved in the writing exchanges, teachers were preparing their students for the General Certificate of Secondary Education (GCSE), the assessment that determines graduation from high school. At the time, the GCSE offered the option of portfolios of student work and clearly was an examination worth teaching to. But the GCSE curriculum had produced many unintended negative side effects, depressing the teachers' ability to negotiate the curriculum and the amounts and kinds of writing students did. The exam also affected their interactions around the writing from the United States and resulted in striking differences between the writing of the British students and their counterparts in the United States. In general, the examinations decreased the amount of attention teachers paid to the writing students sent to the U.S. classes and inhibited their responses to students' writing. Ultimately, however, the British teachers considered good curriculum, good teaching, and high standards for student performance as issues quite unrelated to the national tests or to national standard-setting efforts.

Finally, there were important differences across classrooms in both countries in students' interactions with and response to the writing from abroad. Although some of these differences could be attributed to the British students' focus on the exams, others could not. Generally, students in classrooms where interactions with the writing from abroad were most serious and where they received the most specific responses to their own writing did the best writing for the exchange.

Past Comparisons of Learning to Write in Britain and the United States

There have been other cross-national studies of learning to write, but none has focused on teachers' interpretation and implementation of the theories that guide their teaching and learning. The first cross-national comparison of British and U.S. approaches followed the month-long 1966 Anglo-American Conference at Dartmouth College, which brought together major figures in the teaching of English and the language arts from the United States, Canada, and Great Britain. The goal of the Dartmouth conference was to pool the expertise of the assembled scholars in discussions of "the aims and methods of English teaching" (Squire and Britton, 1975, p. xviii). Two attendees, Dixon (1967, 1975) and Muller (1967), wrote reports about the conference from the British and American points of view, respectively. As Dixon summarized it in his report, the representatives all proposed "a new interest in the learner, his development, and the processes of using language to learn" (1975, p. 112).

Immediately after the Dartmouth conference, the U.S. Department of Education funded Squire and Applebee's (1968b) major study of teaching English in Great Britain as an extension of an earlier parallel study in the United States (Squire and Applebee, 1966, 1968a). As these researchers embarked on their new study they noted, "though the two countries share a common language, no detailed study of the teaching of English in Britain and the United States has yet been published" (p. 8). In their project researchers observed classrooms in 42 schools, both private and state-supported, in England, Scotland, and Wales to supplement the 158 high schools they had observed in the United States. They found sharp cross-national contrasts, particularly in the teaching of writing. In Britain they observed more writing across the curriculum, less emphasis on formal language study, less direct teaching, and more emphasis on fluency and practice than in the United States (pp. 2, 183–190, 325–326). They also found more frequent informal conferences about writing between students and teachers in the course of a school day that was filled with more frequent breaks (for example, morning coffee and longer lunch periods) and more sharing of written work with peer audiences than in the United States (pp. 194–199). The schools in the United States showed a predominant pattern of "write-correct-revise," the corrections being red-ink notations written by the teacher. In Britain, however, there was little in the way of teachers' written corrections or student revisions after marking; rather, the British teachers opted for "less frequent annotation and more extensive writing" (p. 192). As Squire and Applebee noted, "one of the major insights gleaned from the study of these [British] schools is an awareness of the contribution which expressive uses of language can make to skill in using the language in all contexts" (p. 324). They concluded that schools in the United States could benefit from the British example. In particular, they claimed, "after their observations in these schools, few members of the project staff would challenge J. N. Hook's conclusion that 'Americans err in stressing expository writing so greatly, especially with young children'" (p. 324).

The only recent cross-national project focusing on written language has been the international study of achievement in written composition initiated in 1980 by the International Association for the Evaluation of Educational Achievement through the International Education Association (IEA) (Degenhart, 1987; Gorman, Purves, and Degenhart, 1988; Gubb, Gorman, and Price, 1987; Purves, 1992a). The IEA studies were designed primarily to compare the writing competence of students in fourteen countries, including the United States and Great Britain. Although an individual country report has been published in England (Gubb, Gorman, and Price, 1987), no cross-national comparisons have been completed, and the British report only considers fifteen-year-old students. No report is available from the United States. Recently, Purves (1992b), one of the directors of the study, deemed it a failure because of the difficulty in obtaining reliable cross-national judgments of writing. The IEA studies were designed primarily to yield comparative information about student achievement. Only a small amount of information about teaching and learning was gleaned from brief questionnaires given to students, teachers, and school personnel.

Although not comparative, some information about the teaching and learning of writing is available from status surveys of teachers and students in both the United States (Graves, 1978, for elementary teachers; Applebee, 1981 for secondary teachers; Applebee et al., National Assessment of Educational Progress reports with student surveys and eighth-grade teacher surveys in the latest assessment,

1986a, 1986b, 1987, 1990a, 1990b) and Great Britain (Bullock, 1975; Medway, 1986; Gubb, Gorman, and Price, 1987). These surveys of typical classrooms show schools out of sync with the new emphases in the professional literature. They present a rather dismal picture on both sides of the Atlantic: there is great stress on mechanics in both countries, students perform poorly on complex tasks in the United States, and students are denied opportunities for discursive writing and given insufficient feedback in Britain.

Besides its potential to contribute to theory, a new comparative study is particularly timely now, since over the past twenty years both the United States and Great Britain have seen substantial changes in schooling in general and in the teaching of English in particular, especially in the teaching and learning of writing (see Squire and Britton's introduction to the 1975 edition of Dixon's *Growth through English* for a midpoint review of some of those changes). In Britain extensive reforms in the schools almost totally abolished the eleven-plus examination, which had streamed 11-year-olds into "grammar" schools leading to college or careers in commerce (20 percent) and the so-called "secondary modern" schools, whose students expected, at best, careers in industry and in semiskilled occupations. In their stead, the reforms established comprehensive secondary schools for students of all ability levels. In addition, the usual age for completing school rose from 15 to 16. In contrast with the United States, the usual school-leaving age of 16 (grade 10) for about 70 percent of the British population still comes earlier than the U.S. completion age of 18 (grade 12); national examinations still determine entry into universities and careers; and there remains a strong tradition of private education for the upper- and now upper-middle classes. Furthermore, in Britain today current shortages of funds and emerging government policies are eroding past reforms that were moving schools toward democratization.

In the United States, although the formal structures of schooling have changed little in the last two decades, educational philosophies have changed a great deal. The country has seen a move toward accountability and "basic" education. The educational community at large has called for a more professional and literate teaching force, for rewarding excellence in teaching, and for structural reforms in schools, such as site-based management and increased teacher and community decision making (for example, *America 2000*, 1991; Boyer, 1983; Carnegie Forum, 1986; Goodlad, 1984; Holmes Group,

1986; Sizer, 1984, 1992). In the area of writing, the National Writing Project and other in-service programs for teachers have been pushing schools toward a national goal of higher standards of literacy.

Simultaneously, a revolution in writing theory and research has taken hold in both countries. In England it began when Dixon (1967), Barnes, Britton, and Rosen (1969), Barnes (1976), and Britton and his colleagues (1975) presented ideas with major implications for changes in practice. In the United States it began when Emig (1971) published her research on the writing process. In both countries the literature urged teachers to support students through an extended writing process, allowing them time for planning and substantive revision as they solved complex problems and produced multiple drafts of a piece of writing. There is also a growing interest in both countries in the sociocultural contexts of writing, which undoubtedly influence what writers write and how they learn (see Dyson and Freedman, 1991).

The Cross-National Study

As we planned the design of the questionnaires and the writing exchanges, we took into account both our theoretical concerns about learning to write and what we had learned from previous cross-national studies. In addition, we encountered a number of practical issues, which controlled some of the decisions we made. In fact, some of those practical issues—selecting the teachers for the questionnaire study, wording the items on the U.S. and British forms of the questionnaires, and selecting exchange classrooms—were a direct result of cross-national differences. These practical considerations, which are described in the following sections, provide a first look at cross-national contrasts.

Designing the National Surveys

Our plan was first to collect questionnaires from a national sample of particularly thoughtful and successful teachers of writing and of students at the secondary level. Cross-national differences in the structure of schooling in the two countries made it necessary to gather the samples differently and to adjust both the kinds of questions we asked and the wording of a number of the questions.

Gathering the sample in the United States proved relatively straightforward. Many teachers across the nation participate in the National Writing Project (NWP). Every summer local site directors work with a cadre of these teachers, who are selected to become Writing Project teacher-consultants and often offer workshops for other teachers. It was easy to get a U.S. sample by asking each of the 116 site directors to identify six of the most outstanding teachers of writing in his or her region, two at the elementary level (grades K–6), two at the junior high or middle school level (grades 7–9), and two at the senior high level (grades 9–12).[3] One junior and one senior high teacher from each site, both randomly selected, helped gather the student sample by asking four of their students to participate, two high achieving and two low achieving, with each pair including one male and one female.

The British had recently launched the British National Writing Project (BNWP), but it was new and did not follow a model that could identify successful teachers for our sample. Rather than giving workshops in the schools, teachers in the BNWP worked together at a particular school site to make changes and to create materials that other teachers could use. Alex McLeod and I turned to other networks to gather a sample that would parallel the U.S. group. We decided to consult the National Association of Advisers in English (NAAE), a type of organization that did not exist in the United States. In Britain, each Local Education Authority (LEA), the governing body for state-supported primary and secondary schools in England and Wales, employs an English Adviser to work with teachers in the LEA. These advisers, who were at one time teachers of English and were likely to have been department heads, are well-respected teachers and known authorities in the teaching of their subject area. They were able to identify outstanding teachers in their LEA since they conduct and organize in-service programs in the local schools, negotiate national educational policies (for example, the examination system), advise administrators in the evaluation of teachers, aid new teachers ("probationers"), and write reports for the Local Educational Committee (roughly equivalent to the U.S. school board) to keep that committee informed of local events and to recommend action regarding teachers in their subject area.

We began with the NAAE executive board, which has one member from each of eight geographical regions in England and Wales: London and the Southeast, the Southwest, the North, the West Midlands, the East Midlands, Yorkshire and Humberside, the East, and the Northwest. Each of the eight board members selected three English

Advisers within his or her region who were then asked to recommend six teachers: two primary, two lower secondary (Forms 1–3 or grades 6–8), and two upper secondary (Forms 4–Upper 6 or grades 9–12). Through other networks, we collected samples from: (a) Scotland (the Scottish Curriculum Development Service for twenty-four nominees from state-supported and independent primary and secondary schools); (b) various parts of the private sector in England (the Headmasters' Conference for eight nominees from secondary schools for boys; the Girls' Schools Association for eight nominees from secondary schools for girls; the Incorporated Association of Preparatory Schools for eight nominees from primary schools for girls and boys; and recommendations of national authorities on education for eight nominees from alternative private primary and secondary schools); and (c) a supplementary group of eight nominees from state-supported schools in the densely populated London area (recommendations of national authorities on education). Students were selected in Britain just as they were in the United States: a randomly selected half of the secondary teachers distributed questionnaires to four students, two higher achieving and two lower achieving, and within each category one male and one female if the school enrolled both genders.

Although we made every attempt to select parallel samples, the different cultural contexts and the different networks in the two countries produced samples that are undoubtedly somewhat different. The U.S. teachers, who were all part of the NWP network, shared a common professional reference point and were likely to identify themselves as teachers of writing. Because of their Writing Project connections, they were used to being regarded as specialists by other teachers and educators. Because only teachers affiliated with the Writing Project were included, however, the U.S. sample was limited. Many successful U.S. teachers are not part of the Writing Project and may even disagree with its philosophies (for example, see Delpit, 1986, 1988). By contrast, the British teachers at the secondary level provided a broader base but were more likely to identify themselves as teachers of English than of writing, and primary teachers would probably think of themselves simply as classroom teachers. Nevertheless, many British primary teachers in our sample would also be likely to claim a particular interest in language development. And for British secondary teachers the focus on written language has been strong within the teaching of English since at least the 1920s, if not longer. English teachers and those interested in language development are well versed in issues pertaining to the acquisition of written language.

In spite of the teachers' general knowledge about writing, I was not as confident about the overall level of expertise in the British sample as I was about that in the U.S. sample. In gathering the British sample I could not ask directly for "excellent" teachers as I had in the U.S. In Britain, it is considered immodest and inappropriate to apply that label either to oneself or to others. Alex McLeod guided me in choosing the phrasing "successful" and "especially thoughtful." Even with this more culturally appropriate wording, many British teachers objected when asked to reflect on what made them successful. In a randomly selected group of twenty-five, six issued qualifications: one began, "If I am successful"; another explained, "I'm a successful teacher of writing in a fairly limited way"; a third hesitated, "I'm not sure how successful I am—certainly not all the time nor as often as I would like." Two others qualified their comments: "While you are kind enough to consider me a successful teacher of writing, I should say I have much to learn" and "I am quite flattered that I am considered as a 'good' teacher of writing"; and the sixth protested impatiently, "Oh come off it." In thinking back on the different ways the National Writing Project was organized in the two countries, I suspect that this reluctance to identify excellence may also have played a role in shaping the BNWP. All data are interpreted with these considerations in mind.

Designing the Writing Exchanges

After collecting the national surveys, Alex and I turned to the writing exchanges. The exchanges provided an opportunity to observe students engaged in parallel writing activities that often occurred simultaneously in the two countries, to observe interactions across the two countries as students sent and received writing, and to observe a process of instructional change being put into place in two countries. And the exchanges allowed us to observe all this from multiple perspectives: those of the university research teams, the teachers, and the students. We focused on the teaching and learning conditions at the eight school sites and their consequences for classroom life, for the ways the teachers set up their classrooms to support their students' growth and development, and for the writing the students did.

In each country we identified four "experienced and thoughtful" teachers of writing who were known to be successful in the classroom and who were enthusiastic about collaborating with us and having one of their classes participate in a writing exchange with students from abroad. Besides being committed to the theoretical stance behind the study, they were interested in contributing to our knowledge of what is involved in translating theory into practice. In addition, they were working with students in grades 6 through 9, making the transition into secondary school. Table 1.1 shows how teachers were paired. The sole criterion for pairing teachers was the age level of their students, which we wanted to be as similar as possible.

Table 1.1 also lists the tracking labels of the participating classes. In London, where there has been a strong and effective movement against tracking, all classes were of mixed ability. Although we wanted to select parallel groups in the United States, we had difficulty locating mixed-ability classes in the San Francisco Bay area, where classes are typically tracked. Nancy Hughes's seventh-grade group was one of the few we could find. Working within this tracked system, in addition to the one mixed-ability class we selected two lower tracks so that we could study students who were labeled "at risk for school failure" (both ninth-grade groups fell into this category) and one "gifted" class, Carol Mather's sixth-grade group.

Although all students in the classrooms were full participants in the research, we focused on four students in each classroom who showed the range of response to the exchange activities exhibited by the different students in the class.[4] These focal students provided detailed information about how a range of students learned.

Each pair of teachers, together with their students, planned a number of writing activities, and these formed units of work. Students completed some of these writing units in just a few days, while they worked on others over weeks or even months. At the end of each unit,

Table 1.1 Classroom exchange pairs

United States	Great Britain
Carol Mather (gifted, grade 6)	Fiona Rodgers (mixed, grade 7)
Nancy Hughes (mixed, grade 7)	Peter Ross (mixed, grade 8)
Ann Powers (low, grade 9)	Gillian Hargrove (mixed, grade 9)
Bridget Franklin (low, grade 9)	Philippa Furlong (mixed, grade 9)

they mailed their writing to the partner class in the other country. Although there were differences in the ways different pairs of classes conceptualized their exchanges and in the degree to which they coordinated their writing activities, all exchanges shared four principles:

1. In no case did the writing exchange consist solely or even mostly of letter writing. Although personal writing was encouraged and even facilitated, the main academic business of the exchanges was to provide an occasion for students in the two countries to write substantial pieces for a distant but real whole-class audience. The writing included, for example, autobiographies, books about their schools and their communities, fiction and poetry, essays about books they had read, and opinion pieces about important and often controversial issues.
2. Students in the paired classrooms exchanged writing across a year's time, although the amount and type of writing varied within and across exchange pairs.
3. The paired classes worked together to make their writing programs for the year center on the exchange activities, although teachers varied in how completely they turned over their program to the exchange, both within exchange pairs and across pairs.
4. The paired teachers worked collaboratively to decide on some parallel topics for writing, but the degree and nature of the collaboration varied across pairings, as did student involvement in this collaboration across classrooms.

Questions and Answers

The following chapters address three broad questions from the point of view of the research teams, the teachers, and the students:

1. What institutional supports and constraints are associated with writing in school in the United States and in Great Britain—at the national, district, and school levels and at the classroom level?
2. As students acquire written language within the classroom, what characterizes the culture in which they report and interpret their ideas and their wider cultural experiences and how are their broader social needs integrated with their academic needs?
3. In each country, how does student writing develop across time?

Chapter 2 presents the findings from the national surveys. Chapter 3 describes the institutional contexts of the classrooms involved in the writing exchanges and supplements the results of the national surveys with additional information from the exchanges to address the first question. Although both Chapters 2 and 3 touch on classroom practice, they deal mainly with the school structures that shape and influence that practice and will be of special interest to those involved in school reform and restructuring. Readers who are more interested in the exchanges and their classroom applications may want to skip Chapters 2 and 3 and turn directly to Chapters 4, 5, 6, and 7, which are situated squarely in the classroom. They supplement the information from the questionnaires to address the last two questions. Chapters 4 and 5 explicate a British philosophy of teaching that involves an exchange of responsibilities between teacher and students and show how this way of teaching relates to British ideas about student development. Chapters 6 and 7 focus on assessment issues as they affect the classroom placement and the life chances of students in the United States and the similar effects of national examinations in Britain. Chapter 8 revisits the theories that drive how we structure and restructure our schools and underlie our everyday practices. It suggests ways to reconceptualize these theories in order to provide useful frames to guide ongoing school restructuring and help us rethink everyday classroom practice, especially in the area of writing and literacy.

Chapter 2

⟿ Learning about Policy and Curriculum

The National Surveys

I would like to say I'm glad I was able to do this survey, it was an enjoyable experience. Like I mentioned before I enjoy writing very much thanks to my dear sweet teacher whose name I won't mention; but I would like to thank her and you for making it possible for [me] to do this survey. I also would like to thank her for introducing and really helping [me] into the world of writing. I know she won't see this but I still would like to thank her and I will do just that. (U.S. student)

My English teacher makes our lessons very interesting because she is interesting, interested in what we have to say, good fun and willing to have discussions. She is a fair marker and understands problems that I have in my work, when I have them. She is excellent at explaining work and a very nice lady. (British student)

In both the United States and Great Britain, the students completing the national questionnaire surveys were often moved to offer their thanks and to include spontaneous positive comments about their teachers. They seemed genuinely to appreciate having an audience for their opinions. The teachers completing the questionnaires were also gracious in their responses and seemed pleased to have an opportunity to be heard. Overall, students and teachers revealed that the cultural context of learning to write in both countries was characterized by sometimes similar but more often divergent patterns—in terms of the schoolwide institutional supports and constraints associated with learning to write, and in terms of the classroom cultures these teachers and students constructed. I will briefly describe the questionnaire forms and the respondents, explain the questionnaire analysis, and then turn to what the questionnaires revealed about school institutions and the cultures of the classroom.

The Survey Forms

Teachers in both countries answered questions about (a) their educations; (b) the teaching conditions at their schools; (c) how often and how much their students wrote; (d) their reasons for teaching writing; (e) their teaching practices, including the types of writing they emphasized, the most frequent and most successful activities in their classrooms, and how they responded to their students' writing; and (f) how they thought they achieved their success. The secondary teachers were also asked to focus on a specific class they were currently teaching as well as their classes generally. As appropriate, students were asked parallel questions designed to elicit their points of view on those same issues. Separate forms for the British and U.S. participants reflected the language conventions specific to each country and included questions sensitive to the different school contexts. In all, there were six parallel forms for the questionnaires: one for U.S. and one for British primary teachers, one for U.S. and one for British secondary teachers, and one for U.S. and one for British secondary students. Complete forms used for the British teachers and their students can be found in Freedman and McLeod (1987); the U.S. forms can be found in Freedman (1987).

Analysis, Response Rates, and the Sample

The analysis compared the differences in the answers of primary and secondary teachers, teachers and students, higher- and lower-achieving students, and most critically, teachers and students from the United States and those from Great Britain.[1] In both countries the response rates were excellent. The teacher return rate of 75.4 percent in Britain, although lower than the U.S. rate of 87 percent, was quite satisfactory.[2] The larger U.S.-based sample of 560 teachers and 715 students and the smaller British sample of 135 teachers and 187 students corresponded well with the sizes of the school populations in the two countries. The characteristics of the different samples also reflected national demographics. The students came mostly from middle- and working-class backgrounds, but also included those from the most wealthy to the most poverty-stricken families (Freedman and McLeod, 1988, pp. 10, 12). In Britain, the private school population was slightly oversampled (Freedman and McLeod, 1988, p. 7). Also, there were significantly more nonnative speakers in British than in U.S. primary classes, most likely because in Britain they tended to be mainstreamed rather than placed in separate classes as they often are in the United States (Freedman and McLeod, 1988, pp. 10–11; McKay and Freedman, 1990).

As for the teachers, their backgrounds differed in ways consistent with the educational norms in their respective countries. More U.S. than British teachers held M.A. degrees, but British teachers had postgraduate training in the form of special certificate programs that have no equivalent in the United States. In addition, British teachers were significantly more likely than U.S. teachers to have majored in English than in education (Freedman and McLeod, 1988, pp. 7–8, 12) and at the secondary level were more likely to be younger (in their thirties rather than their forties) and male (22.8 percent in the United States and 41.5 percent in Britain) (Freedman and McLeod, 1987, p. 21).

Institutional Supports and Constraints

The questionnaires uncovered important institutional supports and constraints in the teaching and learning of writing that followed from both school-based and national policies. The results led to considerable differences in school sizes, grade configurations, and ways of scheduling classes. Such contrasts are important in the teaching and learning of writing because differences in size and scheduling can affect the amount and kinds of attention individual learners receive.

At the level of national policy, British national examinations tended to control the curriculum, especially in Forms 4 and 5 of secondary schools (grades 9 and 10), affecting both the content and organization of learning.[3] Besides profoundly affecting students' futures, the British examination courses led to differences in grading practices and elective course options and to early specialization in particular academic areas.

School Policy: Size and Scheduling

Overall, the schools in which students learned were smaller in Britain than in the United States. Both primary and secondary schools in

Great Britain were configured differently from those in the United States, and these configurations affected the size of the school and the number of students in different year groups or grade levels in the school.

At the primary level the British usually subdivide their schools into infant schools (equivalent to kindergarten and first grade) and junior schools (grades 2–5). The most usual configuration for the U.S. elementary school is K–5 or K–6. Given the subdivisions of the British primary schools and the fifth-grade cut off, it is no wonder that British primary teachers reported working in schools that were substantially smaller than those of their U.S. counterparts.

While British primary schools housed fewer age levels than U.S. elementary schools, British secondary schools housed a greater range of ages, usually covering the equivalent of grades 6–12, yet they were about the same size as the subdivided U.S. secondary schools, which housed three or four years in middle or junior high schools (grades 5–8 or 7–9) and senior high schools (grades 9 or 10 through 12).[4] The result was that in British secondary schools, each grade level or year group was smaller than that in U.S. secondary schools. Also, there was a greater range in the size of the U.S. secondary schools than of their British counterparts. No British secondary schools in this study approached the size of the largest U.S. secondary schools, which enrolled over 2,500 students.

Whereas school size and year-group size were generally smaller in Britain, class size was roughly equivalent, as was the teachers' general workload. The median class sizes ranged from 25 to 29, and primary classes were significantly larger than secondary classes in both countries.[5]

At the secondary level British teachers taught more separate classes than teachers in the United States, but they taught each one for fewer hours per week, again making their teaching time roughly equivalent.[6] In Britain core subjects like English or math generally met only three to four periods each week, each lasting about an hour and distributed across two, three, or four days in even or uneven proportions. By contrast, in the U.S. core subjects generally met five periods per week, usually for close to one hour every day. Whereas most U.S. teachers taught a five-class load, most British teachers taught a six-class load, and quite a few taught seven or more classes. It could be argued that the British job of teaching more classes, albeit for fewer hours each, is more difficult.

In spite of their similar teaching loads, a major organizational difference helped British secondary teachers get to know their students. In Britain, secondary teachers routinely taught the same class of students for more than a year, frequently for two years or more.[7] In the United States it was relatively common for secondary teachers to report keeping the same class for only a semester, something that was virtually unknown in Great Britain. Gubb, Gorman, and Price (1987) found that for their British sample of teachers of fifteen-year-olds, "two-thirds of the teachers reported that this was their second year with the group assessed and a further 11 per cent said they had taught the class for longer" (p. 113). In addition to having the same teacher for several years, the students stayed together as a class from one year to the next and thus had the opportunity to bond as a class group over the years. Also, for the first three years of secondary school the class group stayed together through much of the school day.

In sum, the British schools were smaller than U.S. schools at the primary level, but at the secondary level they were the same size; since the British schools covered more grade levels, however, the size of the year-groups was smaller. Teachers had roughly equivalent work loads in both countries, heavy ones according to most professional standards. For example, in the U.S. the English Coalition Conference resolved that teachers should teach "no more than four classes per day with a maximum of 100 students at the secondary level; no more than 20 students for [the] elementary [level]" (Lloyd-Jones and Lundsford, 1989, p. 48). In Great Britain the National Union of Teachers (NUT) published "Our Overcrowded Classrooms" in September 1991. NUT notes that in 1986 all teachers' organizations in Britain agreed on recommendations for a maximum class size of 26, with lower numbers for the early elementary years, for mixed-age classes (21), and for the examination classes (18 in GCSE examination courses and 10 for A-level classes) (p. 5). NUT surveys of class size showed that in primary schools 67 percent had "more than the objective of 26 pupils" (p. 6), and in secondary schools 46 percent did (p. 10); in mixed-age classes 84 percent had "more than the objective of 21 pupils" (p. 7); in GCSE examination courses 75 percent exceeded the recommended level of 18 pupils, 51 percent having less than 26, 19 percent between 27 and 30, and 5 percent between 31 and 35 (p. 11); and in A-level courses 60 percent had more than the recommended 10 students (p. 12). These findings, although more detailed, are consistent with the reports of the British teachers completing the questionnaires for this study.

In the end, because of differences in the way classes were scheduled, both within the school day and from one year to the next, British teachers worked in organizational structures that gave them more support for creating tightly knit classroom communities and for getting to know the needs of their developing student writers than did their peers in the United States.

National Policy: Examinations and Their Effects

At the secondary level the British national examination system has had profound effects on the organization of schools and on the curriculum, especially in the last four years of secondary school. Students are prepared for the national examinations in two-year examination courses, usually taught by the same teacher for both years. They take the first set of examinations when they are 16+, after they have completed examination courses during the equivalent of grades 9 and 10. The results of this set of examinations provide information for employers and help universities select which students they will admit. They also determine which students are advised to complete secondary school and go on for additional education. After these examinations, about 70 percent of students leave school (*Statistics of Schools*, 1989, p. 133).

For this first set of examinations, students usually take English language and math, along with another one or two compulsory subjects depending on the requirements of their school. In addition to the compulsory subjects, they choose four or five other subjects to make a total of about eight. Until 1986, students were placed into either Ordinary level (O level) (required for college entrance and employment in many vocational pursuits) or Certificate of Secondary Education (CSE) (non-college-bound) courses; students could take O level in some subjects and CSE in others. About half of the students completing the questionnaires, regardless of achievement level, had taken or were planning to take the O-level exam in language (53.5 percent) and the O-level in literature (49.2 percent); 17.3 percent had taken or were planning to take the CSE. The others were part of a new examination system. In 1986, the two-tiered system was abolished so that students would be able to keep their options for higher education open longer. Instead of college and noncollege courses, all students would take the same two-year examination course, the General Certificate of Secondary Education (GCSE), and scores on the GCSE would determine future possibilities. The first GCSE examinations were administered in 1988. Of the students responding to these questionnaires, 20.5 percent reported that they would take the GCSE in English language and/or in English literature.

Some of the students who remain in school go into another two-year examination course called Advanced level (A level) during the equivalent of U.S. grades 11 and 12 or into one of several new courses. A-level results determine eligibility for university entrance. Of the 30 percent who continue in school, only about 20 percent actually take A levels (*Statistics of Schools,* 1989, p. 133). At A level, the emphasis is on specialization, not breadth, so students often take only math and science or only humanities. Normally, they take three or sometimes four A-level courses in subject areas of their choosing. The use of a new examination, the Certificate of Pre-Vocational Education (CPVE), is growing rapidly in many schools, generally as an option for post-GCSE students not thought able to attain the A-level standard.[8]

Consistent with the fact that only 20 percent of the population takes A levels, 23.8 percent of the students completing the questionnaires said they were planning to take A levels. Somewhat inconsistently, however, when asked at what age they planned to leave school, 54.3 percent optimistically said they planned to stay until age 18.[9] Some undoubtedly planned to attend vocational schools rather than go into the A-level courses.

Upon leaving school the British and U.S. students had significantly different plans. Most U.S. students expected to go to a four-year college (66.2 percent), especially those students labeled high achieving (78.8 percent); 40.2 percent of the British students had similar expectations, although it is unclear how half of them would attain their goal without taking A levels. Also, more British (28.3 percent) than U.S. (18.4 percent) students said they had no plans after secondary school.[10]

Since the British exams certify students, the grades individual teachers give are not so important in determining a student's future. Perhaps for this reason, British secondary teachers did not always give grades, and they often did not grade every piece of writing. Some 15 percent of the British students said that their teachers never gave them grades on individual pieces of writing or at the end of the term. In response to one item on their questionnaires, which asked the students how frequently their teachers gave them grades on final versions of their writing, the U.S. students reported that they virtually always received grades, while the British students reported receiving grades significantly less frequently.[11] When the teachers were asked how frequently they gave grades on final versions, the U.S. teachers reported giving grades more often than the British teachers, but teachers in both countries claimed to give grades less frequently than their students claimed to receive them.

When British students got grades, they found it more difficult to make an *A* than their counterparts in the United States.[12] Since few students receive high enough grades on their first set of examinations to move into the second two-year examination course and since *A* was a very rare examination grade, British teachers may have felt they could not afford to raise their students' expectations unrealistically.

Given the fixed curricula of the examination courses, it is no surprise that in Britain, English was almost always a required class.[13] In the United States the higher percentage of electives in English indicates that there still may be remnants of the elective system begun in the 1960s, which allowed students to choose what they wanted to study (for example, the American novel, Shakespeare, romance in literature) in lieu of, say, an eleventh-grade survey of American literature.

Classroom Cultures

The questionnaire results also shed light directly on the classroom cultures within these schools. The teachers explained the basic philosophy that guided their teaching, their reasons for having students write, including the kinds of writing they promoted, and their approach to fostering and supporting student writing. The secondary students also provided their views of the classroom culture, describing the kinds of writing they did and commenting on how their teachers fostered and supported their writing growth.

In responding to open-ended questions, which asked them to reflect on how they achieved their teaching success and what advice they would give other teachers of writing, the teachers revealed something of the basic philosophy about student learning that undergirded their teaching. For these free-response questions, a content analysis was performed on all 135 of the British teachers' replies and on 135 randomly selected replies from the U.S. group. Coding categories were derived from the data. Only topics that were mentioned by at least 35 teachers were included in the coding.[14]

The teachers discussed their roles in the classroom, the traits they felt successful teachers possess, and their pedagogical emphases. A look at which topics the teachers mentioned most often shows that, while both U.S. and British teachers claimed to work collaboratively with their students, their sense of what constitutes a collaborative environment and their view of the nature of collaboration differed.[15] The U.S. teachers seemed to focus most of their energy on the curriculum—in particular on their use of a process approach, on writing with their students and sharing that writing, and on their willingness to take risks in their teaching. A typical U.S. secondary teacher wrote: "I think of myself as a writer. I emphasize the writing process rather than the product . . . I write with my students when we write in journals. We use peer writing groups when students are competent enough to be successful with them."

By contrast, the British teachers focused on their students, on getting to know them as writers and as people so that they could build their instruction on what the students knew and could do. More than the U.S. teachers, the British teachers mentioned the importance of giving support while challenging students and understanding their needs. They talked about nurturing their students' creativity, focusing on their meaning-making, and helping them write in a variety of ways. The following comment is typical: "I'm interested in and responsive to the individuality of pupils' creative work. I'm excited by language and I'm reasonably fertile in suggestions which can open new directions from what pupils spontaneously produce without making them feel that their work is being taken over by an alien sensibility."

In addition to these differences in philosophy, the teaching approaches also differed in the two countries. Consistent with their focus on the curriculum and a process approach, the U.S. teachers explicitly taught and valued the writing process more than the British teachers did (Freedman and McLeod, 1988, p. 26). Along these same lines, the U.S. teachers reported that they thought responding during the writing process was significantly more helpful to their students than responding after a piece of writing was finished (Freedman, 1987, pp. 59–61). By contrast, the British teachers reported that they saw no significant difference in helpfulness in terms of the timing of the response.

In contrast to their teachers, the students in both countries emphasized the importance of the teacher's response to their writing after they had completed it, in the form of both written comments and grades. They valued their teachers' response to completed pieces of writing much more than the help they received in the process of writing itself.[16]

The British and U.S. teachers also revealed important differences in the kinds of writing they promoted. These differences occurred mostly at the secondary level. In Britain a strong focus on imaginative writing remained prominent, continuing the strong focus in the British primary school. In the United States in the later grades the critical, analytical essay replaced the imaginative fiction that was prevalent in the U.S. elementary school. Remarks made by secondary teachers on their questionnaires make this contrast vivid: "I feel that successful writing is usually produced by descriptive and narrative assignments of a highly concrete kind which can be met in very literal-minded terms, but give scope for fantasy" (British teacher). And "I base most of my assignments around the essay, a form of writing that demands both a mastery of facts and a willingness to be creative. This form tends, I find, along with essential teacher enthusiasm to motivate student writers" (U.S. teacher).

This cross-national difference first surfaced in the questionnaires when the teachers indicated why they had their students write. Two lists of items asked them about their most important and least important reasons for teaching writing. The six items on the first list asked whether they taught writing to help students learn to transmit information or share personal experiences, and the six items on the second asked whether they taught writing to help students understand content or develop skills. (Appendix 2 contains a full description of the lists and the rationale for their construction.) For each list of six items the teachers were to check two that represented their most important reasons for teaching writing and two that represented their least important reasons. The frequency of those items checked as most important was then compared across the samples.[17]

In Britain, teachers across all age levels placed the most importance on sharing imaginative experiences through writing (73.5 percent checked this item). Their other major concern, although to a lesser degree, was to allow their pupils to express their feelings when they wrote (58.3 percent checked this item). In the United States, the teachers' reasons for teaching writing shifted in major ways across the grade levels. The elementary teachers were much like their counterparts in Britain: they emphasized having students write to share imaginative experiences (68.8 percent) and to express feelings (66.7

percent). Unlike their British peers, the U.S. elementary teachers, aligning themselves with U.S. secondary teachers, also stressed forcing students to think for themselves (65.8 percent). The secondary teachers emphasized writing to understand content, saying that what was most important was to force students to think for themselves (68.8 percent) and then to correlate their personal experience with their topic (57.6 percent).[18] The strongest cross-national differences in the teachers' values, then, were between the British and the U.S. secondary teachers: the British group were most interested in having students write primarily to share their imaginative experiences, while the U.S. group focused on teaching writing to force students to think for themselves. The British teachers also emphasized proper form more than their U.S. counterparts, but neither group checked this item especially often.

The teachers' and students' replies show further that the students actually did the kinds of writing their teachers valued. These questions asked teachers and secondary students to assess the relative amount of time the students spent on various types of writing. In Britain, consistent with their reasons for teaching writing, the teachers said their pupils most frequently engaged in writing to provide a poetic experience (poems, plays, short stories).[19] Next in frequency was writing to convey personal experiences. In the United States, the elementary teachers said that their students most frequently wrote to convey personal experiences and then to provide a poetic experience, while the secondary teachers focused on conveying personal experience, writing to discover ideas, and writing to analyze and synthesize information.[20]

The British secondary students confirmed their teachers' reports, saying that they wrote mostly poems and plays. But unlike their teachers, they also said that they wrote to analyze and synthesize. Interestingly, the British students claimed to be doing more analytic writing than their teachers reported they were doing. The U.S. secondary students also confirmed what their teachers said. They claimed to write mostly to analyze and synthesize information, then to convey a poetic experience, and then to convey personal experiences.[21]

Particularly telling of the British emphasis on imaginative writing are the kinds of writing required on the GCSE examination. Whereas in the United States tests of writing at the upper secondary level do not normally call for imaginative forms, the GCSE asks for stories, poems, or plays alongside critical analyses of literary works and opinion pieces. One student, for example, who included two short stories in his GCSE packet, wrote one in the style of a detective story, as his introductory paragraph illustrates:

> I glanced at my watch. it was only four in the morning. The sky was black and empty, just like my wallet. The street was as bare as my drinks cabinet. My head was still spinning from last night. I put on my long black coat and dark blue trousers. As I stumbled down the stairs and opened the large oak door, my thought turned to the call I'd just received. Everyone knew about Jack Mahony, but no-one had ever tried to take him on before. I guess it was my job to do just that, and no I wasn't looking forward to it.

This British emphasis on imaginative writing throughout the secondary years, identified by Squire and Applebee in 1968, still differentiates writing in U.S. and British secondary schools.[22] These results also are supported by Gubb and her colleagues (1987), who found that for British fifteen-year-olds, the personal story and personal essay were the most common types of writing, followed at a close distance by the short story and the statement of personal views.

Connections between Institutional Policies and Classroom Cultures

The responses of the teachers and students who completed the questionnaires pointed to several important differences between the institutions of schooling and of classroom cultures in the United States and those in Great Britain. In the first place, the teachers evidenced deeply rooted philosophical differences about how students learn. The U.S. teachers focused their attention on the curriculum, on developing techniques for teaching writing as a process and on being certain to set a good example by writing alongside their students. The British teachers focused on their student learners, on getting to know their needs and then developing activities to meet those needs. The institutional structures in the two countries supported these different philosophies. In particular, the British tradition of keeping the same class of students with the same teacher for several years at the secondary level made it possible for British teachers to learn things about their students that were qualitatively different from what the U.S. teachers could learn in only one hour per day over five to ten months. In some sense, the rapid turnover of student groups forced U.S. teachers to focus on the curriculum, since they must depend on what other teachers have done for continuity, and the questionnaires confirm this focus. In the same way, in Britain the smaller school sizes, the smaller sizes of year groups within the schools, and keeping the same classes of students together across the years personalized secondary education.

We know little about the advantages and disadvantages of either focus, and certainly both must be viewed within their institutional contexts. It is true that when British educators talk and write about the importance of getting to know students and making their instruction sensitive to student development, they talk about possibilities that are different from those in the United States within current school structures. But U.S. educators also write about the importance of individualizing instruction and getting to know student learners. For example, Graves (1983), writing for elementary teachers, who in both countries usually have the same group of students for the entire school day, even if for only one year, equates notions of teaching the writing process with attending to student development. As he explains, "teachers will need immediate information that will help them aid children in the midst of the writing process, not when the paper is completed" (p. 247). Graves then advises teachers about how to watch their students develop as writers. Recognizing that teachers cannot know where every child is at every moment, he continues, "the challenge is to have enough of an observation and record-keeping system to know which children need help that is timely" (p. 286). Graves tells the story of his visit to a British primary school:

> Several years ago I visited a primary class in Oxfordshire, England. The teacher had thirty-eight children to teach, yet she could discuss child progress in detail. I asked how she managed to know such information, especially in writing. She replied, "Oh, you are wondering about records." Her reply carried the implication Americans were always asking about record-keeping systems. I said, "Well, yes, I am interested in how you do it." She turned to a large carton where each child had a folder containing a collection of all of their writing. With a wave of her hand she said, "There's my record-keeping system. The folders speak for themselves. Take a look in any folder and you will know how the children are changing." (p. 295)

He goes on to extol the value of collecting folders and suggests how teachers might use them to watch their students develop.

In a similar vein, Jaggar and Smith-Burke (1985) assert:

The key to effective teaching is building on what students have already learned. The best way to discover this is to listen and watch closely as children use language—spoken and written—in different settings and circumstances. Careful observation over time will reveal individual styles and patterns of language use. As patterns emerge teachers can reflect on them, comparing the observations to past observations and to their knowledge of language development, to determine what their students know (competence) and can do (skill) with language. (p. 5)

Likewise, Moffett (1973) explains why it is important that secondary teachers get to know their students: "The main points are to let students do the same things at different times and to get the teacher out from under lesson-planning and direction-giving so that he or she can afford to do all the things that really make education work—the individualized coaching and counseling, the small-group arranging, and so on" (p. vii). And more recently, "What you do not do is set yourself up as sole problem-solver. You note problems, keep your own record of the kinds of experiences each student is having, and then guide her into new areas when she's ready. Your goal is to keep the process alive, not necessarily to intervene to improve the end products that the students are working on. This play-it-by-ear teaching style requires an involved interaction with students that takes energy, patience, interpersonal awareness, and courage" (Moffett and Wagner, 1992, p. 54).

The problem, especially at the secondary level, is that few U.S. teachers work within contexts that support these ideals. Hence, on these questionnaires at least, they remain in the background. In addition, lacking a tradition of watching students grow, U.S. teachers have difficulty explicating development when they collect folders across time (Calfee and Perfumo, 1993). Also missing in the U.S. notion of curriculum is any clear way of building across time. Teachers focus on strategies that can be used across ages—mainly the writing process and related activities, including writing with students and peer response groups. We are left wondering how U.S. teachers manage to move their students in "new directions," and, given the students' desires, how teachers can bridge the gap between their own values and those of their students.

We still know little about the precise consequences of emphasizing imaginative writing rather than writing that forces students to think for themselves. In the analysis of the teachers' questionnaire responses regarding their reasons for having their students write, it became clear that the common distinction between "encouraging imaginative writing" and "forcing students to think for themselves" must be considered carefully. Sometimes, especially in very high quality student writing, the imaginative and critical thinking functions are both present and, in fact, reinforce each other. In imaginative fiction or in the historical reconstruction of people's lives, for example, a student may be making significant critical comments on moral or social issues (McLeod, 1992).

These best-case scenarios aside, we still need to know whether these varied emphases affect how writing functions for the students in the two countries—both cognitively and socially. Does the U.S. emphasis mean that teachers neglect imaginative writing and if so, is such neglect detrimental to secondary students? Does the British emphasis mean that teachers neglect synthesis and analysis of ideas, and if so, is such neglect detrimental? Are these differences in emphasis encouraged by the fact that U.S. teachers are charged with preparing a large and diverse portion of the school population for higher education and may feel that they must begin early teaching those functions of writing that are most valued in the university? What are the effects on students of the U.S. teachers' discontinuous values from elementary to secondary school, and are these value shifts appropriate or disconcerting?

Medway (1986) has begun a study that offers a preliminary critique of the way writing is commonly taught in Britain. Consistent with our questionnaire results, he found that in 346 assignments given to twelve-year-olds in twenty-one classrooms in the north of England, "a third of the assignments were stories" (p. 23). After looking closely at the sorts of assignments to discover what kind of thinking they required of the students, he found that what was valued was not the writers' unique thoughts but rather adhering to fictional discourse types. He also found that students were asked to stay mostly at the level of the specific and had little opportunity to analyze and generalize. Medway concluded that the ordinary English class in England "is a good place in which to recreate or imagine experience, but a bad place to be curious" (p. 37). Although he did not base his conclusions on a study of especially thoughtful teachers, nor has any similar close analysis of what is actually called for in the writing of U.S. students been performed, there is growing evidence in the United States that much of the writing designed to evoke critical thinking does not succeed (Bereiter and Scardamalia, 1987; Flower, 1989; Langer and Applebee, 1987; Nelson and Hayes, 1988; Nelson, 1990). Finally, in the last years of secondary school the British national examinations literally dictate the curriculum. Again the questionnaires reveal little either positive or negative about the effects of the examinations.

Putting aside these differences, it is clear that the successful teachers in this study, in both the United States and Great Britain, regardless of the function of writing they valued and promoted or how they promoted it, considered writing to be more a way of gaining deeper understandings than a skill to be transmitted or a vehicle for learning.[23] The real educational issues do not focus on the discourse type promoted (story, essay) but on how these varied discourse types function in the ebb and flow of teaching and learning. These teachers held that writing can allow students to transform knowledge for themselves, whether that transformation takes place mostly through an orientation toward critical thinking, as in the United States, or through an orientation toward imaginative thinking, as in Great Britain. As one of the U.S. secondary teachers said of her class, "we work toward higher levels of thinking in our writing."

The issues raised by the contrasts in the responses on these questionnaires and the teachers' relative levels of success in achieving their goal of knowledge transformation will be revisited in greater depth in the following chapters as we look inside the schools and classrooms that are part of the writing exchanges.

Chapter 3

∽ Comparing Local Contexts

Exchanges among Teachers, Schools, and Classrooms

The Teachers

The British teachers in the exchanges had much in common with their U.S. counterparts in educational background, amount of teaching experience, and reputation as successful teachers. However, there were striking differences between the two groups as well, especially in professional opportunities and daily work lives, differences that have profound effects on education as a whole and on literacy education in particular in the two countries.

Portraits of two of the exchange teachers, Peter Ross of Garden Hill Community School in an outer London borough and Carol Mather of San Francisco's Webster Middle School, provide a starting point for probing some of these similarities and differences.[1] These portraits are intended to reveal something of the teachers' educational backgrounds, their career paths, and their work lives, and to show the full range of their professional opportunities and contributions.

Peter Ross in London

British exchange teacher Peter Ross was born and raised only a few miles from Garden Hill, where he has spent his entire eighteen-year teaching career. He attended the College of Saint Mark and Saint John in London, a well-known institution that has since moved to Plymouth. Peter's four-year college course led to a B.A. and teaching credentials in three curriculum subjects, one of which was English.[2]

Five years after coming to Garden Hill, Peter was appointed head of the English department, a position reserved for outstanding faculty members who are effective teacher-leaders. In this post, Peter received extra salary and a reduced teaching load in return for supervising seven other English teachers and taking charge of overseeing and supporting student teachers in English who were sent to Garden Hill from the University of London Institute of Education and from other London colleges. Four years after becoming department head, Peter was seconded[3] full-time to take the diploma in the Role of Language in Education at the Institute of Education. After receiving this diploma, Peter remained department head but was also promoted to the additional post of senior teacher, a school-level appointment for which there is no equivalent in the United States. In England senior teachers are directly over the department head and directly under the deputy head, who is much like an assistant principal. As senior teacher, Peter received another salary raise and his class load was reduced to allow him to coordinate in-service education for all Garden Hill teachers, not just those in English. He also supervised the work of all new teachers at his school.

Along with his administrative duties, Peter produced school plays and at his reduced load taught five classes of English a week, one fewer than the usual British six-course load reported in the national questionnaires. Peter taught each course to a different age level. Besides his Form 3 (grade 8) class participating in the exchange, Peter had a Form 4 (grade 9) GCSE class, a Form 5 (grade 10) GCSE class, a Lower Sixth Form (grade 11) class that was not taking A levels but was taking the one-year Certificate of Pre-Vocational Education; and an Upper Sixth Form (grade 12), A-level literature class.[4] Each of these classes met for two or three sixty-five-minute periods each week, and Peter also had two scheduled periods during the week when he was "on call" to support other teachers who were having difficulty with their classes. Sometimes he was also asked to cover classes for teachers who were absent, and once a week he voluntarily ran an extra class before school for his A-level literature group.

In addition to his job at Garden Hill, Peter was active in other areas of education. He published a book on curriculum and change in Great Britain with another teacher-leader. He also played important roles in the London Association for the Teaching of English (LATE) for over a decade, serving in major offices in the organization and on the executive committee, which determines policy and plans and organizes conferences and other events. Well-known for his thoughtful and innovative ideas, Peter clearly stated his commitment to the teaching and learning of English in an interview conducted by one of his students and sent to the exchange class in the United States as part of a book about Garden Hill School: "English is probably the most important subject because English is the subject where people deal with their own lives, their own feelings, the world that they live in. It's where people can read what other people have got to say about the world, and hope that has some sort of effect on the way we think, and the way we feel. It also gives me a lot more freedom than other subjects, I'm not tied to a lot of knowledge that I have to get across." Peter received a two-week paid study leave from his school to come to the United States to participate in the Bay Area Writing Project's summer invitational program and to work with the research team on the exchange project.

Carol Mather in San Francisco

In 1988, the year the writing exchanges began, Carol Mather had been teaching for twenty-three years. She had taught at Webster Middle School for eighteen years and before that at another inner-city San Francisco middle school for five years. Like Peter, Carol was born and raised near her school. In fact, like her mother and uncle before her, she had attended Webster. A picture of her as a schoolgirl at Webster claimed a prominent spot on her classroom bulletin board. After completing her B.A. in English at San Francisco State University, she did most of the coursework for her M.A., with a specialty in the English department in women's literature and women's studies.

Whereas Peter had received a number of promotions during his career, no promotions were available to Carol. Carol wanted to remain in the classroom, but U.S. classroom teachers, unlike their British counterparts, have little opportunity for professional mobility. Still, Carol was well known for her contributions to the Gifted and Talented Education (GATE) program at Webster, which had been in operation since the early 1970s. She had taught GATE classes since the late 1970s and acted as program co-director since the mid-1980s. Carol used to be released from one class to work in the GATE program, but shrinking education budgets had taken away such perks. Cutbacks had also caused the loss of one teacher in the program, and Carol and her remaining colleagues had absorbed rises in class size.

Beyond her uncompensated leadership in Webster's GATE program, Carol also pioneered work in women's studies and received official recognition when she received a California mentor teacher award. Established in 1983, California's Mentor Teacher Program each year provides funds to school districts to award extra salary to a select group of teachers with special expertise and interesting ideas for projects. The awards allow but are not specifically designed to encourage teachers to focus their projects on improving programs at their own schools. For her mentor project, Carol developed and tested curricular materials for women's studies in her classroom, offered workshops to teachers in the San Francisco Unified School District, gave other presentations, collected curricular resources other teachers could borrow, and conducted a year-long workshop for teachers for two years running in which participants met monthly to discuss issues in women's studies. This mentor award, unlike Peter's promotions, lasted only one year and focused more on district than school-based activities.

Carol's work in women's studies led to a number of outside consulting jobs, both for local conferences and workshops and for national summer programs. A successful entrepreneur, Carol also had received grants to obtain films, a computer for her classroom, and a class set of women's biographies. She got these extras pretty much on her own, with little support from school or district administrators.

Just as Carol's professional opportunities were different from Peter's, so was her school's organization and therefore her work day. During the exchange year, Carol taught the same five classes every day: three fifty-minute morning periods with the sixth graders in the exchange—for language arts, reading, and social studies—and two afternoon periods, one of English and one of social studies, with seventh and eighth graders. The long interdisciplinary morning block was designed to provide the sixth graders with a smooth transition from elementary to middle school. The last two periods were usually organized as nine-week special topic units (for example, Shakespeare, Rebellion and Conformity, Greek Mythology, American Women Making History); students and topics could potentially change every nine weeks, and some of her sixth graders would likely cycle back through some of these nine-week blocks in their seventh- and eighth-grade years.

A year after the exchange project, Carol was awarded a one-year sabbatical leave. During that year, she says with excitement and enthusiasm, "I found my writing voice." With that voice, she completed a sometimes touching and often humorous book entitled *Teaching Stories* (Logan, 1993).

Themes across the Exchanges

Backgrounds

Both Carol and Peter came to teaching with undergraduate majors in English, their subject specialty; both had some postgraduate education; both had been in the classroom for many years and were dedicated to their schools and their jobs. In these ways they were much like the other teachers in the exchanges, although they were the only two born and raised in their schools' immediate neighborhoods.

With the exception of Fiona Rodgers, Carol's partner in England and the youngest of the exchange teachers, all had taught for over ten years, and more than half of the group had, like Peter and Carol, taught for close to twenty years or more (Table 3.1).

Most of the U.S. exchange teachers had also either completed or partially completed an M.A. degree. In England most either had an M.A. or had completed a special certificate or diploma program, as Peter did at the Institute of Education (see Table 3.2). In the United States, the M.A. seems to be the only formal and sustained university-based postgraduate option for practicing teachers, although there are some specialist credential programs, for example, in reading or counseling. In Britain there were more varied postgraduate options for certified teachers, the diploma course that Peter took being only one. Thus, it is not surprising that on the national questionnaires more U.S. teachers than British teachers reported having M.A.'s. When all was said and done, on paper at least, the exchange teachers' educations seemed roughly equivalent. It is beyond the scope of this study to probe the substance of their educations, but undoubtedly there were cross-national differences.

Professional Opportunities

Of all the cross-national differences in Peter's and Carol's situations, the most striking was the promotion system. The British teachers

Table 3.1 Teaching experience

| | U.S. teachers | | | | | | British teachers | | | | | | |
	Carol Mather	Nancy Hughes	Ann Powers	Bridget Franklin	Total	Mean	Fiona Rodgers	Peter Ross	Gillian Hargrove	Philippa Furlong	Total	Mean
Years teaching	23	20	14	23	80	20.0	5	18	20	12	55	13.75
Years at current school	18	17	5	13	53	13.2	5	18	3	5	31	7.75

Table 3.2 Educational background

	U.S. teachers				British teachers			
	Carol Mather	Nancy Hughes	Ann Powers	Bridget Franklin	Fiona Rodgers	Peter Ross	Gillian Hargrove	Philippa Furlong
Undergraduate								
Degree	B.A.	B.A.	B.A.	B.A.	B.A.	B.A.	B.A. (Honors)	B.Ed. (Honors)
School	San Francisco State University	University of Southern California	University of California at Berkeley	Seattle University	Queen Mary College, University of London	College of St. Mark and St. John	Goldsmith's College, University of London	Thomas Huxley
Major	English	Education	English	English	English	English and 3 teaching credentials	Sociology	English and drama
Graduate								
Degree (or certificate)	Coursework for M.A.	—	Began M.A. program	M.A.	P.G.C.E.	Role of Language Diploma	Began M.A. program	M.A.
School	San Francisco State University	—	Breadloaf School of English, Middlebury College	University of California at Berkeley	University of London, Institute of Education	University of London, Institute of Education	University of London, Institute of Education	University of London, Institute of Education
Major	English and women's ...	—	English	Education	English	English	English	Language and literature

enjoyed a system that had no equivalent in the United States. In fact, every British exchange teacher had received an important promotion and had a job title to mark that promotion. For the British exchange teachers, these leadership roles were essential to the running of the academic programs at their schools and fully integrated with those programs. Teachers received financial compensation and recognition from peers at their schools and from the culture at large, which bestowed promotions for expertise. These promotions were accompanied not only by higher salaries but also by decreases in classroom teaching loads; in contrast, the teaching loads of the U.S. teachers remained fairly constant across their careers. The national questionnaires reflected these differences: in Great Britain 1.6 percent of the secondary teachers taught four classes or fewer, 23.8 percent five classes, 44.4 percent six classes, and 30.2 percent seven classes or more (see Table 2.4 in Appendix 1). Although the norm was six classes, the spread was great. Of the U.S. secondary teachers, 5.4 percent reported teaching four classes or fewer, 66.7 percent five classes, 26.9 percent six classes, and 1.1 percent seven classes or more. In essence there was a norm for U.S. teachers: almost all taught five classes, with an extraordinarily heavy six-class load creeping into over one-fourth of the schools. The British exchange teachers followed the spread shown in the British surveys. By contrast, all four U.S. exchange teachers taught five classes like most of their secondary counterparts across the nation.

It appears at first that, although the British teachers' class loads were variable, they were on the whole extraordinarily heavy, since administrative duties were piled onto already onerous teaching loads. However, in Britain, as Peter's experience illustrates, classes met fewer times per week and for less time, leaving space for the teachers to teach more separate classes. Table 3.3 shows how often each teacher met with the exchange class each week. It also shows that, on average, students were in class for less time than in the United States. Although the British system is not as onerous as it at first appears, it could still be said that teaching more different classes required more work, even though those classes met for less time. In the end, one might argue that teaching loads were too heavy in both settings.

In spite of heavy teaching loads, the British promotion system and the accompanying flexibility in scheduling had multiple effects on schools and schooling. In the first place, the promotions provided teachers with major school-based academic leadership roles, giving them both responsibility and recognition. Most of these roles had no equivalents in U.S. schools, leaving what the British would consider to be gaping holes in U.S. academic programs. The promotions made it possible for Peter's school to take advantage of his talents in designing and executing university-based teacher education programs, inducting first-year teachers into the profession, and organizing in-service education. Carol's school had few ways to fully exploit her potential.

Table 3.3 Exchange schedule

	Length of class period in minutes	# Periods/week (# Days/week)	Total time/week (Mean time/week)
U.S. teachers			
Mather	50	5 (5)	250
Hughes	50	5 (5)	250
Powers	54	5 (5)	270
Franklin	56	5 (5)	280
Total	—	—	1,050 (262.5)
British teachers			
Rodgers	50	4 (4)	200
Ross	65	3 (2)	195
Hargrove	55	4 (3)	220
Furlong	70	3 (English) (3) [1 (Drama) (1)]	210 [70]
Total	—	—	825 (206.25)

In the area of teacher education, Peter assumed a number of important duties that not only affected his own work life but also reflected the nature of British teacher education programs. He arranged for student teachers to observe in the classrooms of a number of experienced teachers, and for each one to have several different student teaching experiences, adjusting those experiences as necessary. He also led formal seminars in his office for the student teachers in which they discussed the application of theory to practice and issues related to their teaching experiences at Garden Hill. Garden Hill supported teacher education by paying Peter to conduct school-based programs and activities.

The involvement of Carol and the other U.S. teachers in teacher education was limited. When student teachers were assigned to them, the student teachers worked solely in their classrooms; they did not have varied practice teaching experiences with different teachers in the department. The U.S. teachers helped their student teachers with day-to-day classroom concerns but played no other official role in their education. Carol reports helping her student teachers get their first jobs and spending much time counseling them early in their careers, but she provided this help as a volunteer effort without formal institutional support or recognition.

Since the U.S. student teachers were not, by policy, clustered at particular schools, they often felt isolated from their novice peers during their school-based experiences. In addition, they had no teacher-led school-based seminars, an activity that would make no sense, since often there was only one student teacher in the school's English department.

Peter's duties in inducting new teachers into the profession were largely unknown to U.S. teachers. In Britain newly qualified teachers in their first year of teaching are officially on probation; full certification depends on satisfactory performance over this first year. During the probationary period the new teacher is on full salary but has a reduced teaching load and meets regularly with other "probationers" in group seminars where they hear guest speakers and discuss issues of common concern. At the end of the year, a teacher in charge of probationers for the department,[5] the department head, the head of the school, and the local education authority advisor evaluate the progress of the probationer. Probationers normally pass or may have the probation period extended; only in rare cases do they fail.[6] U.S. schools have no uniform mechanism for inducting new teachers, who are often exploited rather than supported. Low on seniority, they may receive the most difficult teaching assignments and then be subject to extra evaluation. Not surprisingly, 10.2 percent decide to leave teaching after only one year, another 12.9 percent leave after two years, and another 10.6 percent leave after three years (Bobbitt, Faupel, and Burns, 1991, pp. 4–5). In Britain the attrition rate has been lower, with 9.8 percent leaving within two years of qualifying (*The Supply of Teachers for the 1990s*, 1990, p. 10).

Whereas Peter was in charge of in-service programs at Garden Hill, Peter's exchange partner, Nancy Hughes, taught at a school where in-service programs were handled quite differently. As seventh-grade chair she determined some but not all in-service programs. Either the school principal, who sometimes consulted with teachers, or district-level administrators, who rarely consulted with teachers, determined the schoolwide programs. Nancy described a typical example from a neighboring school district: "At the beginning of the year they [the teachers] had four days [of in-service]. They had no choice at all. They had to be there and this was the agenda. And I know there was . . . lots of kicking and screaming: 'They could have done it in two days. They could have given us time in our classrooms. They could have given us time to look at materials.' You could go on and on" (Interview, November 28, 1990). The other U.S. teachers had similar feelings. All thought that if teachers had more say in planning their own in-service programs, the programs might be more useful.

Like Peter, the other British teachers' promotions gave them other responsibilities that were foreign to the U.S. teachers and delineated other roles the British promotion system supported. Gillian Hargrove was Head of Communications, assuming responsibility for coordinating language policy and for all language teaching in the school, including foreign and community languages and English as a Second/Other Language (ESL). Philippa Furlong was Head of Drama and Second in Charge of English, and after the exchange year moved to another school to take a post as Head of English. As Head of Drama, Philippa was in charge of drama teaching in regular classes. Fiona Rodgers was Acting Deputy Head of English, and like Philippa, after the exchange moved on to another school to obtain a permanent promotion. As Deputy Head of English, Fiona was responsible for the school-based grading of the students' national examination folders, making sure the school grades were consistent with national standards, and for overseeing the curriculum of the examination courses at her school.

Part of Gillian's job in overseeing ESL teaching was to organize support for ESL students, all of whom were integrated into regular classes. In England most ESL teaching is done through a system that supports students with individualized help as they participate in regular classes. In contrast to the United States, after their initial entry into the country, there are very few special classes in English for them. Even when such classes exist, students spend only a short time in them before joining the "mainstream" class (see McKay and Freedman, 1990). In the United States, some schools provide special ESL classes, while others provide no special help. The system relies on specialized ESL teachers who teach their own classes. There is no room in this organization for a consulting teacher to work with other classroom teachers or with students in their classes. Gillian's work with foreign language teaching led her to collaborate with teachers of all the languages her school offered: French, Greek, Turkish, Gujerati, and soon, if there was enough student demand and available staff, Bengali.

As Head of Drama and Second in Charge of English at her school, Philippa provided drama support for classroom teachers by advising them on ways of using drama in their teaching. Drama is more highly valued in the regular English curriculum in Britain than in the United States and is normally an integral part of all English classes. In the United States, drama, if offered, is, like creative writing and ESL, handled by a specialist within the confines of a self-contained classroom. Philippa's job, like Gillian's, fit into the British tradition of having specialist teachers, but it was not confined to teaching specialty classes. As Head of Drama Philippa also regularly produced plays and musicals for her school, organized theater visits, and worked with community theater groups.

While Fiona Rodgers was Acting Deputy Head of English, filling in for another teacher on maternity leave, she coordinated the national examination courses in literature for both the GCSE and A levels. For the GCSE courses Fiona supervised the grading of her school's examination folders, completed all administrative paperwork, acted as liaison between the examination board and her school, and held meetings for the GCSE literature teachers. For the A levels she performed similar duties. In addition to calibrating the scoring of the A-level examination folders at her school with national standards, she sat on the review panel which set national A-level literature standards.

In addition to these regular jobs, all four British teachers participated in some extra-school professional work. All were active in
citywide and sometimes national professional circles. Like Peter,
Fiona had served on important LATE committees, some with a national focus, and Gillian had been an officer in that organization.
Philippa was active in citywide drama circles. These activities, although professionally important, were necessarily limited, given the
school-based activities that consumed most of their professional time
and energy.

The professional situation for the U.S. teachers was strikingly different from that in Britain. Because there was no school-based system
of promotions, the U.S. teachers depended on professional networks
outside their schools for supplementary financial compensation and
professional recognition. Through these networks, all the U.S. teachers organized and/or gave workshops for other teachers and participated in professional organizations. Although all the U.S. teachers
used their professional involvement to improve their own teaching
and in some cases even shared some of their knowledge informally
with other teachers at their schools, the schools provided no institutionalized way for them to share their expertise with their peers.

While Carol Mather conducted workshops on women's studies, the
other U.S. teachers, Nancy Hughes, Ann Powers, and Bridget Franklin, were teacher-consultants for the Bay Area Writing Project
(BAWP). In this capacity they provided in-service programs for teachers at distant school sites or in distant districts. The programs were
made up of a series of five to ten workshops, all focusing on a coherent
topic such as writing across the curriculum, writing assessment, or
process approaches to teaching writing. As teacher-consultants, they
led individual workshops within the series. All three also planned and
coordinated these in-service programs—selecting the teacher consult-
ants; attending all sessions; helping the participants weave the threads
into a greater whole; critically assessing the series, including the success of the individual presenters; and planning follow-up programs
upon request. After the exchange year, Ann and Bridget were selected
by BAWP to lead teachers doing classroom research. Ironically, these
workshops and other professional efforts were appreciated more by
the greater Bay Area professional community than by officials or
colleagues at their respective schools. These professional activities also
took these teachers away from their classrooms. Their travel to distant

school sites, and sometimes to national meetings, often created resentment at their schools because they had to miss class.

With a similar lack of local recognition and local benefit, the U.S. teachers participated in professional organizations at the state and national levels. Bridget, Ann, and Carol gave speeches at meetings, and Nancy worked on several district-level curriculum committees and was active in the "State-of-the-Art Middle School Program," a California project that had selected Nancy's Central Middle School as one of the one hundred participating schools.

Like Carol, Ann and Bridget, who both taught in the Richmond Unified School District, also took advantage of the state of California's Mentor Teacher Program. The Mentor Program was specifically designed to make up for the lack of a professional ladder for U.S. teachers. However, as was the case for Carol, their experiences and the philosophy of the program fell far short of those in the British promotion system. When the California Legislature established the program, the goal was explicit:

> The Legislature recognizes that the classroom is the center of teaching reward and satisfaction. However, the Legislature finds that many potentially effective teachers leave the teaching profession because it does not offer them support, assistance, recognition, and career opportunities that they need.
>
> It is the intent of the Legislature in the enactment of this article to encourage teachers currently employed in the public school system to continue to pursue excellence within their profession, to provide incentives to teachers of demonstrated ability and expertise to remain in the public school system, and to restore the teaching profession to its position of primary importance within the structure of the state educational system. (California Education Code, Article 4. California Mentor Teacher Program, 44490)

Specific criteria are set locally and applications are judged by local teachers and administrators. For Carol's award the San Francisco Unified School District required her to conceptualize an "Action Plan" that would identify proposed service with a balance among the following areas:

- assistance to new teachers or experienced teachers
- staff and curriculum development

- mentor teacher professional development (*SFUSD Mentor Teacher Handbook,* 1991, p. 6)

In addition, Carol was required to donate "180 hours of service per year in the three areas of duties and responsibilities . . . These hours of service are in addition to the mentor teachers' full time, regular assignment" (*SFUSD Mentor Teacher Handbook,* 1991, p. 6). Carol's individual proposal was to work on curriculum in women's studies with teachers across the city, not specifically at her own school.

In the Richmond Unified School District, Ann and Bridget could apply to work either on a self-initiated project, as in the San Francisco model, or on a project predefined by the district. Half of Richmond's awards go to each type of application. The predefined awards for 1991 included typical activities: developing curriculum at the district level in math and science, working at the teacher's school site in four elementary schools only, or providing workshops at schools beyond one's own "in areas such as classroom management, assertive discipline, lesson planning, cultural diversity, instructional materials, organization, etc." (Richmond Unified School District, Mentor Teacher Announcement, September 20, 1991). At the elementary level, where teachers could focus on their own schools, the district office suggested projects that could easily be handled by paraprofessionals and that did not remotely relate to professional mentoring or to building stronger academic programs in the school. For example, the district suggested that school site mentors might engage in

- Supervising after-school dismissal if such duty is over and above what other teachers are assigned
- Scheduling yard duty, prep, library, music, computers and other scheduled teacher activities
- Supervising the lunch room (optional)
- Coordinating duties of aides, yard supervisors, volunteers, etc.
- Coordinating testing (Richmond Unified School District, Memo, September 7, 1991)

Clearly the district's vision of how to use teachers' talents productively seems clouded.

In this context, both Bridget and Ann applied for self-initiated projects, and both attracted some support and involvement from teachers at their schools. Bridget led an ongoing workshop for district teachers that examined research on at-risk youth. Eight teachers participated, four from her school, Los Padres, and four from another district high school. In 1991 Bridget received a second award to lead workshops in the district on productive uses of talk in the classroom. Ann also received two awards. Her first, in 1987, focused on writing across the curriculum. She worked with teachers across disciplines on integrating writing into their teaching both at her school, Costa Mesa, and in the district. For the first districtwide workshops, thirty teachers participated, five of them from Costa Mesa. The follow-up workshops consisted of only Costa Mesa teachers. Ann's second mentor project focused on a cadre of student writing coaches, both juniors and seniors, whom she had trained to guide and assist freshman and sophomore writers. In groups of ten or more, they went into classes to help younger students with drafts of their writing before the teacher evaluated them. Besides giving an oral response, the writing coaches provided written comments on drafts and helped with editing. For her project Ann involved students from the Costa Mesa Write Team in helping teach twenty-five teachers from other schools who were interested in establishing coaching programs.

Although the Mentor Teacher Program officially augmented the U.S. teachers' professional opportunities, the temporary professional functions of the mentor teachers were not equivalent to the permanent posts of the British teachers. According to Bridget, with few exceptions most of the mentor awards in her district have contributed little to academic programs: "Most produce a report or curriculum guide that's useless because there's no context for them. They're produced in isolation. You just throw them out. They're worthless" (Interview, December 17, 1991). In spite of the lack of institutional support for U.S. teachers to improve the academic programs at their schools, all were involved in activities that contributed to their schools' growth. Most volunteered their time to improve school programs, but with no official role they had little power to make major changes. Carol's leadership role in Webster's GATE program and in gifted education outside her school fell into this category. Nancy, as seventh-grade chair, received a small stipend for some administrative responsibilities that directly affected her school. Similarly, Ann contributed as department chair, but since she received no compensation in either time or money, her duties were limited, and she received little recognition. Both Bridget and Ann, through their own choice, used their mentor awards to stimulate school-based change.[7]

In reflecting on the greater integration and recognition of professional activities in British schools, Nancy remarked:

> I wish something like that would begin to happen. You know we've talked about this before. Because in this country there's no place for a teacher to go except for out of the classroom and into administration, so you have a dichotomy. You don't have a union of, of you don't validate good teaching in this country. The bottom line is if you do a good job in the classroom, so what . . . They can kick and scream about why they don't have teachers in this country. They're running out of teachers. Who in their right mind is going to go and stay in the classroom and never be acknowledged for your ability to teach. It's very rare. I mean you have to get out. (Interview, November 28, 1990)

The Schools and Classes

Many of the differences in the teachers' work lives were tied to differences in their schools and their classes. Descriptions of Peter Ross's Garden Hill Community School and Carol Mather's Webster Middle School, and of the places of their exchange classes within their schools, illustrate a number of important contrasts in the schools in the two countries.

Garden Hill Community School and Peter Ross's Class

Garden Hill, with approximately nine hundred pupils, enrolls students in Forms 1 through Upper Sixth (the equivalent of U.S. grades 6–12). It is located in a working-class residential and commercial neighborhood in an eastern London borough. The nearby dwellings, in which many of Peter's students lived, are mostly small row houses built eighty to a hundred years ago, nearly all of them modified and modernized in the past two decades. There are also some 1960s vintage "tower blocks" (apartment buildings of more than twenty floors). The borough is industrial as well as residential and is laced with major highways to the eastern counties and with railways and railway yards. There are small factories and industrial enterprises near the railways and main roads. The borough's southern boundary is the river Thames, and it includes an area that was once a major part of the port of London and had large factories, electric power stations, and coal and gas manufacturing plants nearby. Nearly all these enterprises, including the docks, are now semiderelict; the port of London is at Tilbury, about thirty miles down the river. The dock area was being redeveloped for housing, leisure activities, shopping malls, commercial office buildings in the American style, and an airport for executive jets and short-haul commercial flights.

Built in the late 1960s of red brick, Garden Hill Community School is conspicuous for its newness in relation to the surrounding row houses and commercial buildings. The school is on a relatively small site beside the busy main line railway and not far from two major roads. Ringed by high cyclone fences, the Garden Hill grounds are mostly concrete, with very little grass. The school has an asphalt playground with lines marked for tennis, netball (a game similar to basketball), and rounders (a game similar to baseball). A second playground, called a "dry play," is used mainly for cricket and football (soccer). There is a small grassy area at the back of the main building. The playgrounds are nowhere near as large as those at Central Middle School, where Nancy, Peter's exchange partner, taught. After seeing the pictures of Nancy's school, Charlie, one of Peter's students, wrote to the U.S. class, "Your school looks alot more Bigger then our school." Still, Garden Hill students had a certain pride in their school in spite of the obvious limitations of the grounds.

The main Garden Hill building is three stories built around an interior assembly hall and stage. One inside wall is covered by a huge and colorful jungle mural painted by the students. Having seen pictures of Garden Hill in one of the exchange packages, Quirk, one of Nancy's students, noted that from his vantage point it "seemed like they were more into arts and crafts than we are here, which I wish we were, 'cause I am really interested in that stuff . . . They had huge things on the walls or all over the place, or things that people had done like murals and stuff and lots of art classes and stuff from what I saw" (Interview, March 29, 1988).

Peter's office was in a special annex separate from the main building. This annex contained the modern language department, the Sixth Form classrooms, and the Sixth Form student lounge. In British schools pupils in the Lower and Upper Sixth Forms, the last two years of secondary school, generally have special privileges that may include some separate facilities and a lounge, called the "Sixth Form common room." They may also have specially designated study areas as well as a library, because it is quite usual for sixth form students to have individualized timetables with several possible "study periods," during which they work unsupervised on class assignments.

Garden Hill had the special status of being a "community school." In England, the idea of the community school came about in the 1970s when a number of Local Education Authorities and some of their schools set out to make strong links between those schools and the public they served. The borough took on the idea in the 1980s. A community school receives extra funding to extend its activities and services. It also strives to be open to the community, including parents and others, with signs to welcome visitors in several languages. Garden Hill forged community links first of all by setting aside two community rooms in the school building where classes are held during the day for members of the community. In addition, regular classes for the GCSE and for A levels are open to community members. In the evenings the entire school can be used by and for the community either for classes or for meetings of community organizations. Garden Hill also housed a nursery where parents could bring their preschool age children when they attended class or when they needed child care for personal purposes. The nursery, supported by community funding, was free. Garden Hill also strived to build its regular curriculum around community needs, but Peter felt that this aspect of Garden Hill's efforts had been only partially achieved.

Garden Hill's nine hundred students were subdivided into smaller academic units as part of the British system of "pastoral care." "Pastoral" in the British system is complementary to "academic" and focuses attention on the students' personal welfare in the school setting. The first subdivisions were into "year groups" and then, within each year, into five "tutor groups," which remained intact across the students' first five years of secondary school. A teacher designated "head of year" looked after the year group for all five years of secondary school, and another teacher, a "form tutor," was assigned to each tutor group. The year groups met once a week for twenty-five minutes, and the tutor groups met several times a week. Students took most of their classes with their same tutor group for their first three years. The students in Peter's exchange class, then, were in the same tutor group. Since students at Garden Hill were not grouped by ability, the exchange class consisted of learners of mixed abilities.

At Garden Hill it was common for subject matter teachers to continue with the same class for several years. Peter was in his third year with the exchange class, having started teaching them English when they entered Garden Hill in Form 1. He looked forward to teaching them for another two years, until they completed Form 5 and their GCSE course.

Peter's brightly lit classroom was located on the ground floor of the main building. Student writing from all of Peter's classes was displayed on bulletin boards alongside the writing and photographs received from Nancy's class. As Figure 3.1 shows, students in his

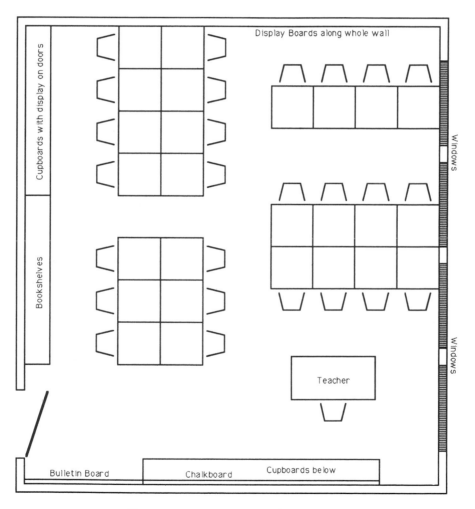

Figure 3.1 Peter Ross's Classroom

exchange class sat at tables, not at individual desks. They chose their own table groups, which most often resulted in their sitting with their friends. There was little change in who sat where from one day to the next and often from one year to the next. This room arrangement was meant to promote student talk and allow for easy and natural group work.

During the exchange year Peter experienced some shifts in class enrollment. He began the year with twenty-nine students and ended with twenty-six. Six students left the group and three joined. Most who came and went were from East Asian immigrant groups. At the end of the year, eleven of Peter's twenty-six students, or 42 percent, were white, and twelve, or 46 percent, were bilingual students from South Asian countries, mainly India and Bangladesh. There was one student from a Greek family and two black students, one from a bilingual Nigerian family and the other African-Caribbean. The bilingual students ranged from recent arrivals in England with limited proficiency in English to those who were born in England, had grown up with two languages, and were fully literate in English. Peter's class did not reflect the school population well in that it contained proportionately more white students (42 percent) than the school (19 percent), fewer Asian students (46 percent) than the school (65 percent), and fewer students of African origin (8 percent) than the school (15 percent). Only 1 percent of the school's enrollment consisted of students from Greece, Turkey, or Cyprus.

Peter started the year with nineteen boys and ten girls and ended with a similar ratio. This gender imbalance was probably related to the fact that many South Asian families, who lived nearby, preferred to send their daughters to the two all-girls' schools in the neighborhood. In England there has long been a system of parental choice in the state-supported schools. The choices include single or mixed gender schools, schools with and without religious affiliations, and schools in or outside one's neighborhood.

Webster Middle School and Carol Mather's Class

Webster Middle School for grades 6–8 had a school population of 850 (close in size to the 900 enrolled at Peter's Garden Hill, which housed the equivalent of grades 6–12). Located near the center of San Francisco, Webster is surrounded by four diverse neighborhoods that feed in a nearly complete cross section of the city's population. An area to one side is home to the largest Chicano/Latino community in the San Francisco Bay area, while on another side is a primarily African American working-class area. Webster is also bordered by one of the largest gay communities in the city, with singles and families living there as well. On its remaining border is a middle-class, mostly white, family area. In all of these neighborhoods, corner shops and restaurants abound, and shopping streets and commercial areas are mixed with housing.

Built in the late 1920s, Webster features a Spanish style of architecture prevalent in California. Its three stories of creamy stucco with floral insets are covered by a terra-cotta tile roof, and painted Spanish tiles decorate the facade. A concrete play area behind the school merges with the playground of a neighboring elementary school, the two separated only by a fence. Webster faces a busy city street.

Upon entering the school building, one meets a calm and quiet unusual in city schools. Even when children change classes, the principal monitors the halls to ensure silence. The silence is modulated with the periodic muted murmurs of ongoing teaching and learning inside classrooms, which, on the whole, are quiet places. In addition to the GATE program in which Carol did all of her teaching, Webster had a federally funded program (Chapter 2) for students scoring below the fiftieth percentile on tests in reading and math; bilingual programs in Spanish, Chinese, and Tagalog; programs in English as a Second Language; and a Special Education program.

Carol Mather's classroom, on the second floor in the back of the building, had a number of unusual features. Figure 3.2 shows the layout. Formerly a library, the spacious, open room was shared by Carol's classes and a class for students designated as having learning difficulties in reading, writing, and mathematics. No walls separated the two classes, and generally Carol and Marsha, the other teacher, taught simultaneously. Noise was an obvious concern. Carol and Marsha had to coordinate their schedules so that while one was lecturing or having another potentially noisy lesson, the other was supervising a quiet activity, such as reading time. Since the converted library was large, the two teachers were able to keep a fair amount of space between their classes, which met at either end of the room. The meeting areas were separated by a couch, bookshelves, and a round table arranged to keep the students out of each other's line of vision.

Carol's students sat at tables of four, arranged in four rows of two

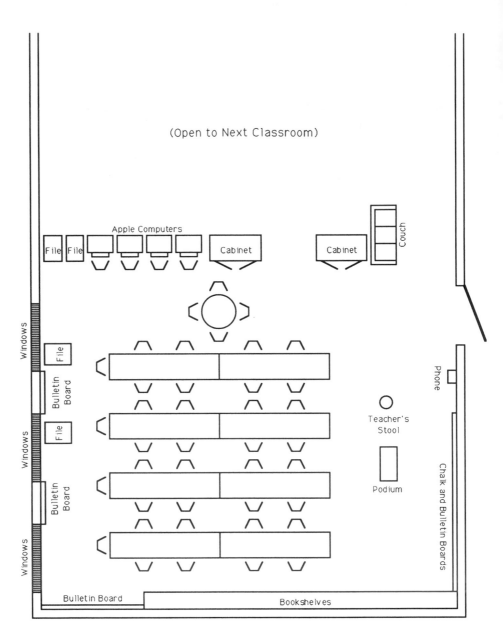

Figure 3.2 Carol Mather's Classroom

tables each, and faced one another rather than the front of the room where Carol often stood. This arrangement promoted more student talk than rows of desks facing the front would have, but it did not provide the small working-group feel that Peter's separated tables promoted.

Behind the rows of student tables a bank of windows, made of a cloudy, nonbreakable glass, looked out from the back of the school on the hills of the city and the backs of neighborhood houses. From these windows Carol could see the hospital in which she was born and the house in which she was raised.

Although Carol's sixth-grade exchange class was labeled GATE, almost half of the students had not been officially designated as gifted by the school district.[8] These nondesignated students were admitted into the GATE program because of parental pressure or, if they came from private schools, because they had been recommended by a teacher although not officially tested by the school district or recommended by a district teacher. The GATE staff also invited some students, especially ethnic minorities, into the program on a trial basis because the staff thought these students would do well. Some students in the class were there for no discernable academic reason but because it fit their schedule or they had been placed there in error.

Carol's class had the highest enrollment of all those involved in the exchange, a stable thirty-seven students across the entire school year. Since GATE parents could choose programs in schools outside their neighborhood, half of Carol's exchange class came from other parts of San Francisco. Students who were not in the GATE program, however, did not have a choice of schools; they were expected to attend the school in their neighborhood. This choice program skewed the ethnic composition of Carol's class in favor of students from white, middle-class families (56 percent in her GATE exchange class as compared to 18 percent for the school). The exchange class was also 25 percent Chicano/Latino, slightly below the school population of 35 percent; 14 percent African American, just below the 18 percent for the school; and 6 percent Asian, much lower than the 30 percent for the school.

Themes across the Exchanges

Just as Garden Hill Community School and Webster Middle School and the classes within them are organized somewhat differently, so are the other British and U.S. schools and classes. All four British schools were structured to create close whole-school learning communities that integrated diverse students from diverse backgrounds while honoring, promoting, and maintaining the students' specific cultural identities.[9] The U.S. schools, however, had no systematic approach to handling diversity; teachers were essentially on their own.

In addition, a strong philosophy of mixed-ability teaching dominated the British schools, while three of the four U.S. schools tracked students by ability. Initially, we tried to locate mixed-ability classes for the U.S. study but could find only one, since secondary schools in the San Francisco area are highly tracked.

During the exchange year, Gillian Hargrove's and Philippa Furlong's Form 4 (grade 9) classes were preparing for the British national examinations. These examinations controlled the classes' curriculum. They also determined what opportunities for higher education, if any, would be available to many British students. The U.S. students in Ann Powers's and Bridget Franklin's classes had no equivalent experiences.

Before I look at these three aspects of the educational system in the two countries in more depth, I want to provide more details about the enrollment patterns of the exchange schools and classrooms and more background about the ethnically and intellectually diverse groups of learners who participated in this study.

Enrollment Patterns

Table 3.4 summarizes the ethnic makeup of the exchange classes and the schools in which they were situated. We worked in urban schools as much as possible, in areas with high concentrations of students of color from working-class backgrounds. These schools were not selected to be representative of all schools in either country. Rather, they were selected because they are typical of those schools in both countries that are facing daunting challenges. In all the exchange classes except the single mixed-ability class in the United States, at least half of the students were identified by their schools as members of "ethnic minorities."

At the same time, however, those belonging to the dominant ethnic groups were different in each country. In Britain, the Asians came mostly from Bangladesh and the Indian subcontinent, and African-origin students' families originally came from the Caribbean and Africa. In the United States, Asians came mostly from China, Japan, and the Philippines, and most of the blacks were African American

Table 3.4 School and class ethnic percentages

		Webster M.S. (Mather) Broadbent (Rodgers)		Central M.S. (Hughes) Garden Hill (Ross)		Costa Mesa H.S. (Powers) Manderley Grove (Hargrove)		Los Padres H.S. (Franklin) Hampden Jones (Furlong)	
		School	Class	School	Class	School	Class	School	Class
	US	(N = 850)	(N = 37)	(N = 586)	(N = 30)	(N = 1,486)	(N = 27)	(N = 1,500)	(N = 19)
	GB	(N = 1,200)	(N = 25)	(N = 900)	(N = 26)	(N = 900)	(N = 17)	(N = 1,100)	(N = 22)
Ethnic group[a]									
African American/African Caribbean/other African origin	US	18	14	12	10	30	37	46	68
	GB	30	24	15	8	50	53	43	38
Asian[b] and Asian subcontinent	US	30	6	20	8	0	0	0	0
	GB	15	16	65	46	0	0	12	14
Chicano/Latino	US	35	25	5	10	10	15	4	11
	GB	0	0	0	0	0	0	0	0
Greek/Turkish/Cypriot	US	0	0	0	0	0	0	0	0
	GB	25	20	1	4	25	18	0	0
Other white	US	18	56	63	73	60	48	50	21
	GB	30	40	19	42	25	29	45	48

a. Different reporting methods in the two countries reflect different immigration patterns; therefore, no Chicano/Latinos are reported for British schools, no Greek/Turkish/Cypriots are reported for U.S. schools, and the label Asian refers to different Asian groups in the two countries, as does the label African origin. In addition, British schools do not always keep statistics about schoolwide ethnic origins. Therefore, in some cases, British school figures are estimates provided by the teachers.

b. Powers and Franklin's school district does not report Asians separately but instead groups them with Chicano/Latinos.

and were not immigrants. In addition, in some British schools there were also sizable numbers of Greeks, Turks, and Cypriots, while in the U.S. schools there were sizable numbers of Latinos and Chicanos.

Besides these cross-national differences in ethnic groups, the schools in each country were characterized by different enrollment patterns. In Britain, Peter's Garden Hill had fewer black students than the other three schools, and Fiona's Broadbent had fewer than Gillian's Manderley Grove and Philippa's Hampden Jones. The Asian population was greatest at Garden Hill, while only Broadbent and Manderley Grove had a sizable representation of Greeks, Turks, and Cypriots. In the United States, the dominant ethnic group at Ann's Costa Mesa High School and at Bridget's Los Padres High School was black, at Webster Middle School there were two dominant ethnic groups, Asians and Chicano/Latinos, and at Nancy's Central Middle School the dominant ethnic group was Asian. In all cases other groups were also represented. Central Middle School and Costa Mesa High School both had white populations of about 60 percent; at Costa Mesa, most of the whites came from low-income, working-class backgrounds, while the whites at Central were more often middle class.

As Peter's and Carol's experiences show, the exchange classes did not always perfectly represent the ethnic makeup of their schools. The British mixed-ability philosophy included balancing classes in every respect. For the most part, the exchange classes reflected school philosophies, Peter's class being the only real exception. It is not surprising that disproportionate numbers of white students populated Carol's highest tracked class and that disproportionate numbers of nonwhites populated Bridget's and Ann's classes, which were the lowest tracks. Nancy Hughes's mixed-ability class also had a higher proportion of white students than her school. Theoretically, her class should have reflected the demographics of her school; however, during the year the exchange took place, the district allowed parents to request teachers, and white, middle-class parents made the largest number of requests. Naturally, the classes of a popular teacher like Nancy filled quickly, with the result that a disproportionate number of her students came from white, middle-class homes. The numbers might have been even higher, but the district, in an effort to prevent such "de facto" ability grouping and segregation, allowed only fifteen parental requests for a given teacher. After these requests had been honored, the counselors and teachers tried to balance the classes with students of mixed backgrounds and abilities. Beginning in 1990–

1991, two years after the exchange year, the district stopped accepting parental requests, and classes began to reflect the school population.

Community Structures

"If you want something to happen in a large organisation, you must structure it to happen." (Northumberland Park *Teachers' Guide*, 1986, p. 4)

The British schools that participated in the exchanges were deliberately structured to support teachers in creating close classroom communities. These community structures helped the teachers to learn about their students' academic and social needs and to design ways of meeting them. All the schools featured (a) subdivisions into smaller working units; (b) small class and school size; (c) long spans of time for teachers to work with the same group of students; (d) teachers' communities (classrooms were arranged in discipline-based clusters and there were substantive department meetings); (e) students' classroom communities (students sat at tables with four to six of their friends); and (f) in two cases, community schools. For the most part, the U.S. schools did not support such structures. In the main, community-building activities in the U.S. schools were purely social, focusing on sports events or school dances. Nevertheless, all of the U.S. exchange teachers worked to create strong classroom communities and through their efforts managed to build supporting structures to varying degrees.

Subdivisions within the Schools. To help teachers get to know their students, all the British schools, like Garden Hill, had systems of pastoral care that involved the creation of smaller units by year and then tutor groups within each year. At Manderley Grove, where Gillian Hargrove taught, the school was also divided into four "houses," each of which included students across age groups; students stayed in the same house from their first through their fifth year of secondary school. K.C., in a letter to the U.S. exchange class, explained the system:

> I suppose you're wondering why Crowland Building is also known as the Yellow House Building? Well, it's a part of our grouping system.
> We have what is called a House System. Four Houses or Groups of pupils. (and staff) Each have a colour.

Yellow, (that's mine) Green, (our rivals) Red and Blue. Then, all the staff and pupils are divided within the Houses. I'll take Yellow House as an example:

First. The whole group of kids, from eleven to sixteen years are split right down the middle, creating the first state of classes. Classes one and two. Then it is decided what House or colour, they are going to be. In this case, Yellow.

Then finally, according to the age of the pupils, they are set into years. Elevens and Twelves are first years. Thirteens are second years. Third years are Fourteen, and Fourth years are Fifteen, and the sixteen year olds are in the Fifth year.

I am a fourth year in class one of Yellow House. That's what the 4Y1 at the beginning of the letter means. Fourth year, Yellow House, class one.

I don't know what your system is. So would you tell me please? It would be so helpful!

In the United States pastoral care was left to the school counselor and to individual classroom teachers, who sometimes voluntarily took on pastoral-type duties. The U.S. pastoral focus was more on helping individual students with individual problems than on building secure and supportive learning communities. None of the U.S. schools had formal schools-within-schools that kept smaller groups of students together for academic and social enrichment. The closest equivalent was the GATE program at Webster, which, however, provided only a subset of the most academically talented students with a smaller community. GATE students took most of their classes with their fellow GATE students, and usually only six teachers at the school taught in the GATE program. Those teachers often saw students in more than one class over their three years at Webster, and students saw one another in their different classes.

Class and School Size. Although class size did not differ from one country to the next according to the national questionnaires, it did differ for the teachers in the exchanges: the U.S. teachers had significantly higher enrollments than their British counterparts. Extrapolated from Table 3.4, the average British class size was 22.5 (all teachers reported that the size of their exchange classes was normal). By contrast, the average U.S. class size was 28.25 (Bridget and Ann reported abnormally small groups).

As for school size, on average U.S. middle schools, grades 6 through

8 or the equivalent of the first three forms of the British secondary
school, are smaller than U.S. high schools and provide a more pro-
tected environment. However, Garden Hill in Britain, which housed
nine hundred students in the equivalent of grades 6 through 12, was
not much larger than Webster Middle School with its 850 students.
None of the British secondary schools was as large as either of the
U.S. high schools (see Table 3.4).

Keeping Classes across the Years. The national questionnaires showed
that it was normal for British secondary teachers to keep the same
group of students for more than one year. This was true for the British
exchange teachers as well. Just as Peter Ross was in his third year
with his Form 3 class, Philippa Furlong was working with her Form
4 class for the fourth year running. Both Peter and Philippa would
keep their groups through Form 5, for a total of five years with the
same class. Gillian Hargrove was in her first year with her Form 4
exchange class but would continue to teach them throughout the
two-year examination course. At Broadbent, Fiona Rodgers was in
her first year with her Form 2 class. She had taken over from a new
teacher who, in his first year, found the class difficult to handle and
thought the students would benefit from a change of teachers. Fiona
taught this same group for another year after the exchange was over
and then had to turn them over to another teacher when she took a
maternity leave.

In the U.S. schools, teachers normally kept the same group for one
year only. Carol Mather did see some of her students again as they
passed through varied elective blocks in the seventh and eighth grade,
but not as a class group. Ann Powers, taking note of the British
example, decided she wanted to keep her exchange class for a second
year and managed to persuade Costa Mesa's administrators to make
the complex scheduling arrangements that would allow her to do so.
She has written about the enormous progress she was able to make
with these students during her second year with them (see Reed, in
press).

It is notable that both Carol Mather and Nancy Hughes had concentrated time with their students. As middle school teachers, they
taught their exchange class for a three-period morning block. This
schedule was meant to help ease the students' transition from elementary school, where the same teacher has the same group all day, to
middle school, where students change teachers and are in class with

a new group of students every hour (see Freedman and McLeod, 1988).

Teachers' Communities. In many ways, the physical layout at Garden Hill—Peter's office was in a different building from his classroom—was unusual. At the other British schools, the teachers' classrooms were mostly clustered in suites alongside other members of their departments and close to the department offices and libraries. This physical clustering of discipline-based teachers was done deliberately to facilitate communication.

At all four British schools, department meetings were substantive events where curriculum was discussed and debated and where theoretical orientations and the needs of various students were considered. This structuring of professional collegiality supported teachers' efforts in working with their students.

In some ways, the PACT program (see note 7) at Los Padres High School provided Bridget Franklin and her colleagues with similar intellectual support. In particular, the collaborative research project focused the team on the needs of low-achieving students and their progress. At PACT meetings also, teachers had a chance to discuss their students and the issues important in teaching them. The other U.S. teachers had close colleagues and important collegial conversations, but their efforts were not formally supported at the schoolwide level.

Students' Communities. A look at the seating charts for the different classrooms reveals a fairly standard seating arrangement for British students (see Figures 3.1, 3.3, 3.4, and 3.5). Peter's students sat with their friends, sometimes the same ones from one year to the next, and so did the students in the other British exchange classes. They also saw these same friends in other classes throughout the day, since they were in the same tutor group. The table groups were designed to help the students feel comfortable seeking and receiving academic help from their tablemates.

In the United States the teachers also arranged their classrooms to stimulate student talk, but these arrangements showed more variation: Carol Mather's students faced one another rather than the front of the room (see Figure 3.2), Ann Powers's classroom looked much like those of her British counterparts (Figure 3.6), and the desks in Nancy Hughes's and Bridget Franklin's classrooms provided for fluid movement (Figures 3.7 and 3.8). With the exception of Ann's table

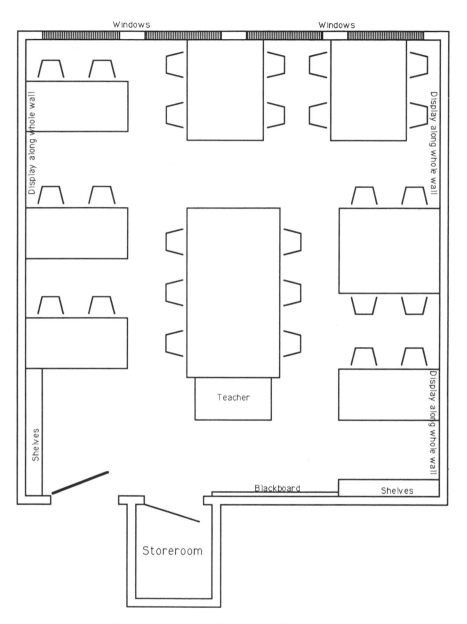

Figure 3.3 Fiona Rodgers's Classroom

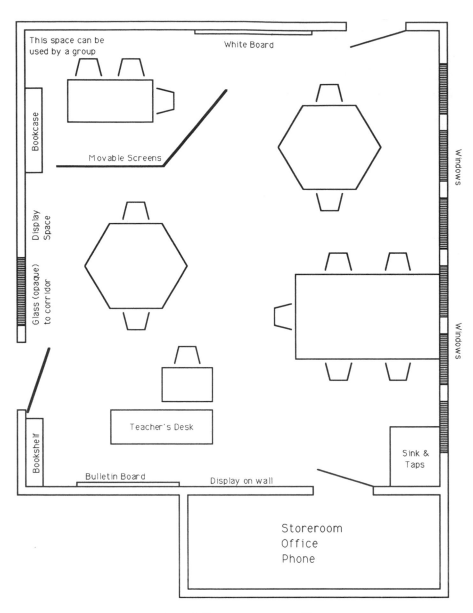

Figure 3.4 Gillian Hargrove's Classroom

groups, the other U.S. teachers could and did arrange the seating to accommodate up-front teaching as well as small group talk. At the same time, however, although some of the students might have known one another socially, they did not spend consecutive years together in all their classes.

Community Schools. Like Garden Hill, Manderley Grove, where Gillian Hargrove taught, was also a community school. Community school structures were meant to help the teaching staff get to know

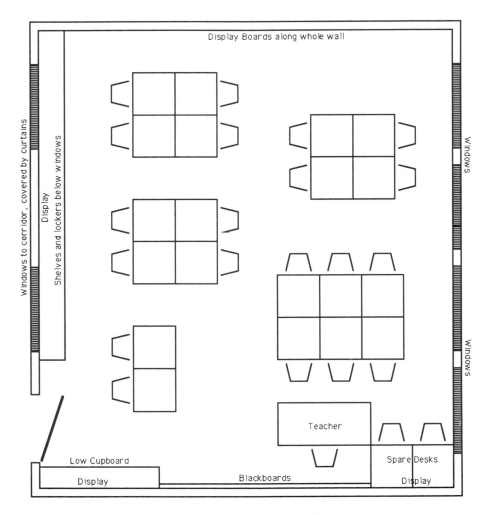

Figure 3.5 Philippa Furlong's Classroom

their students in the broadest sense. At Garden Hill and Manderley Grove, the families of students from diverse backgrounds gathered routinely at the school site for many activities, which promoted a close, familylike atmosphere. Both schools found that their community orientation helped with dropout and attendance problems, and with opportunities for ongoing interactions with community members, school staff learned about the needs of the varied communities their schools served. Besides making the schools comfortable gathering places for community members, the school staffs were responsible for designing programs that would appeal to the community. To create effective programs, the teachers built them from the base of their growing knowledge about the community. In this way, they got to know how their students' lives outside the classroom might impinge upon their learning in school. In the process, they also had natural opportunities to welcome their students' families into the educational process. When the Manderley Grove students wrote their first letters to their U.S. exchange class, some anticipated that the community school structure was unique to England and explained it to the U.S. students:

> You may wonder why we have the word community in it's name because the school is open to anybody and everybody. We have lots of different clubs after school. The school has a very friendly atmosphere, were the teachers are fair in most cases. (Leabow)

> You may have being wondering why the word "community" is in the title of my school. Even if you haven't I will still tell yhou. The reason is, people from outside school can come during and after school hours. There is a part of the school called the "Community Building". Kids from the school go there and hold clubs. As I said before, people outside school go there and hold pensioners clubs and mother and toddler clubs. (Deenie)

Ability Grouping

Another major contrast in the ways the two countries organize their schools centered on ability grouping or tracking policies. Three of the four U.S. classes tracked their students, while all the British classes were mixed ability. These grouping practices had implications for organizing instruction inside classrooms, a topic that I will explore in more detail in the next chapter.

As at Garden Hill, mixed-ability teaching was taken for granted at the three other British schools. It was considered neither remarkable nor a subject of debate. In fact, in recent years mixed-ability teaching has become institutionalized in many British schools, especially in the London area. The shift to mixed-ability teaching brought with it a major reorganization of the classroom to allow teachers to meet the needs of varied students at once. In the exchange classes in particular, instruction usually took place in a workshop atmosphere in which students did much of their writing in class and received help from their teacher and their peers as they needed it. Teachers rarely talked at length to the whole class; even discussions of literature took place most often within small table groups. Whole-class discussions were common only at the start and end of the lesson, as a framing device. In general, classrooms were filled with student talk as students worked together at their tables. If students completed work ahead of their peers, teachers assigned extra reading or writing while giving other students extra time to do their best job. Many British educators feel that this radical shift in classroom organization—away from structures dominated by teacher talk and away from requiring all students to engage in the same activities at the same time—has reformed teaching and learning at least as much as, if not more than, the change in ability grouping itself.

In the United States, Nancy Hughes and her fellow teachers at Central Middle School were pioneers in structuring classrooms for mixed-ability teaching. They had to feel their own way, quite unlike the British teachers, who over the years had worked out ways of organizing the classroom to accommodate students of varied abilities. In addition, community support for mixed-ability classes was not unanimous at Central, and Nancy's school labored under strong pressure, mostly from its middle-class parents, to place their children in the classes of particular teachers. By acceding to those requests, the school found itself inadvertently undermining its educational philosophy, something it took some time to discover and rectify. On the U.S. national scene community groups and some teacher groups may be resisting shifts to mixed-ability teaching precisely because a vision of classroom reorganization has not been coupled with calls for detracking. The British experience and Nancy's experiences at Central show how crucial it is that a school-level shift in tracking practices be accompanied by support for fundamental shifts at the classroom level.

In the three U.S. schools with tracked classes, the differing educa-

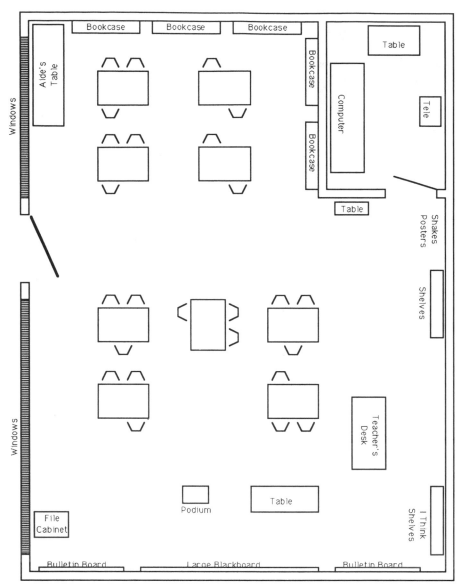

Posters of American Writers (along wall near top)

Figure 3.6 Ann Powers's Classroom

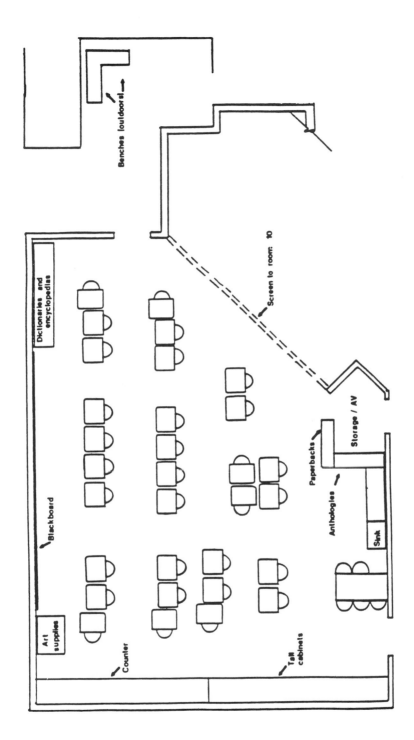

Figure 3.7 Nancy Hughes's Classroom
(figure prepared by Greenleaf, 1990)

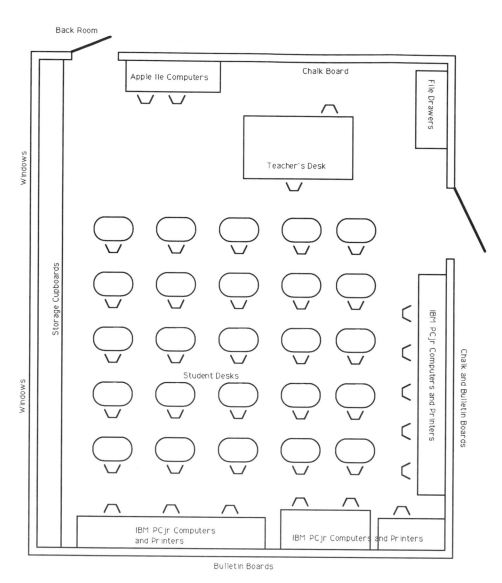

Figure 3.8 Bridget Franklin's Classroom

tional histories and experiences of the students, from one U.S. class to the next and compared to their British counterparts, emphasize the potentially deleterious effects of tracking, especially for students like those in Bridget Franklin's and Ann Powers's classes, who had spent year after year in the lowest tracks. The school system had few expectations for them as they amassed report cards and school records that carefully documented their history of school failure. Not coincidentally, they were largely students of color. When placed all together in one class, many subscribed to a peer culture that shunned education. Bridget and Ann faced the difficult challenge of inventing a productive classroom culture that would motivate these students and support their learning.

Because of Los Padres's PACT program, Bridget's students received more positive support outside her classroom than Ann's students did. Bridget, and many of her fellow teachers and administrators, did not consider her students as remedial or treat them as such. As Los Padres worked toward schoolwide reforms that would lead to mixed-ability classes, tracking labels began to lose their institutional meaning. A superb teacher, Ann expected her students to learn and did her best to teach them, but without such school-level support her task was more difficult. During the exchange year her students tended to play out their "remedial" roles with erratic attendance patterns and high attrition rates. During her second year with this same class, however, many of these counterproductive behaviors diminished.

The permutations of ability grouping in the four U.S. classrooms and how this contrasts with the British classes raise important issues for U.S. educators. The next few chapters will delve more deeply into the classrooms themselves to consider the differential effects of tracking for students labeled gifted versus those labeled remedial and which instructional contexts best meet the needs of all students in a mixed-ability setting.

The British National Examination System

The third major institutional contrast is the national examination system, which had long been in place in Great Britain but had no equivalent in the United States. Both Gillian Hargrove's and Philippa Furlong's students were in their first of two years of preparation for their GCSE examination. Their entire curriculum for the two years, the equivalent of grades 9 and 10, would focus on the examination syllabus. In their exchange classes everything they did had to move them toward taking and making their best mark on the examination. Both Manderley Grove and Hampden Jones subscribed to examinations that consisted of coursework only (portfolios) for the English language exam (speaking and writing) and the English literature exam. Some of the students took both exams; others took only the language exam. At the end of the two years, Philippa's and Gillian's students would present a portfolio containing a range of their best work in one or both areas and would receive a single letter grade for each portfolio they submitted. Their grades across their six or more different examination subjects (for example, besides English language and literature, such subjects as mathematics, geography, drama, Spanish, French, Russian, physics, chemistry, biology, and so on) would determine their future. Those with good results (about 30 percent of the test takers) continue in school to prepare for university or other postsecondary education, or leave with a fair chance of employment. Those with poor results generally leave school, though there is a growing tendency for them to return to try to improve their grades.

For the British students the pressure of preparing their examination folders in English was in the background of all they produced in class, including what they wrote for the exchange. At first, both Gillian and Philippa thought it would be possible to combine the exchange with the preparation of the coursework folders, but events during the year forced them both to modify this view. When the British students or their teachers had difficulty combining the exchange audience and the GCSE examiner audience, the high stakes of the exams necessarily gave the examiner audience priority. Their experiences showed that even well-designed examinations meant to encourage and flow from good instruction were restrictive in many ways. In the end, because the exams restricted the curriculum, they had some negative influences on the instructional program.

The examinations also created a national sorting mechanism, which effectively determines that only about 20 percent of students continue on in school and have a chance at university entrance. By contrast, even students in the lowest tracks in the United States are expected to stay in school until they are eighteen, and they have more opportunities to enter higher education than their British peers, even those in the lowest tracks.

Philippa's exchange partner, Bridget Franklin, speculated about the effects of the British examinations on the exchange when she summarized her feelings about the year: "I think there were some bugs, to tell you the truth, in this, because I really believe in exchanges, and I would like to get a really good exchange going, but we didn't get as much as we sent." It is important to note here that when Bridget remarked "we didn't get as much as we sent," she was comparing what her "remedial" students produced to the output of Philippa's mixed-ability class. Bridget continued: "it would be really wonderful if . . . you really could get a whole set of papers and get to know them as writers, real writers . . . I got the feeling . . . that they just kind of put other things in their folders [for the examiner], and they didn't send us those things or something, which was unfortunate" (Interview, December 13, 1988). In reflecting on her own year she says, "We were very lucky because we don't have those tests."

Issues to Explore

This chapter reveals significant differences between the working conditions and career opportunities available to teachers in Britain and in the United States. In many respects, the career ladders for British teachers and the kinds of responsibilities they are expected to assume would seem to support the conclusion that teaching is considered a more serious profession in Britain than in the United States.

In addition, the British teachers worked in contexts that supported the building of academic communities. U.S. schools focused on building social communities, something many of the British students we interviewed yearned for. They found cheerleaders, school sports competitions, and proms and other school dances all very romantic and were envious of these aspects of the U.S. school, just as they admired and lusted after the natural beauty and the good weather in California. What the contrast points out for U.S. educators, however, is the small amount of energy that these U.S. schools spent on building academic communities.

Another striking contrast between the British and U.S. schools was the implementation of mixed-ability grouping. The British experiences provide guidance to U.S. schools that are moving toward mixed-ability teaching, showing especially something of the kinds of classroom organizations that promote higher achievement for all students. This issue will be explored in more depth in the following chapters.

Problematic for the British classes was the national examination system, which interfered with Philippa's and Gillian's ability to engage their students in writing seriously for a foreign peer audience. Although the exams were not designed to constrain teachers and students in this way, in practice they did. The experiences in these two British examination classes raise questions for groups in the United States, such as the New Standards Project, which are calling for and working on developing a national system of perfomance-based examinations they hope will reform instruction in positive ways and raise instructional standards for all (Simmons and Resnick, 1993; Tucker, 1992). In these efforts, it will be important to track the actual effects of examinations (for example, see Loofbourrow, 1992). The experiences of the two examination classes will be explored further in Chapters 6 and 7.

Chapter **4**

↶ Sharing Responsibility, Releasing Control

Carol Mather, Fiona Rodgers

> I just hope it [the exchange] doesn't end, that's all. That we became good enough friends, enough that we won't have to just kind of have it be only in class and only for an assignment that we're writing to each other. (Elizabeth, Interview, March 24, 1988)

Like many of the students in Carol Mather's and Fiona Rodgers's classes, Elizabeth didn't want her writing for the exchange to end at the close of the school year. She felt that she had come to know the British students in Fiona Rodgers's class through their writing and that friendships had developed. She didn't want to lose her new friends. In both countries the students in this exchange showed enthusiasm, excitement, and good will toward one another.

In spite of this commonality, the exchange between Carol's and Fiona's students provides a close-up view of one of the major contrasts revealed by the questionnaires (Chapter 2): U.S. teachers emphasize the curriculum while British teachers emphasize student development.[1] The orientation to curriculum on the one hand and to development on the other emerges through two simultaneous analyses. The first focuses on the classrooms in which these adolescent writers develop their ideas and write. The second explores how particular students' social and academic needs are met as they acquire written language.[2]

On the surface, the classrooms of Carol Mather and Fiona Rodgers were similar. Alex McLeod and I saw no obvious differences in the teachers' pedagogical theories or philosophies and few differences in their students' work. In fact, the students' mutual enthusiasm proved to be the dominant theme. But at our last interview with Fiona a year after the writing exchanges, when we showed her our draft report stressing the two classes' similarities, she felt strongly that we had missed an important difference in how she and Carol approached teaching. Fiona saw her British curriculum as less fixed and therefore "more messy" than Carol's. These perceptions emerged during and after the exchange, when she and Carol became friends and spent time together in London and San Francisco. They naturally discussed their teaching. Through these conversations, Fiona's ongoing and regular communication with Carol, and her comparisons of the writing of Carol's students with that of her own, Fiona sensed this underlying distinction.[3] Her observations stimulated us to look more closely at the data from these two classes, and our reanalyses confirmed what she had observed. We found further that the focus on curriculum over development led to subtle but interesting differences in the students' writing.

Fiona accurately characterized how her teaching at Broadbent differed from Carol's at Webster: "I tend to work much more by a kind of negotiation." In essence, in addition to the cross-national writing exchange, Fiona created curriculum through a dynamic process of exchanging responsibilities with the students in her classroom. Fiona's curriculum evolved according to the developmental needs of her particular class. Over the course of the year, following the British emphasis on student development and having no feelings of obligation to particular curricular activities, Fiona helped her students assume increasing levels of responsibility for making classroom decisions. Her goal was to motivate students by allowing them to make choices that would inspire a strong commitment to their writing.

In spite of her approach, which valued the importance of creating sound curricular activities, Carol worked hard to make her assignment frames flexible enough to accommodate individual student interests. Like Fiona, she tried to help her students make personal connections to their writing. However, like the U.S. teachers who responded to the national surveys, she focused so much attention on curricular activities that Fiona considered her curriculum rigid. From her vantage point, Fiona thought Carol's students "all do the same thing." She perceived that Carol had her students write on the same topics at the same time and in similar ways. Carol's teaching seemed more preplanned than hers. But Carol felt that she shared a great deal of responsibility with her students.

In the end we found that Fiona and Carol both shared responsibilities with their students, but that Carol gave her students less say in structuring their curriculum. What the British teacher saw as teacher dominated, the U.S. teacher saw as a shared and interactive exchange. To understand both teachers' orientations requires looking closely to compare how they planned the writing exchange, their ability to account for their students' intellectual development given the differences in the support structures at their schools, and the writing activities their students engaged in.

Perspectives on Curriculum

Carol's students started each year by introducing themselves through "name papers" in which they reflected on how they got their names and nicknames and how they felt about them. Later, they made up "spooky tales" for a yearly Halloween contest, and in the spring they entered essays on "women in history" in the annual citywide National Organization for Women (NOW) essay contest, usually taking top prizes. When Carol agreed to be part of the writing exchange project, she wanted to maintain her tried-and-true activities and, where possible, to use them as part of the cross-national writing exchange. For the most part the writing exchange caused her to make few changes. As Carol explained: "I always start off my year with a names paper, as a way for the kids to get to know each other, because that's a good structured way to begin, to introduce the process. Of course, I was still open to what Fiona wanted to do, but to tell you the truth I don't think there's much that she sent me that has changed what I already did" (Interview, January 18, 1989).

Fiona had no set activities; nothing in the curriculum was pre-planned. Her theoretical framework told her that activities must be planned anew with each class to meet their particular needs. What she had was a general framework for her curriculum. She believed it important to foster "reading, writing, talking, listening, the basics of English," which she would "approach in a variety of ways across the year." She also noted, "I have certain things in my head about what I want to do, the kinds of learning experiences and books to discuss" (October 28, 1990). Fiona's general framework allowed her to incorporate Carol's preset activities as long as her students found them motivating. And her class did write name papers and women in history papers, which Carol initiated. In addition, at the end of the year when Fiona's students decided to write magazines, a number of them chose spooky stories as one of their magazine features. Ultimately, Fiona's decisions were based on her students' reactions to each proposed activity and to their suggestions for activities. Carol's students, however, did not feel it was appropriate to provide this level of input into their curriculum.

Perspectives on Student Development

Carol and Fiona both put a high priority on getting to know their students and accounting for their development, but they each learned about different aspects of their students' lives. With thirty-seven students in her class at Webster, Carol reported that those with very severe problems took precedence. To Carol, severe problems were life-threatening. In a recent academic year, for example, five of her students had attempted suicide. Since Carol found the counseling services at Webster inadequate, she spent substantial amounts of time supporting these students and their families and making the appropriate psychiatric referrals. Carol next concentrated on her "stars," who knew how to seek and get teacher attention, the ones she found "easy to get to know." She feared that she neglected many of the students that were in the middle but would have benefited greatly from additional support. She felt somewhat guilty about how hard it was for her to meet her own high standards for nourishing her students' intellectual development. She was deeply discouraged by the institutional difficulties she faced but still blamed herself whenever she knew her students were missing something.[4] Carol's guilt and regret came out most strongly when she expressed nervousness about the research team's plan to interview individual students about their work: "It's sort of assumed that I was able to get around and have an individual connection with each person and that I was somehow on top of what they were doing as individuals, whereas the reality of it was that most of the stuff was done as a group . . . In some ways I thought that maybe Sarah knew and Marcia [one of the project's research assistants] knew more about what some of the kids were thinking than I did" (Interview, January 18, 1989). It is important to stress that, in spite of her fears to the contrary, Carol knew a great deal about the students in her class, more in fact than most teachers. And her students appreciated her personal concern about them. They consistently portrayed her as an inspiring teacher. The British students soon knew that the U.S. students liked their teacher and learned much from her.

Fiona, on the other hand, had only twenty-five students and worked within the British pastoral system, which she could rely on for support, especially with students who had personal or emotional problems or learning difficulties. This school structure allowed her to concentrate on the students' intellectual development, since she could attend to their other needs much more easily than Carol could. Fiona explained how she would deal with her students' personal problems: "I would refer any problems I had to the tutor or to the head of year, unless it was something that came out of something we were doing as a class, and then we could either address it or talk it through as a group or deal with it on an individual basis" (Interview, August 20, 1992). When she found "a student in distress," she would "have a word with her or him": "I would say to the child, 'Well you know, have you talked to your tutor about this? It's something you could talk to your tutor about.'" She found the exchange class "a very, very stable class" and "got on with the class very well." For these reasons, she says, "I didn't actually play a huge role in actually supporting them emotionally, although I hope that through the way I was teaching I would support them emotionally in terms of building up their confidence with their work."

Effects on Student Writing

The student writing and the surrounding activities show the subtle effects of Carol's and Fiona's ways of developing curriculum and their takes on student development. Figure 4.1 charts the flow of the year's writing for Carol's and Fiona's exchange classes. On the surface, the writing from both classes seems equivalent, but a further look reveals interesting contrasts, not in quality or quantity but in approach.

For a better sense of the amount of writing flowing back and forth between the exchange classes, we counted the number of words in two relatively parallel pieces for four focal students in each class, who were selected because they displayed a range of writing abilities. Table 4.1 compares the length of the four focal students' autobiographies and women in history papers.[5] Carol's students wrote slightly longer pieces than Fiona's.

Both classes were impressed with what they received. They didn't dwell on the "quality" but rather on how much they enjoyed reading

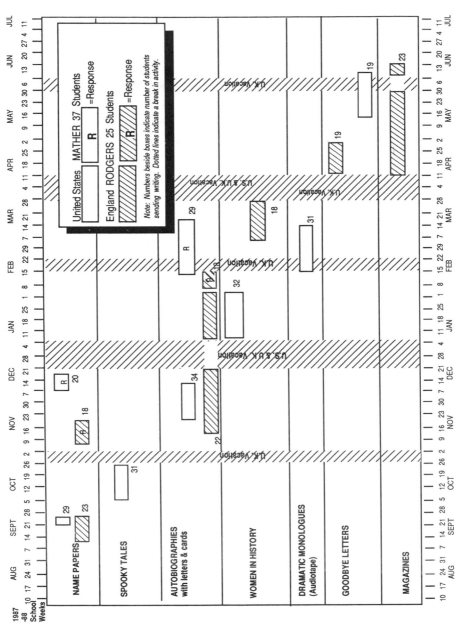

Figure 4.1 Timeline for the Carol Mather–Fiona Rodgers Exchange

what came from abroad and what they learned from it. They also discussed the importance to their writing growth of having a foreign peer audience. As Farah, a British student, put it, "If you've got an audience, you don't want to do rubbish work. You do your best. Do you get what I mean?" (July 1988). On a similar note, Belle, a U.S. student, explained: "I think I'm more concerned about my writing when I send it off to England because I know that those people over there are going to be looking at my papers and . . . you're like an impression on them from America . . . You're writing to somebody and you don't want to send your worst piece of junk over there. You want to send a good piece of work so they can enjoy it and be able to read it too" (Interview, March 24, 1988).

Name Papers

In the first writing the students did for the exchange, the name papers, the most obvious differences surfaced in the style of the pieces. The U.S. students wrote with more formality, keeping a greater distance from their readers. To illustrate, one of Carol's "star" students, Elizabeth, wrote about wanting to change her name:

> If I could change my name I would change it to Nicole for two reasons. One is I like the name. The other is becouse Nicole is a name that

Table 4.1 Autobiography and women in history: Focal students' word counts

	Autobiography	Women in history	Total words
Mather (US)			
Belle	935	658	1,593
Torch	2,815	477	3,292
Elizabeth	2,949	1,096	4,045
Iggy	1,714	243	1,957
Total	8,413	2,474	10,887
Rodgers (GB)			
Farah	2,016	518	2,534
Daniel/Veronica	2,429	803	3,232
Helen	2,144	366	2,510
Christos/Kenneth	1,282	357	1,639
Total	7,871	2,044	9,915

sounds like how its spelled so its easy to pronounce correctly unlike my name.[6]

In her name paper, Fiona's student Farah told about how her parents selected her name:

> My parents chose my names with ease, so my mother tells me, they didn't really argue, if they did my dad might have got a few blackeyes! Note: My mum does not dominate my father.

Continuing on about her nicknames, Farah is even more disarmingly honest:

> My nicknames I don't mind, Faty or most people call me pig as if to make fun of me. I just dont take any notice of them. Or I give them a piece of my mind. Not that it results in violence. I suppose I got these nicknames because I'm fat. Half the boys in my class take the micky out of me being fat but as I said, I dont take any notice. People I know who dont call me [nickname] are what I call friends.

Farah revealed more of herself, and in a more passionate voice, than Elizabeth, although it is possible that Elizabeth's writing seems constrained because she was following a common expository technique often advocated in the U.S. writing curriculum: put forth a proposition and then give reasons. Farah's approach is more like a narrative.

Interestingly, neither Fiona's nor Carol's students perceived these differences. When asked directly about contrasts between British and U.S. writing, Farah gave the usual reply, "I don't really think there are any differences" (Interview, May 1988).

Another contrast, which was not mentioned by the students or their teachers in any of their conversations with members of the research team, occurred at the level of mechanics. Carol's students exhibited more control than Fiona's, especially over punctuation and capitalization. Carol's Elizabeth misspells *because* as "becouse"; otherwise her sentence boundaries are marked correctly even though the syntax is far from graceful. Fiona's Farah has many more surface errors. She begins with three sentences that are separated by commas instead of periods and continues with a sentence fragment before the conjunction "or" ("My nicknames I don't mind"). She inserts a second sentence fragment ("Not that it results in violence") and omits the apostrophe in *don't* three of the four times she uses it.

As it turns out, Fiona, like all the British exchange teachers, did not edit her students' writing in the way the U.S. teachers often did. According to Alex McLeod, in Britain it is inappropriate to work too explicitly on editing. British teachers feel ethically compelled to get their students to work on mechanics independently, since when the students put together their GCSE examination folders, their teachers may not correct mechanical errors. Teachers can advise students by saying something like "This paragraph has a lot of errors. You should check them." Or they might correct a sample paragraph and then leave the rest to the writer. But if teachers provide more comprehensive help, the student can be marked down or even disqualified from the examination and not allowed to pass. In fact, several pieces written under testing conditions ("set pieces") are included in every examination folder as a check against what students produce as part of their coursework. If there is a discrepancy in the mechanics of the "set pieces" and the coursework pieces, then examiners get suspicious and may drop the folder by an entire letter grade (a significant drop) or even two. In part because of the ethical standards surrounding the examinations, teachers, even of younger students, feel reluctant to correct students' failures in mechanics. Fiona explains: "Teachers mustn't go round and proofread, but general . . . comments being made are [allowed] . . . At the end I'll say, 'You know, you need to look at punctuation here or whatever,' and I might even proofread some of it, like say the first bits of it" (Interview, August 20, 1992).

By contrast, Carol, like all the U.S. teachers, was not inhibited about correcting her students' mechanics. Especially if student writing was going to be read outside the classroom, the U.S. teachers felt it was their job to see that students clean up their surface errors, and they provided whatever help was necessary to accomplish this goal.

Autobiographies

In the second writing exchange, the autobiographies, another difference surfaced. Although both classes produced interesting and exciting autobiographies, Carol's students structured theirs in a similar way, while Fiona's showed much more variety. We traced this contrast to subtle differences in Fiona's and Carol's classroom approaches.

At the start, both Fiona and Carol helped their students make this rather daunting autobiography project easier by dividing it into what Fiona called "manageable chunks." In a letter to Carol written during their first year of work together, Fiona explained:

I did not think that they could cope with being asked to write anything extensive in the way that I understood Autobiographies to be written (starting at birth and proceeding step by chronological step to the future). I felt that for many they needed a clearer structure from within which to work and create. In the [English] department's resources there are two worksheets for use with this kind of work which divides up the idea of writing autobiographically into various chapters. (Letter, November 27, 1986)

When asked how her teacher introduced the autobiographies, Farah explained what Fiona had said: "I want some suggestions what you're going to put in it, write it down on the board. And take it from there what should be put down. We could ask about it and talk about it and find yourself finding out more topics to write about" (Interview, May 1988). In a similar way, Carol's students came up with ideas for chapters during an in-class brainstorming session.

The differences became more apparent when Carol's students proceeded to write chapter by chapter, while Fiona's used her initial structuring as a starting point "from within which to work and create," molding the structure to fit their purposes. For example, Helen, in Fiona's class, wrote an autobiography that is among the longest. It includes eight section headings and sometimes subsections:

"About me and my surroundings" [which also includes subsections "My character," "My background," "My features," replete with sketched self-portrait, "My hobbies," "Where I live," with a drawing of her room and a floor plan of her house];

"My Schools";

"Friends and Family," with subheadings for friends and family;

"Likes," which include subheadings for television, music, books, animals, and food;

"DISLIKES," written on a computer and containing subheadings for food, music, people, my town, and political parties;

"My school journey to France," a five-page section of daily journal entries including a long entry telling how a classmate accidentally hit her in the head with a rock and how she suffered a concussion and was taken to the hospital, making the entire group miss their boat back;

"My Pets," a section divided between text and drawings of her goldfish, kittens, gerbils, and tortoise; and

"My Future"

In contrast, Susanna, another of Fiona's students, used a different structure and chose a different set of topics, as her table of contents shows:

1. My private file
2. Likes and Dislikes
3. My character
4. My Hobbies
5. My Beginnings
{6. My Background
{7.
8. My Earliest Memories
9. Important people
10. Speacial events
11. Sports
12. Holiday pictues
13. My future

She concluded with descriptions of her family members.

In Carol's class every student followed the chapter topics the class generated during the brainstorming session. Table 4.2 shows the U.S. focal students' chapter topics; each wrote on seven to fourteen different topics. Carol did not intend that her students interpret the brainstorming session to yield a rigid set of rules. Indeed, some thought they had complete freedom of topic choice for their autobiography, while others saw Carol as unilaterally assigning everything and still others fell somewhere between these two extremes.

As Belle explained, she created the topics for the different sections of her autobiography all by herself: "*I* just put the stuff in that *I* thought was important to me" (Interview, March 24, 1988, emphasis mine). The result was that Belle wrote on more unique topics than any of the other focal students (see Table 4.2).

Elizabeth, on the other hand, thought that she had collaborated fully with Carol and her classmates to determine the topics: "The first thing *we* did was write some ideas that *we* thought would be good ideas to write about . . . Then *we* made a long, list of . . . interesting topics to write about . . . She just, like, assigned us a paper to do on, like she'd just say, well okay tonight, why don't *we* write about my hobbies and special interests" (Interview, March 24, 1988, emphasis mine).

Another student, Torch, claimed that he wrote on teacher-assigned topics but that he could select from among topics on a larger list: "*She* gave us a list, a suggestion on what things *we* should send to them, and *I* did most of the list" (Interview, April 5, 1988, emphasis mine). But Iggy felt that he had to write on a particular set of topics assigned by Carol: "Well *she* gave us the assignments" (emphasis mine). Iggy described his autobiography as "all these other assignments that I did a long time ago, that I put together." When the interviewer asked what he meant, he revealed that he lacked "ownership" of his writing: "Well it's like . . . *she* wanted us to do all these assignments, but *she'll* tell us some. And then *we'll* do them that night, and then *she'll* just say keep them, or *she'll* put them in *her* folder" (April 5, 1988, emphasis mine).

Fiona's students, however, all seemed to know that they had to assume major responsibility for deciding what would go into their autobiographical writing. Farah explained how she decided what to include: "*I* thought about what *I* was going to put into it, thought

Table 4.2 Autobiography topic choice and focal student selection

Topics	Belle	Iggy	Elizabeth	Torch
About me		X		X
"Event of the year"	X			
Favorite teacher			X	X
Favorite person		X		X
Favorite place		X		X
Greatest party		X		
Halloween		X	X	X
Hobbies and interests	X		X	X
I have learned		X		X
I remember when I was most happy	X	X	X	X
I remember when I was angry or mad	X	X		
I used to be . . . but now I am		X	X	X
Important people			X	
My first five years	X		X	X
My house			X	
Pets		X	X	X
Sunday				X
Thanksgiving	X	X		
Trips		X		X
Typical day		X		
When I'm 25	X	X	X	X

about doing my dad's background, my mom's background, what *I* think of my family" (Interview, May 1988, emphasis mine). When asked why she ordered events as she did, she replied, "If it's your autobiography, you've got to go from the day you was born, and you've got to lead up to, lead up to, um, where you are now." Daniel explained that Fiona provided some suggestions and that he had combined her suggestions with his own ideas: "We had a sheet and she said what you could do if you wanted to and . . . I got most of my stuff in that, except about two items and I put about three of my own items in there." Still, Daniel felt in control of these choices: "*I* tried to pick up the good and bad things, you know what *I*'d done, the way you learn and stuff like that . . . *I* wanted to tell them what *I* was like as a child" (Interview, May 1988, emphasis mine). Fiona's other students showed similar levels of independence.

We were puzzled by why some of Carol's students saw themselves doing an essentially teacher-directed task, and this led us to look more closely at how she and Fiona structured their classes. What stood out was Fiona's emphasis on student "responsibility":

It's a project that, after the initial setting up, . . . they are then *responsible* for. And in my experience projects like that, where they are *responsible* for finding information, they've got it all in their heads. They know what they're doing. They can start at any point in the autobiography, any chapter that they like. They can include any diagrams, any photographs, any maps, any pictures. Obviously I make suggestions, but they could be *responsible* for it. They were shaping it. They were, you know, bringing their stuff to the lesson. They knew what they were getting on with, and that is important . . . because it creates that feeling of *responsibility,* and when that's finished, a huge sense of achievement that it's something they've done, that they've been directly *responsible* for. It's not something that the teacher has given them and said, "Answer this. Do this. Do that." They are *responsible* and . . . then as a teacher, you can . . . give suggestions to help them produce something that they want to produce rather than, "I'll give you the answer" . . . And so I'm there as a helper . . . If I say halfway through a lesson or whatever, ". . . Why don't we just have a quiet time now where you can get on with thinking about and working on your own?" . . . You're not kind of like imposing it in a sort of dictatorial way. It's a natural thing. They want to get on with their work, and they get on with it in that way, which is nice. You know, and there were times with the autobiography where they were just completely absorbed in whatever they were doing . . . It was good. It worked. (Interview, May 1988, emphasis mine)

After Fiona's students got going on their autobiographies, they brought their writing to class ("bringing their stuff to the lesson") and worked on it there. Her course took on its own momentum, directed by the students who had work to complete. Farah explained her interactions with her classmates while they wrote side by side: "Well, you was always discussing what you was going to write, what you was going to do, and all that. It was like, 'What are you going to do?' 'I'm writing about so-and-so.' 'Well, I'll write about that.' And goes, 'No, you can't write about that. I'm writing about it.' Stuff like that you know. And then you felt, if she writes it, why can't I?" (Interview, May 1988). Farah took her writing home and put in whatever she wanted. She said she wrote every night: "Every night you felt, I've got to do a bit of autobiography . . . It was, like, you read autobiographies in the library. Here's my chance to do mine . . . I've always wanted to do this." Farah then explained Fiona's role, "To me, Ms. Rodgers's a good teacher. I mean, she's not like other teachers who will just tell you to get on with it and won't help you or anything like that. She can take it further and really explain it more, and that's personally why I like her" (Interview, May 1988). As Fiona explained, she was "there as a helper."

In Carol's class, the students did their writing mostly at home as homework and rarely interacted in class as they wrote. Although involved in their autobiographies, Carol's students did not direct the lessons.

In spite of the differences in these classrooms, the autobiographical writing helped the students make important connections with their partners from abroad. As Carol's student Torch explained: "I learned about them because, like, in their autobiographies, they, like, tell certain stories about their life. So, like, in that, I learned scenes from their lifetime" (Interview, April 5, 1988).

Women in History Papers

This contrast in the two teachers' approach to exchanging responsibilities with their students took an interesting turn in the "women in history" papers. Fiona began introducing this topic in the usual British fashion by discussing the idea for writing on it with her class. However, once the students had decided that they wanted to write about women in history, Fiona discovered that neither the school nor local libraries had very many books about women. What was readily available focused mainly on the royal family, Florence Nightingale, and the suffragettes, and there were virtually no books on famous black women. With these limited resources, Fiona's students had difficulty finding subjects they felt connected to; if they chose to write about someone other than a member of the royal family, Florence Nightingale, or the suffragettes, they could find little to read. As a result, many became frustrated and felt detached from this writing.[7]

By contrast, Carol's students wrote about famous women from the past every year for a National Organization for Women (NOW) essay contest. During the exchange year, Carol planned to have her students send the "women in history" papers they wrote for the NOW contest to England. The class had no say in whether or not they would do this writing, but once Carol had assigned the topic, she had plenty of resources to support their choices. She had applied for and received several grants in the area of women's studies, which had allowed her to purchase an impressive array of materials about famous women for her classroom. Her students had easy access to these materials. Given her personal expertise and the resources she had gathered, Carol was able to provide a context that motivated many of her students and then was able to provide numerous possibilities as they tried to decide who interested them. The result was that those students in Carol's class who were motivated by the idea of writing about women in history could negotiate with her until they chose an appropriate topic. Unfortunately, given the large size of her class, some students fell between the cracks. However, as in previous years, two of Carol's students took top prizes for the sixth graders in the NOW contest: Athene won first and Elizabeth second.

Elizabeth shows what happens when a student neatly matches the U.S. teacher's way of exchanging responsibilities with students. Elizabeth wrote about Winnie Mandela because, as she explains it, "I wanted to do someone political, that has . . . influenced my life in some way" (Interview, March 24, 1988). She noticed that Mandela "wasn't in any history books I've ever read." Elizabeth drew selectively and thoughtfully from her reading to construct her essay. She begins "Winnie Mandela: The Soul of South Africa" on a personal note, telling the reader why Mandela is "important to me":

Winnie Mandela has always seemed important to me because she fights oppression. She knew that what was going on in South Africa was wrong and she was prepared from childhood to fight until there was a change. As Winnie Mandela once said in her childhood years, "If they failed in those nine Xhosa wars, I am one of them and I will start from where those Xhosa's left off and I will get my land back." She was speaking about the wars that black people waged against white people and lost. All her life she tried to get the land of all South African's back from white control and she probably will keep trying until she dies. And even then her soul will live on in the thousands of other black people who follow her lead.

Elizabeth's issue-focused essay comes to life as she quotes Mandela and as she creates images of Mandela's soul living on as "other black people . . . follow her lead." The essay continues with a paragraph about Mandela's childhood and her relationship with her parents, and further paragraphs on how she met and married Nelson Mandela, his years underground, his imprisonment, Winnie Mandela's displacement from her home, and her own political evolution. Elizabeth makes her points by giving numerous examples of Mandela's independent political activities:

In Brandfort Winnie made a lot of changes. She went in stores no black went into. At the police station she used the white entrance. She went into the white side of the post office. At the supermarket blacks were supposed to use little windows to do their shopping, but when Winnie started shopping inside the other blacks did too. Some stores even had to close the windows. Also there was a dress shop where blacks had to stand outside and point to which dresses they liked; they were not allowed to touch them. One day, Winnie wanted to buy a dress for her daughter. She and the sales lady had a furious argument. This incident became the talk of the town and the blacks went on strike. Now any black can go in and buy a dress.

In her conclusion, Elizabeth brings her essay back to what is personally meaningful to her:

To me, Winnie Mandela is someone to look up to. I truly believe that even though Winnie Mandela changed only a small part of apartheid in South Africa, she is to be greatly admired throughout the world for her great leadership and commitment in the struggle. She had shown great courage and strength by breaking the law in a country that hates black people so much that they will even jail the children. She had had her husband taken away from her, been banished from her home and banned from communicating with other people, but still she fights. I would like to be like this woman—able to fight, able to care and able to commit myself totally to what I believe in.

As is usually the case in U.S. classrooms, some students remain uncommitted to assigned writing. A number of the boys in Carol's large class resisted writing about famous women, and their writing is much like that from Fiona's class, which illustrates the consequences of a lack of commitment.

Iggy, another one of Carol's students, wrote about Mother Teresa. As he admits, "I didn't try so much in this one." Whereas Elizabeth devoted a month to her essay, Iggy spent only three days on his. When asked why he selected Mother Teresa, he could only say, "I just found somebody . . . that's known, and I did her" (Interview, April 5, 1988). To Iggy, writing this "women in history" paper was like writing a "book report," a kind of writing he defines as boring and unimaginative, involving only the chronological retelling of facts that other people have already written about. He did not make good use of the available resources and relied a great deal on the encyclopedia. In fact, he opens his essay with encyclopedialike facts about Mother Teresa's life:

> On August 29, 1910, a child was born to an Albanion couple living in Skopje, Macedonia, which was to become part of Yugoslavia. This childs name was Gonxha, Agnes, Bejaxhia, a name less easy for Western tongues to pronounce. She was soon to become Mother Teresa.

After presenting a couple more facts about her work, Iggy continues with a list of unsupported opinions and assertions about what he claims to have learned:

> I think mother Teresa is a brilliant woman, I have learned a lot from her.
> I have learned to value life and to cherish all that I may recieve.
> I have learned to help people nomatter if they ar friend or foe.
> She has taught to help people have less than I.
> Mother Teresa is a woman full of compassion.

He ends with a few more facts:

> She has convents all over the wor( )
> Some of the places are Calcutta, Beng( ), and San Francisco.
> I went to the convent in San Francisco. The nuns their were very Nice.
> I think many people have learned things froms mother Teresa's deeds.

As Iggy explains, his mother made him visit the convent, and he volunteers, "I don't know why." Yet in spite of his mother's extraordinary efforts to help him find some connection to his topic, he remains unengaged. His lack of effort coincides with his lack of enthusiasm and illustrates the relative futility of having students write when they aren't interested.

In England, Susanna, in Fiona's class, illustrates a similar lack of commitment. Although she strayed from the library resources and wrote about Janet Jackson, her report is fairly typical in that it is purely a rendering of the facts of Janet Jackson's life. It begins:

> Twenty years ago a little girl was born in to the famous jackson family.she is the youngest out of nine children with six brothers andthree sist ers.

Susanna then tells about Jackson's rise to fame with her hit "Dreamstreet," which was released when she was eighteen and "the brightist new star on telev ison show FAME." She provides some interesting details:

> lately she has a key in the hoop of her earing. some people say it isthe key to her heart and others say it the key to the animal cage(thejackson has a miniature zoo on the grounds around th eir home).

Susanna concludes: "she has been to a disco once at a studio 54 in new york." It is interesting to note Susanna's many typographical and mechanical errors, which likely stem, at least in part, from the fact that she used a computer.

Teen Magazines from Fiona's Class

As their last exchange offering, Fiona's students worked together in small groups to produce teen magazines. The magazines came with colorfully illustrated covers of heavy, laminated paper, giving them a durable and glossy feel. All were bound with three staples along the left side. They are realistic imitations of actual magazines; two covers even contained information about cost (50 pence in one case and 45 pence in the other) and one sported a date and information that the magazine comes out "every Wednesday."

The failure of the "women in history" pieces aside, this last project shows particularly well where Fiona was headed with her notion of exchanging responsibilities with her students. As the year progressed, Fiona expected her students to assume increased levels of responsibility. The students, not Fiona, chose this project. They also decided what to include in their magazines through a process of compromises and some bartering with Fiona, who encouraged the students to use her ideas as well. For example, Fiona pushed her class to write articles about their school and recalled that they "wanted to do scary stories and traditional features of magazines." She explained that, for the most part, her students "decided for themselves what they would put in [these magazines]" (Final Interview).

This set of six elaborate magazines turned out to be major projects of a scope not often seen in this age group. The students worked steadily on them for about six weeks. Each magazine was written by the students in one of six self-selected, single-gender groups, three groups of girls and three of boys. The magazines were the only jointly authored project in either the British or the U.S. class. The girls wrote longer magazines than the boys—the longest, *It's Push*, is seventy-five pages. Another group of girls produced forty-nine pages for their magazine, *Yes*, while the third group's offering, *G'Day to the USA*, was thirty-four pages. The magazines produced by two of the boys' groups—*Hot Max* and *Top Mag*—were only thirteen pages each. Still not approaching the scope of any of the girls' groups, *Gizmo*, by the other boys' group had twenty-three pages.

The table of contents from *It's Push* shows the types of articles common to all of the magazines:[8]

Contents

1   The Plane Crash—story by Nicola

7   Don't Go To Sleep—story by Farah

23   The Hallowe'en Mysterie—story by Bridgetta

31   Fan clubs [lists real addresses for fan clubs for two popular rock groups and two popular singers, with advice about mailing]

33   Posters [cut out magazine picture of a singer dancing to her own music, with lyrics included in magazine]

All six magazines, including *It's Push,* contain elaborate pieces of fiction, many of which paralleled the spooky tales that Carol's U.S. class had sent after Halloween ("Computer Murder" and "The Ever Living" in *Hot Max;* "The Kidnapping of Nelson's Coloumn" in *Top Mag;* "Moving House Murder" and "Guess the Murder" in *G'Day to the USA;* "Milly and the Rats" in *Yes;* "Hijack Story" in *Gizmo*). The magazines also contain the writing about Broadbent School Fiona wanted, often with interviews of school officials. The first two questions in Daniel's interview with Ms. Cashman, the head of the second-year students, give the flavor of this sort of material:

> Now read this: this is a hot hot interview with our head of year, Ms. Cashman just read the following = key Q = Question——A = answer
> Q = Was you surprised when you was asked to be head of year?
> A = Not really because I had taken a large part of looking after the year in the 1st year, It was quite natural really, I am very pleased to take over the 2nd year and I enjoyed it very much.
> Q = Do you like the job?
> A = I do like the job very very much, there is a lot of hard work involved with the job, I'm busy all the time and you can't plan

your day because different things arrive all the time, I enjoy the job because you see lot's and lot's of progress amonst the children, you see development and improvement all the time.

Another example of writing about the school is Brigetta's piece about her first day at BCS in *It's Push:*

> My first day at Broadbent Community School was quite scary. I was nervous. I hardly knew anybody in my class, except for Kelly, Veronica, and Ivan.
>
> I was frightened incase some of the older kids started to cause any trouble. The lessons were really different from juniour school. We had to change rooms to go to the lessons (which we didn't have to do in Juniour School. There were many more people (around 1,100 students) in Juniour School there were only 200 students or so.
>
> It was just really wierd, but I've got used to it now.

The magazines also include advice columns, joke pages, word games, cartoons, quizzes, and articles with titles as disparate as "The Channel Tunel," "Fashion with a Little Help from a Black Dress," and "Fishing in Tottenham." Farah explained the importance of the magazines to the exchange: "I actually put the American people out of my mind for a couple of lessons, just generally wrote down what I would do, you know. Then as you got through the magazine you started to think that there was going to be people who read it, and then you add more and more" (Interview, July 1988).

Reflecting on where her students were at the end of the year, Fiona felt that most of their writing had been relatively personal, "confirming them as writers, people who are effective and [have] got interesting things to say." In their next year she expected them to build on this base and to take on new challenges. "I think that [the personal writing] will hold them in good stead when we go on next year to do more theoretical, more intellectual kinds of work."

Links between Sharing Responsibility, Sharing Control, and Writing Development

For Fiona, curriculum development was part of a complex process of sharing responsibilities with her particular class. By contrast, Carol made decisions about the curriculum before she met her students each year and then adjusted her decisions to the group, relying on her past successes to judge what the current group of students would like. Certain assignments became traditions in her classroom, although there was some room for negotiation with her students around issues of form and content within some assignments. It is important to note that Carol planned activities so that her students would be encouraged to take on increasingly important social and intellectual challenges during the year as they moved from mostly personal to personally based but issue-focused writing. Those students who felt that they were in charge of their decision making made tremendous strides. Elizabeth, for example, who won an award for her essay on Winnie Mandela, exemplified how a sixth-grader can write both issue-focused and personally meaningful prose. During the course of the year, a number of Carol's students wrote on topics that pushed them to question their identities and their cultures.

Traditions of particular writing activities were alien to Fiona. Not only did she assume that tasks would vary depending on the composition of the group, she also assumed that a particular task might not be appropriate for everyone in the group. In addition, Fiona's "negotiated" curriculum included some structured pieces and some of the constants of teaching English, such as drafting for writing and discussions of literature.

This is not to say that Fiona worked out every part of the curriculum with her students or that Carol worked out none of it with hers; the difference was one of emphasis. Although Carol and her students exchanged ideas, she did not consider the students' assumption of responsibility for the curriculum as one of her central or long-term goals. Rather, her central teaching-learning interactions occurred more in the context of helping students develop writing and thinking skills than of completing particular tasks.

For Fiona, student decision making was not just a matter of curricular choice, it was itself a developmental process, a way of learning to take responsibility and assume control. Her approach echoes Vygotsky (1978), who proposed that we learn through interacting with more experienced others who gradually help us work independently. As Fiona handed over more and more responsibility, she expected her students to learn to find information, decide what part of a task to tackle and when, decide what to include, and, ultimately, choose writing tasks to which they would be committed. The closest U.S. equivalents to Fiona's notion of exchanges between the teacher and students in the classroom can be found in the writing of teachers and researchers like Graves (1983), Calkins (1986), and Atwell (1987), who advocate an individualized workshop approach for elementary and middle school students. Graves and his followers hand over the classroom to the students and focus on encouraging them to write only on topics they choose.

Fiona's sense of classroom exchange differs in a number of ways from this approach. First, Fiona gave students a great deal of say, but she did not turn the curriculum over to them completely or suddenly. She expected her students to assume increased responsibility gradually. Second, Fiona never expected her students to make all their own choices. At the start of the exchange year, she gave assignments but expected her students, with perhaps a few exceptions, to personalize them, making individual choices within the framework she set. When students had trouble making choices, Fiona helped them. This approach broke down within the frame of the "women in history" writing, when Fiona did not have the materials available to support the students' choices. Nevertheless, by the end of the year, students were deciding what kinds of writing the U.S. students would enjoy receiving. Third, Fiona placed no special value on individualization. She involved as much of the group as possible in the same activity at the same time because she wanted to use the force of the classroom community to motivate students and push their learning. Even at the end of the year, the class decided what to write as a group. Within the framework the students chose, she pushed them to take on new challenges, concentrating on "boosting individuals to take themselves one step further in whatever activity" (Interview, August 20, 1992). She was resentful of "the national curriculum" because it "believes that teachers don't do that [push students forward] rigorously enough": "It's not like . . . within that negotiation there's complete anarchy . . . There's a certain level of negotiation which is between them and myself about choosing something which, yes, is interesting, but also sometimes it's choosing something which will stretch them as learners. And so you're working together to develop and push them to higher standards and to produce better material and, and more interesting work."

Chapter 5

↪ Managing Mixed-Ability Teaching, Raising Standards

Nancy Hughes, Peter Ross

Nancy Hughes's mixed-ability seventh-graders and Peter Ross's mixed-ability Form 3 (eighth-grade equivalent) students also responded in different ways to the writing exchange project, but these differences were not subtle, as they were for Carol and Fiona. Like Fiona, Peter used his curriculum to foster his students' writing development. Nancy, however, had a completely separate agenda for the writing exchange: she wanted her students to use the opportunity to establish social connections with Peter's class, but since Peter's group did not reciprocate socially, it was difficult for her to accomplish this goal. Peter focused primarily on the academic opportunities offered by the exchange. As a result, Nancy's students were frustrated in their attempts to connect socially, while Peter's group complained that they didn't receive substantive work equivalent to what they produced.

These differences in goals led to striking differences in students' writing. Peter's students wrote lengthy academic pieces, taking several months to craft each one, while Nancy's students wrote frequent short personal pieces. The writing in these classes reflected the teachers' divergent curricula. In spite of these differences and frustrations, the students in both classes enjoyed participating in the writing exchange.

Reflections on Curriculum, Community Building, and Writing Development

When the writing exchange began, Peter had been teaching the same group for three consecutive years and expected to continue to teach them for their remaining two years of secondary school. For this reason, he could think about his students' development over a five-year period and organize the curriculum accordingly. The types of writing on the GCSE examination (discursive, analytical, narrative, responding to texts) served as a guide for the writing and thinking skills he wanted his students ultimately to acquire. He relied on a spiral curriculum that cycled through each type of writing year after year:

> The GCSE has provided me with a range of types of writing . . . And you can actually, in a spiral curriculum you can bring those down from a fifth-year example to the first year . . . I see my job as to provide the right context within which language develops and takes place rather than someone who has in the back of their head a set of skills that has to be offered to the kids at any particular time . . . The context could be a book or a movie that we share together. It could be . . . something like writing a book for a younger audience. (Interview, October 30, 1990)

Peter asked himself, "What context can I provide that will enhance their language development and provide options for the whole range of writing?"

Counting on this five-year period with the same students, Peter saw it as his job to set contexts that would motivate his students to want to try various types of writing. He did not worry if a student was not motivated at a particular time to do a particular kind of writing. He let the student choose a more motivating activity. But he assumed responsibility for helping that student find a motivating context for the kind of writing he or she wasn't interested in originally.

Peter saw important differences between his sense of curriculum creation and what he observed in the United States, basing his opinions on his experiences with Nancy and her class as well as on observations during a study leave to attend the Summer Invitational Program of the Bay Area Writing Project (BAWP). He was surprised by the BAWP teachers' focus in their proposed in-service presentations on using their successful classroom practices as models: "They all seemed to be program models as to . . . how you take it from me and . . . use it in your classroom . . . I couldn't do that 'cause I don't offer a program" (Interview, October 30, 1990). Peter's goal was to get to know the needs of his community of students and provide motivating contexts for them, not to create program models. He didn't even keep files of teaching activities from one year to the next because he felt that each particular group of students shaped the activities and how they unfolded.

For Peter, curriculum developed out of the interaction of students with each other and with their teacher. He depended on the spirit of the classroom community to formulate the curriculum and its force to motivate the students. His curriculum was not the same as a "learner-centered" curriculum, which he associated with the 1960s. He found that philosophy inadequate, since to him it carried the implication that teachers concern themselves only with individuals and not with the community as a whole. From his point of view, the learner-centered curriculum in itself does not take account of the way teachers should provide for the discussions, the activities, and, frequently, the writing that emerge from the interpersonal exchanges integral to the classroom culture.

According to Peter, exchanging responsibility with students is crucial to success in teaching mixed-ability groups or, for that matter, any group of diverse students. Such exchanges demand that the teacher create a tightly knit classroom community while acknowledging that each class will have its own character and that the members of the community will be diverse: different students will bring different strengths and talents that must come together to advance the group's academic ends.

In this classroom community, the teacher attends to the developmental progress of students at different levels, and the classroom is designed to allow teachers this flexibility in meeting students' developmental needs in a communal environment.

Peter did not see how a fixed program aimed at an idealized whole group—or even an individualized program—could motivate students and respond to their varying needs. With the exception of teachers who offered wholly individualized (learner-centered) programs, Peter observed that most U.S. teachers, even though they allowed some variety to meet individual needs, did not seem to have this notion of diversity embedded in their approach to teaching. As he remarked, "If you [in the U.S.] are focusing on a particular area or a particular type of writing, you seem to make all the kids do that type of writing at the same time."

Effects on Student Writing

Over the course of the writing exchange, the contrasts in the goals of the two teachers led to major differences in the scope of the students' writing. As Nancy explained: "Peter's projects tended to be a lot more elaborate than mine . . . That was one of the things that the kids noticed too. We tended to do maybe shorter, less in-depth kinds of projects" (Interview, December 15, 1988). Table 5.1 shows just how significant this difference was. Although Peter considered the autobiographies a relatively minor project, even calling them "snippets," his students wrote on average three times as much as Nancy's. For the short stories the difference was even greater and reflected the kind of extended projects Peter's students tackled as the year progressed.

Figure 5.1 charts the flow of all writing for the exchange during the year, showing that Nancy's class spent relatively short amounts of time on a number of pieces while Peter's class spent long stretches on one major project per quarter, supplemented by a few other shorter efforts.

Peter and his students thought the writing from Nancy's class was much like what British students did when they were younger. Dickens, one of Peter's students, articulated this point of view: "I suppose they haven't got to the stage where they can begin to put more detail in,

Table 5.1 Autobiography and short story: Focal students' word counts

	Autobiography	Short story	Total words
Hughes (US)			
Elise	614	326	940
Bambi	432	217	649
Quirk	361	202	563
Billy	339	177	516
Total	1,746	922	2,668
Ross (GB)			
Dickens	1,204	5,166	6,370
Nikita	935	2,315	3,250
Anita/Ince	670	1,522	2,192
Catherine	807	4,422	5,229
Total	3,616	13,425	17,041

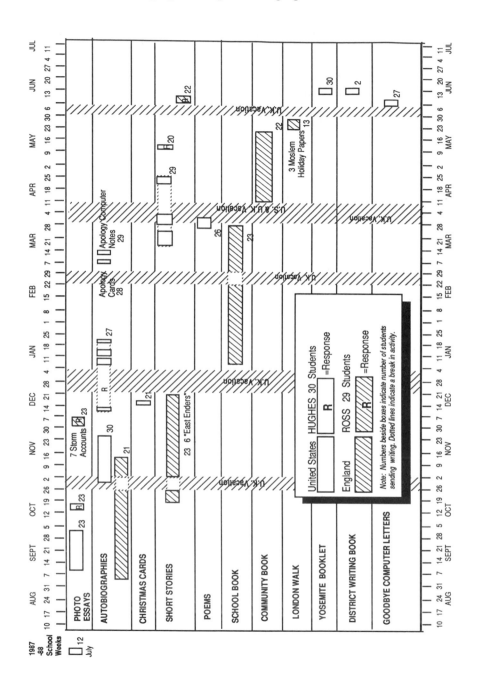

Figure 5.1 Timeline for the Nancy Hughes–Peter Ross Exchange

that I suppose they're sort of compressing it and not, you know, sort of saying everything they could do. And they're probably having a lot of help from their teacher, just like we did then" (Interview, July 19, 1988). Catherine was more generous in her assessment of why the U.S. class wrote such condensed pieces. Although she would have liked to have received "a normal story to read," she concluded that Nancy's students sent condensed stories because "they had to rush" (Interview, June 4, 1988).

Peter's students thought that school in the United States was easy and that U.S. students did not work as hard as British students did. As Dickens put it:

> It's a bit of a breeze compared to us . . . They seem to get a lot more time out of school than we do . . . I'd think it was pretty easy compared to back here . . . Most of them aren't too worried about school. Like it's just there, you know. It's just nothing to worry about. (Interview, July 19, 1988)

Nancy and most of her students preferred their own writing, finding what came from England boring and hard to follow. At the end of the year Nancy asked her students to reflect on their experiences. Fifty-four percent (thirteen out of twenty-four) reported that their writing was better than the writing of the British students and/or that they were more motivated writers than the British students.[1] Guy's response was typical:

> I thought (trying to be as polite as possible) that our writing was better. It was more descriptive, [m]ade more sence, to us, had better stories. We better used the English language. They may have had good stories but you couldn't tell because they misspelled everything and didn't put sentences together correctly.

Lizzie remarked, "I think that our writing is right to the point, while theirs wanders in all directions and takes a while to get to the point." In the same vein, Tae wrote:

> I would say that our class writes better (not more but better) stories and other papers. Maybe it's because here we seem to focus on descriptive writing, interesting papers, and trying to use things like 'magic words' and there they might place a higher priority on how much you get done and the length.

However, Cow voiced the minority opinion: "They wrote tons more.

I was getting rather sad that we seemed to be sending so little compared to them . . . and now, they send us a 50 page book filled with
interviews. Its getting pitiful." Cow underestimated the length of the
book, which in fact was 183 pages. Bruno agreed with Cow, "I think
that the kids in England are encouraged to write more and I think
they enjoy writing more than American kids."

During the exchange, Nancy remarked on these deeply ingrained
differences in the students' writing, "One of the things I think that
. . . the kids discovered is that . . . the approach is a little bit different.
It seems to me, and . . . this is just our own conclusions, that . . . they
tended to write longer pieces, and I don't know if, that was . . . part
of what they are expected to do, or just part of their natural . . ." and
Ellie O'Sullivan, who was interviewing Nancy, added, "I think it's a
bit of both, actually" (Interview, December 15, 1988).

In spite of the differences in how their classrooms were organized
and in the writing they did, Peter's and Nancy's students found having a foreign peer audience a positive experience. Peter's student
Catherine said, "First class was a bit boring, but we started writing
to them and they started writing back. It got more interesting" (Interview, July 19, 1988). Later on in her interview she elaborated:
"When you do your old bench work, you just have Mr. Ross read it
and that was it. You know, you have your work marked and move
on to something else. But with this, you wrote to somebody and you
got some things back and you could read it and have a laugh and it
went on." Similarly, Dickens explained: "It's been more sort of interesting than other things we've been doing in English because the last
couple of years before this one, well if we was told something to do,
develop the idea and present it in a certain amount of time, sort of
thing, and you know there's no one really is going to see it apart from
Mr. Ross and maybe the people in the class. But this time I think
you've got a chance to really show other people what it could do in
their countries, how we learn, and really make new friends as well,
sort of, in the correspondence" (Interview, May 24, 1988).

Dickens continued about how the exchange affected his writing:
"You've got to think about what they'd like to read . . . I'd want to
give them something they could understand and relate to quickly."
Nikita agreed: "When you're writing for somebody else, it gives you
something to write for. It's got to be quite good because other people
are going to see it. It's got to be of a higher standard than your normal
work" (Interview, May 25, 1988).

Nancy's students voiced similar feelings. Quirk explained, "It's nice to be writing to someone with a purpose" (Interview, March 29, 1988). Billy, a reluctant writer, said, "Since we have to do writing, at least we get to send it somewhere, and someone else gets to read it." Otherwise, "just the teacher" sees it "and it's kinda boring" (Interview, March 29, 1988). And Elise remarked, "I think it's [the exchange] fun. If you have to, you know, write stories and stuff, it's nice that other people get to hear them. You get to know other people and other classes, what they're like" (Interview, April 13, 1988).

A journey through three of the exchange projects, spaced across the year, shows how the writing unfolded: first, the autobiographies, completed in the fall in both classes; next, the short stories, completed in the late fall in England and in the early spring in the United States; and finally, the community books and London walks in England and the Yosemite booklets in the United States, completed at the end of the year. This progression shows how the curriculum and the students' writing diverged across time in these two classes.

Autobiographies

Whereas Peter's students devoted two months to their autobiographies, from the start Nancy was concerned that the autobiographies not take too much time. At a meeting with the U.S. teachers, she was alarmed when the research team and the other teachers framed the autobiography as a major project. Nancy asked how long she should spend on the autobiography. When a member of the research team estimated that a span of at least three weeks would be needed, Nancy quickly decided three weeks would be the "maximum" for her class.

In Nancy's class Bambi reported that she originally expected the autobiography to be an elaborate project: "I thought she was going to have us write a book when she first mentioned it. Like, she goes, you guys are going to be writing autobiographies to England. I thought it would be like a big humungous book that would take like the whole year to make . . . 'Cause I thought it would be a book like, about that big, from, like, when I was a baby until, like, seventh-grade life, and what I expected in my future. But it wasn't" (Interview, March 29, 1988). When Bambi discovered that Nancy expected "just your seventh-grade life," she said, "I didn't know really how to feel" (Interview, March 29, 1988).

The autobiographies in Nancy's class functioned much like letters of introduction, except that they were presented inside a cover decorated with drawings and included a photograph of the writer. They ranged from one and a half typed pages to four and a half handwritten pages, with lists and lots of space. The writing began with general salutations—"Hi there" from Elise, "Hello" from Billy, and "Hi" from Bambi and Quirk. With only a couple of minor deviations, each contained a short introductory paragraph of general information about the student's life and family, information about the writer's hobbies and interest in sports, a description of a typical school day, and in many cases a memory from childhood. Four students chose adjectives for each letter of their names and called these listings "poems." The U.S. autobiographies read like a television news brief—disconnected ideas with little development. They were much shorter than the British "snippets" (see Table 5.1).

Each writer in Peter's class typically focused on one topic: six wrote about a hobby (karate, computers, collecting comics, and the like), eight about a trip, four about an event, and three about favorite things to do or about their school day. The narrowed topics made the writing detailed and led students to demonstrate some depth of understanding about their topics. The British students also seemed to have a serious personal investment in their writing.

Examples from average U.S. and British autobiographies show differences in development, depth, and detail. Nancy's student Bambi begins with her name, height, and weight and then continues in her first paragraph:

> I love football, parties, and going out with my friends. I don't do sports much all exscept for at P.E. {Physical Education} and when I play football. I love math, English, french, and P.E best. I like to write stories, talk on the phone, and listening to the raidio. I also, like to read, my favorite book are (the doll and one boy to many). I love to draw roses.

She continues with her daily schedule:

> When I wake up it is 6:30. I take a 15 min. shower. I do my hair, makup, and get dressed in a half hour. then I brush my teeth, make my lunch, and pack my back pack in 10 min. I leave at 7:30. And get to school at 7:45. This gives me 15 min. to talk to my 8th grade friends before they go to class. And At 8:00 my 7th and 6th grade friends.

Bambi adds her school schedule to this paragraph and ends it by recounting her leisure activities. Following a paragraph about her family life, she concludes with a memory:

> I remember when my mom broke her arm. My sister and I had to work together to make my mom better. We had to clean the house, make dinner, dress my mom, and a lot more. It was hard but it gave Jenny {my sister} and I a chance to get to know each other a little better. We talked, argued, laughed and talked about boys. I love Jenny and I'm almost positive that she loves me.

In Peter's class, Nikita briefly introduces herself but quickly turns to an elaborate sharing of her passion, karate:

> I'm Nikita I live in the U.K.. What you're about to read now is all about my hobbies. my main hobby is karate. Karate is a form of martial Arts. It is practised all over the world and it is a form of self defense. A great sport.

She explains when and where she practices, the style of karate she specializes in which she says is called "Higashi kai," the rating system of different colored belts, and then the nine Dans or levels for black belts. She shows where she, as a purple belt, fits in. She then tells what it feels like to be involved:

> The most scaring part of karate is either the thought of being killed or badly injured if you are fighting with a person of a higher belt or if somebody makes a wrong move.
>
> Also the gradings are pretty scaring because you have to stand up and perform and practise in front of your class and everyone is watching to see what you do wrong and at the end if you are good enough you will be graded. In other words put up to a higher belt.

Nikita next describes her travels to compete and the two types of competition, "kata . . . where there is alot of moves all put in together and it makes a sequence" and "sparring (fighting)" between two contestants. She illustrates this explanation with a sketch of who is where on the mats during each style of competition. Nikita tells about her older friends in her karate club, whom she admires. Finally, she includes a tribute to her instructor who "is known through out the world."

Like Nikita, Peter's other students also developed their ideas in some depth and, in the process, revealed a strong personal commitment to their writing. How did Peter encourage and support this personal commitment? It was not just a matter of freedom of topic choice. Students in both countries felt that they could choose what to include in their autobiographies. The difference seemed to be in how Peter guided his students to write on topics that motivated them and that they cared about. Nikita explained her enthusiasm and her connection to her subject, karate: "Well I writ about karate 'cause that's all I ever talk about. Um, I suppose I'm quite good at it, and it takes up most of my, all my week. I go on a Tuesday and a Thursday and a Saturday and a Sunday sometimes. So that's [what] I do all week. I ain't got no other hobbies apart from swimming" (Interview, May 25, 1988).

The missing ingredient for Nancy's students was this level of involvement in their writing. In talking about his autobiography, Quirk, for example, shows his detachment: "I just put down stuff, like the first part is a generalization. There's like these sections on family, hobbies, what I do, and friends. And then, just anything, stuff. And then you just arrange it. You think what looks good or sounds best" (Interview, March 29, 1988).

On both sides of the Atlantic mismatches between the writing students sent and received produced disappointment but also led to an appreciation of differences. Elise, in Nancy's class, described how she felt when she first received the British students' writing: "When we first got their autobiographies, it was kind of confusing because they weren't like our autobiographies. They weren't like, well we like to do this, and this is what our schedule is, and stuff like that. It was an incident, that's how we got to know them, through that incident kind of thing . . . I was kind of disappointed because I really wanted to know more about them personally, than about, you know, a moment they had" (Interview, April 13, 1988). Nonetheless, Elise appreciated the depth of the British students' revelations: "The thing that was really interesting is when they sent us, like, their autobiographies about stuff they were interested in . . . I thought that was kind of neat. They were kind of interesting because you got to know, like, what they like to do, you know. We kind of know that Catherine likes to play the clarinet now" (Interview, April 13, 1988).

In a cover letter to Nancy, Peter apologized for what he considered a weak effort on the part of his students: "We worked on autobiographical 'snippets' so as to avoid the bulkiness of fully-fledged autobiographies but they're not as detailed as I would have liked and some of their ideas about what makes up autobiographical writing are pretty outlandish!! Anyway I thought it was best to get them off to you in this pretty 'raw' state and at least the photographs will bring some of the deader ones to life."

Short Stories

In November, Peter wrote to Nancy and told her that his class would send "an anthology of their short stories." In early January, Nancy acknowledged that her class would send stories as well, but by early March, when she received the British short stories, her class had not yet begun theirs. Nancy felt pressed to have her students respond quickly.

To inspire her students' fiction writing, Nancy decided to use a writing activity she had first heard about through a Bay Area Writing Project (BAWP) workshop. Nancy called the activity "daily writing," and it included exercises modeled on suggestions in Caplan and Keech's (1980) *Showing Writing*. Nancy gave her students a general sentence on four different occasions between March 1 and March 16. These included: "She felt foolish at the dance," "He felt guilty cheating," "It didn't fit," "It was hard to tell him." The sentence was to be the focus of an overnight homework piece in which the students had to use specific details. Nancy hoped that these "daily writing" exercises would teach the students to "show, not tell," to fill their writing with specific details rather than empty generalizations.

After students completed a piece of this writing, Nancy explained that "they got into editing groups and went through the process of working through a story . . . [for a] close look at revision" (Interview, May 25, 1988). Nancy asked each student reader in the editing groups to list two strengths and two weaknesses for each story and to complete these statements: "One sentence I really liked in this paper was . . ." and "One suggestion I have for this paper is . . ." At this point, the students gave the stories to Nancy to keep in their writing folders.

Then, on four separate days, Nancy gave the students their folders and asked them to choose one piece to read aloud for a class critique. About five volunteers read during each session, but if students didn't volunteer, Nancy called on them. As she explained, "We talk about how the piece could be improved, the strengths and the weaknesses" (Interview, May 25, 1988). Our classroom observations showed, however, that the students mostly told their peers what they liked about the story they read.

At this point the students would usually select one of their stories to rewrite. For the exchange, though, Nancy felt there was no time for this rewriting. Students simply chose their best story to type into the computer and send to England via electronic mail:[2] "Because of the time constraints issue we didn't do as much with it [revising the stories] as I've done in the past. A lot of kids took fairly rough stories and put them on the computer [to send to England]. They hadn't really gone through a lot of drafts. And traditionally they did, but we were running behind" (Interview, May 25, 1988).

The dynamics inside Peter's classroom during story writing were markedly different. The short stories were a major project for Peter's class to which they committed two months of class time. Catherine explains how Peter portrayed the short story assignment: "He said we was going to write some stories, so we got down to work" (Interview, July 19, 1988). Not only did Peter commit time to the stories but he helped his students decide on their story focus. Like Peter's other students, Catherine felt responsible for her focus: "I came up with the idea for my story because the previous night I was watching a program on TV. In that space, I came up with this idea, and I asked him if it was all right, and he said yes, and I just had to write it out in class." Ultimately, each of Peter's students wrote unique stories, including science fiction, spy thrillers, romance and horror stories, travel adventures, and stories about school and sports.

For the most part, the students wrote during class. They sat with four to eight friends who, like Peter, provided ongoing feedback.[3] The nature of the peer feedback depended on the individual student and the dynamics of a particular table group. The student writer generally controlled the feedback, deciding the timing and type of feedback friends would give. For example, Catherine requested feedback from her table mates after her chapters were completed. As she explained, her table mates helped her notice when she "jump[ed] from one thing to another," caught her "mistakes," and just generally told her whether or not they liked what she wrote: "I write all that out first of all. Then I wait till my friends are finished. Then we just exchange papers . . . I just let my friends read from chapter to chapter, see if that's all right. And they, they try and read the whole thing, and if they like it, I'm satisfied" (Interview, July 19, 1988).

Nikita explained that at her table she and her friends read "quiet to ourselves" (Interview, May 25, 1988). Nikita trusted her friends' sense of what would please a peer audience: "It's easier to get your friends to read it through than what it is a teacher because your friends are about the age that the story's going over, to people about your age. It's better if you can get people your age to check it . . . You can compare your own work with your friends', and it's easier if you criticize their work. 'Cause the teacher criticizing your work, it's an adult. They might want it to be written differently, but your friends know how . . . they want it written."

Dickens controlled peer feedback by having his friends read only his completed writing: "I'd rather wait until it's finished before I show anyone else" (Interview, May 24, 1988).

While the students worked at their tables, Peter circulated around the room. Nikita explained Peter's role: "We talk to Mr. Ross individually. Like, he would ask us what we were doing. And when we get half way through it ask him if he could check up on it, say what he thinks. If he don't, if he thinks there's something wrong with it, we could perhaps rewrite it or put his ideas into the story as well." Catherine continued: "He'll sort of tell us or make suggestions."

Even though Peter's students wrote for two months, most wanted more time to work on their stories. Catherine explained, "He [Peter] gave us about two months or more," but "he said it had to go on a particular Tuesday and I said I needed some more time" (Interview, July 19, 1988). Likewise, Dickens complained about the "strict deadlines" for the exchanges, which put "pressure on you in a way . . . So maybe if we had more time to do each thing, that might be better" (Interview, May 24, 1988).

Not surprisingly, the U.S. and British stories differed in both form and substance. The U.S. stories contained dialogue, a brief setting, compressed character descriptions, and a single main event; the British stories relayed the writers' passions with thick description, elaborate plots, complex character development, and extended dialogue.

An example of one of the best short stories from each class will illustrate the differences. First, from the U.S., is Quirk's "He Felt Foolish at the Dance."

"I can't wait. I can't wait!"

It was the afternoon before the dance and Willie Afume had just come home from school and was getting dressed up for the dance at school.

Later . . .

It was 6:30 p.m.

"I can't wait to show off this rad new dance! I'll be the coolest kid in the eighth grade. 45 minutes till the dance."

"By Mom!"

Willie stepped out the front door and started walking confidently down the block wearing his new designer shirt, jeans, and underpants. He walked slowly down 27 blocks to the school gate. Delayed by a stop at the 7–11 for a 3 Musketeer's bar, he arrived at the school gate at 7:03pm.

"Right on time."

He handed over his ticket and entered the open auditorium door. After 20 minutes the song he had been waiting for hit the loudspeakers. Willie got out on the dance floor and proceeded to explode into a burst of action, jumping all over the place. After a minute or two he stopped, expecting an awed crowed to be gathered arouned him. Instead he saw about 40 other people doing the same dance. Turning bright red he crept out the door and wasn't seen again that night.

Quirk was not satisfied with his story. He explained that he had not written it for Peter's students and that he felt "it was kind of like a preface to a story." He called it a "rough draft" (Interview, May 10, 1988). His story touches on but does not delve into meaningful issues. Quirk confronts the self-consciousness of adolescence but cannot explore it in any depth without more fully developing his plot and character line.

Peter's students were able to probe more deeply into their topics. An example of a short story from Peter's class is provided by Dickens, who wrote a classic spy story. Dickens's story is packed with action and riddled with death and violence. The excerpts below present only a few scenes from "Commando," which ran to over five thousand words. Dickens begins:

Name: Rex Mason—Codename of Commando: *Striker*
Army No.: 3,61900
Primary Speciality: Ground Assault
Secondary Speciality: Unarmed Combat
Knowledge in Explosives.
Experience: Various Secret Missions In Nicaragua, Grenada. Aided in Storming Hotel Sieged By I.T.M (International Terrorist movement). Gets In And Out Of Any Situation Quickly.

The information printed out on the computer screen. Rex Mason was the best choice for the mission. The American Ambassador to Mexico had been kidnapped by an organization called the Front of Rebel Fighters and he was held captive in an impenetrable fortress. Impenetrable to all, except, a commando. A work force of specially trained soldiers. Only a skilled few could ever become one, and only a few of *those* were skilled enough to go on missions.

The commando Rex, at home and oblivious to the computer screen, has not had an assignment for a number of years. When Dickens changes the setting from the spy operation to Rex's home, he shifts his writing style—from clipped, partial sentences, which telegraph danger and excitement, to a leisurely and contemplative syntactic flow:

> He made himself a quick meal, a juicy steak, succulent chips and [handwriting unclear] of his favourite beer. he didn't know anything of his forth-coming mission . . . He was tired. His thoughts had drifted away from fighting, and killing long ago.

Rex is next summoned to the Pentagon, "the nerve centre of American military operations . . . a quiet monolith of modern architecture. so called because of its shape." There he receives his assignment to rescue the ambassador to Mexico. Rex is instructed to travel to Mexico by train under the alias "Sam Phibbs." His equipment will be dropped for him in "an empty, deserted village, just outside Mexico city."

Natural memory sequences reconstruct past events and provide pertinent background about Rex. One such memory sequence occurs while Rex is waiting in the Pentagon for his weapons. The machine guns and grenades trigger his memories of a previous mission in Afghanistan "to raid a weapons store and eliminate the head of the operation, a man called Kabul." This past mission establishes Rex's expertise as a commando and explains that he has been inactive because of an injury.

At strategic points in the story, Dickens reveals Rex's psychological state. For example, Rex worries before leaving for Mexico:

> Soon he would be in the field, a one-man army against a whole terrorist organization. Every mission (nearly) he had been on was a success, so should this one be, but there was still the risk. The penalty; the consequence for making one tiny little mistake, the ultimate price:

death. Would he die this time. No, he wouldn't. He knew he was too good for anyone to capure and kill him.

Ultimately, after many close encounters with death, Rex rescues the ambassador. Dickens's story concludes in Washington, where Rex receives a medal for his excellence and a permanent post as a commando.

Dickens's plot takes many twists and turns like the plot of a bestselling spy thriller. His protagonist, Rex, is a whole human being who is not only a man of action but a man with feelings, fears, and anxieties. Dickens constructs a strong narrative, presenting a sequence of ongoing events while also reconstructing prior events to provide background information. He shifts his writing style to match his material.

When Nancy's students received the British stories, their responses were mixed. Some were impressed, as was the case with Ashley:

> When I was reading the stories from England, . . . it seemed like they . . . write for themselves, like other kids and us, more than they write for the teacher, which, you know, I do. And I'm sure a lot of other people in our class do. You know, you try and think of the biggest word you can and, you know, make it sound, you know, better . . . And I think that's maybe why they can go on and on and on about one subject, like Lizzie and I were reading this twenty pages, I mean it was actually twenty pages. A twenty-page story from one kid! And it seemed like . . . the writer was actually kind of telling a story to the reader, you know, and you know, stopping to answer questions and doing all of that stuff, you know, backtracking so the person could understand it. (Interview, June 2, 1988)

Most of Nancy's students, including Ashley, wanted the British stories to be more compact. They thought the length of the British writing sometimes created repetition, confusion, or boredom. Ashley later labeled the same twenty-page story "long-winded." Nancy's students completed a response sheet for each British writer identical to the one they used with their own classmates, and one-third of the U.S. students advised the British writers to shorten their writing:

> Cut it down to under 4 pages.
> Compact the story to have all the action on just a few pages.
> He could make it shorter. It's so long that it drags on.
> Too much detail which made it confusing.

The story would be better if you didn't include the part about
 Bonet and Nikita in the beginning. It just makes the story
 longer and a little more boring.
He put in stuff that wasn't needed.
Too much repetition.

When these response sheets arrived in England, Peter's students were
confused by them, since they had never experienced this kind of peer
response. The British students are encouraged to respond positively
to one another, and so the unexpected negative edge in the U.S.
responses proved particularly off-putting.

On the whole, Peter's students were disappointed with the U.S.
short stories. Again they expected writing like their own and thought
the rigid structures of the U.S. writing created an absence of depth.
Nikita said: "All their work was repeated. Just as though they was
copying each other. You know, like the story system was the same.
They had to start on with a line, like the teacher gave them a line, a
couple of words, before they had to start, like 'It was always the same
thing at home.'" Catherine agreed, "When we got their short stories
from school, most of them were about dancing or something like that
. . . I got the idea that the teacher sort of gave them some sort of topic
or some sermon to make them go" (Interview, June 4, 1988).

Peter noted that his students missed the personal nature of handwritten work: "I think however short the handwritten pieces were,
the kids could always see that there was a person there behind it, but
they weren't so sure on the other bits [those that came on the com-
puter]" (Interview, September 19, 1988). Catherine expressed a similar sentiment: "It would be nice for them to do them [the stories] in
their own handwriting, to sort of get personal-like" (Interview,
June 4, 1988).

Taken on their own terms, the stories in both countries achieved
certain goals, yet the task Peter's students tackled was beyond the
scope of what Nancy's class did. The British stories present a vision
of what is possible for eighth graders. Peter's negotiations with his
students led them to produce developed writing to which they felt
committed; their commitment deepened as they tackled complex ideas
and delved into the psyches of their fictional characters.

How does Peter's instructional program support his students'
growth as writers? First, Peter encourages his students' efforts by
ensuring that each student will feel passionate about his or her focus.

After three years, Peter knows all the students and their interests, and this knowledge puts him in a strong position to provide guidance. In the beginning of the writing process, students come to Peter to discuss their focus, and he reaches out to them, ensuring that they all have a clear direction. These discussions also allow Peter to make sure his students are motivated and committed to their writing.

As well as guiding his students to a story focus, Peter creates a cohesive learning community where students receive ongoing teacher and student feedback. The students know when to ask for help, and Peter knows who needs his help. When Peter's students are writing, he is sensitive enough not to intrude but is available if they need him. The classroom is also filled with academic chatter, which Peter promotes by encouraging the students to sit at tables with friends. Whole class, teacher-led discussions are rare. Peer feedback occurs as part of these table-based conversations. The students can ask one another for help as they need it. They control the nature and timing of the feedback, and this helps them retain control of their writing.

Unlike Peter, Nancy assigns one topic to the entire class on each of several days and restricts the students' choices to something from the set she has assigned. Nancy is convinced that her students are motivated and enjoy her paragraph topics. However, Billy's remarks indicate that she is mistaken: "I didn't like writing about them [the topics] because I didn't know much about [them]" (Interview, March 2, 1988). Similarly, Ashley explains: "The ones I didn't like were, like, the ones where Ms. Hughes gave us a topic to write on and then we had to write about it. Especially, you know, 'cause some of the topics I really couldn't relate to or didn't know much about or just didn't know what to do. Like around when we were doing that, around March in our little green writing folders, which she would tell us you're supposed to write about 'It didn't fit'" (Interview, June 2, 1988). Although some students did enjoy this writing, most of them remained relatively detached.

In another contrast to Peter's students, Nancy's students write at home but are given feedback mostly during formal peer response groups and whole class discussions. Nancy asks for volunteers or calls on students to have their pieces of writing critiqued. The students receive encouragement but little substantial feedback, and because editing groups structure peer feedback, students lose control over its nature and timing.

The contrasts in these two classrooms have a profound influence on the students' writing. Peter's British classroom offers a model for what we might expect from eighth-grade students; however, even if we put institutional differences aside, the often negative U.S. response to the British writing shows how complex implementing such a model would be.

A Community Book in Britain and a Yosemite Booklet in the United States

At the end of the year, Peter's class produced two extensive collaborative projects, a book about their school and a book about their community; Nancy's students produced a small photo journal of a trip to Yosemite.

The 183-page community book from England contains three sections, one chronicling the geography of the borough; a second on the Docklands, a dock area under renovation, which the class visited; and a third on the history of the borough. The first section describes each student's home, as well as the student's journey to Garden Hill Community School. The home descriptions are single-author pieces. The first section also contains a street map of the borough, which is precisely marked to show each home in relation to Garden Hill.

The second section is a compilation of one- to two-page papers written by students about the Docklands area. The students left the Docklands after their visit with unique impressions, which they pursued further in their writing. For example, Nikita focuses on the plans for the renovation of the Docklands, whereas Delbert focuses on the history of the area. Nikita describes the planning for "a new shopping centre":

> Inside the centre there will be lots of other shops also a child caring unit where you can leave your children while you shop in the centre. The docklands will also be providing alot more water-sports such as sailing, rowwing, wet bikes and speed boats.

Delbert writes about Mr. Polish's talk on the Docklands' history:

> Mr. Polish . . . gave us a little history about the docks. Here are some facts:
> 1. *The eldest docks:* St. Katherine's docks is the eldest and it was built to take expensive cargo.
> 2. *When and Why the docks closed:* The docks began to close in the

mid-sixties and by the eighties all the docks had. The docks had to close because they were hardly used anymore. This was because faster, cheaper and safer ways had been found to transport the goods.

Delbert continued to unravel Mr. Polish's history of the docks for another page and a half. By this time, Peter's students know how to use thick descriptions to reflect what they find interesting.

The final section of the community book describes the area near the school from 3000 B.C. to the present. The first part of the history section is a timeline co-authored by Catherine and Jane. It begins:

B.C.
3000   Bones, beads and weapons discovered indicate human habitation here by this time.
57   The trinovantes, a tribe of ancient Britons, who lived in Essex and Suffolk are known to have lived in the area.
A.D.
43   The Roma Emperor, Claudius Caeser had a road built from Londen to Colchester. to-day this is Romford Road.
61   The Trinovates joined Queen Boadicea in her struggle against the Romans.

The timeline ends in the present. The history section continues with two maps, one of West Borough and East Borough from 1886 and another of present-day Newborough. Catherine brings the history up to the depression of the 1920s and 1930s and writes about West Borough Hall, which is now a school.

In the last part of the history section, Peter's students included a ten-page piece on the origin of the names of the roads in Newborough, photographs of local landmarks with accompanying explanatory captions, and a map showing where bombs fell during World War II. Sent under separate cover but originally planned as part of the community books are ten student pieces about a class walk around London.[4] Peter used to be a walking tour guide for the city of London. He enjoys taking his students on tours to teach them about their community and to motivate their writing.

One aspect of Peter's exchanges with his students involves motivating them to do various kinds of writing. He had been having some difficulties with Dickens who, given the choice, always preferred writing fiction. The community book provided an opportunity to encourage Dickens to write nonfiction. Dickens's comments about the

London walk are revealing: "I like what I'm doing now, about writing about London because I think the way Mr. Ross planned that was to make it interesting to start with, like taking us all round London . . . You're taking in all the sights . . . I think we treated that day out not as a school trip but sort of more of a leisure trip. I think that might be the way Mr. Ross planned it. So that we'd be more interested in it when we came back."

The Yosemite booklet produced by Nancy's students was not an elaborate project. It contained forty photographs, one per page, with accompanying captions of one to two sentences that named locations in the park or briefly identified the students and activities photographed. One such caption reads, "Here we have two happy campers (Chip and Chuck) writing in their Journals. Notice the Redwood trees in the background."

In his end-year interview Dickens reflected on the Yosemite booklet his class had just received and their reactions to it:

Well when I first saw the thing you know, just sitting on Mr. Ross's desk, I thought well at last we're going to get a very good clear picture of what America's like. But when we got it I was pretty disappointed . . . But I think the main drawback was it was mainly pictures. Like there was a big picture that covered about this much of the page and there was about five or six lines of writing. It said more about the people in the picture than the place itself, whereas when we went on the London walk, Mr. Ross asked us specifically to write in detail about it so that they could get a good picture of London or wherever we go. But I don't think we got a very clear picture with their faces. (Interview, July 19, 1988)

Dickens is less interested in the "faces," that is, in the individual students, than he is in learning about the place.

Giving the Yosemite booklet as an example, Nancy explains that her class could have approached the exchange differently but only at the expense of other activities she felt were important:

Before the kids go to Yosemite, for instance, they do a whole study on the geology of the area and the history of the area and . . . there's quite a bit involved. And then it's basically when they get there, it's the culmination of the activity, so they're walking and keeping journals and things of that nature, but at that point it's, they're to take in the scenery, I guess, would be the best way to say it. But they could have done something like that. Had I known that it was to be a piece, you know we could have been doing ongoing things about writing up the history of the valley and the stages and done some things that had been there. But then you see the ultimate problem with that is the time constraints because, you know, you're trying to get, in the meantime you're teaching this, that, and the other.

Rethinking Expectations for Student Writing

Peter's and Nancy's expectations for their students' writing are reflections of national trends in each country. Although extended pieces are sometimes part of the U.S. English/language arts curriculum, as was the case with Carol Mather's "gifted" class (see Chapter 4), such writing is not the norm. Especially in the middle school, U.S. students do not routinely spend months or even weeks of intensive work on major pieces of writing. By contrast, the kind of sustained writing that Peter's students did as the year progressed has been a feature of British English teaching for the past two decades; British youngsters often start writing extended stories in the early elementary years. It is also noteworthy that Peter's class still writes serious fiction, a common feature of British secondary schools according to the national questionnaires.

In the United States, condensed writing is promoted, albeit inadvertently, in state, district, and local curriculum guidelines that Nancy, as a teacher-leader, participated in shaping. For example, the California Assessment Program, with its accompanying curricular guides, stresses variety at the inevitable expense of sustained work. The eighth-grade assessment requires students to write short pieces, impromptu and in forty-five minutes, in one of eight categories: autobiographical incident, problem-solution, report of information, evaluation, first-hand biographical sketch, story, observation, and analysis and speculation about effects (*Writing Assessment Handbook: Grade 8*, 1986). Teachers are expected to see that their students master these eight kinds of writing, leaving little time for extended work (Loofbourrow, 1992). By contrast, the British GCSE, at the time of the exchanges, required just four types of writing over the two-year examination course.[5]

The latest surveys from the U.S. National Assessment of Educational Progress (NAEP) (Applebee et al., 1990a) indicate how little writing U.S. students actually do. According to NAEP data, even Nancy's students write more than most U.S. eighth and twelfth graders: "The amount of writing that eighth- and twelfth-grade students reported doing for English class was limited. Less than two-thirds of the students in either grade reported they were asked to write one or two paragraphs at least once a week, and only one-third reported writing one or two page papers this often. Just 14 percent of the eighth graders and 9 percent of the twelfth graders reported being asked to write a paper of three or more pages on a weekly basis" (p. 7). Nancy's approach is also consistent with national norms for teachers of writing identified as outstanding by NWP site directors (Freedman, 1987). At the secondary level (grades 7–12) Freedman (pp. 26–27) found that only 13.1 percent of these teachers reported that their students were writing something longer than four pages, compared to 3.6 percent of the usual secondary teachers (grades 9–12) that Applebee (1981) surveyed. Obviously, quantity does not guarantee quality, but without some degree of quantity, extended projects of the type Peter's students produce are not possible. The NAEP statistics, along with Freedman's and Applebee's national surveys, indicate that students in the United States rarely work on extended or projectlike writing in any instructional program.

Peter's sharing of responsibilities with his students keeps them interested in working on a single piece over long stretches of time. Capturing the attention of these relatively young students and motivating them to stick with the same topic for several months is not easy. The students must feel strongly committed to their writing. Through his classroom exchanges, Peter ensures that all his students have chosen a focus for their writing that they care deeply about.

Like Fiona (see Chapter 4), Peter rejects individualized workshop approaches like those currently posed as the alternative to traditional teacher-dominated classrooms in the United States. He calls such individualization the "learner-centered curriculum of the 1960s"; it does not account for the importance of creating an intellectual classroom community. From Peter's point of view, creating this strong intellectual community is essential to his teaching and is especially critical in mixed-ability and multicultural classes, where diverse student voices have so much to offer. He uses the force of the community to motivate his students and his knowledge of their interests and academic needs to be sure they learn.

Also like Fiona, Peter gradually increases the levels of student decision making across the year. For the autobiographies and short stories his students chose their own focus and worked at their own pace, seeking help from Peter and their peers as they felt the need. By the time they wrote their community book, Peter's students made most of the decisions about what to include, and they worked together to coordinate this class-authored effort. During the year, Peter's students also decided to write several pieces spontaneously. These included descriptions of the British television show "East Enders" and accounts of a hurricane that hit London.

Peter's student Nikita offered a few pedagogical suggestions to the U.S. team: "Let them write about what they want to write about as well . . . So far you keep writing the same thing, who we are, what we do, things like that. Try it like, let them write their own things" (Interview, May 25, 1988).

In the United States the major structural reforms widely advocated in education (for example, Boyer, 1983; Goodlad, 1984; Sizer, 1984, 1992) are in need of specific curricular guidance. Along with Fiona Rodgers, Peter presents a picture of alternative institutional structures and changed expectations about what writing is, what it is for, and how it can be integrated with the rest of the curriculum. This picture should stimulate our thinking about new possibilities for writing classrooms as we plan our schools of tomorrow.

Chapter 6

Creating Opportunity, Implementing National Examinations

Ann Powers, Gillian Hargrove

Ann Powers and Gillian Hargrove taught the oldest students in the exchange, grade 9 in the United States and Form 4 in Britain. Gillian would teach her exchange class for two years (Forms 4 and 5) to prepare them for the British national examinations in language and literature. (Chapter 2 outlines the British examination system and Chapter 3 provides preliminary information on Gillian's examination class.)

Examiner versus Exchange Audience

In 1987–1988, the year of the exchange, the British language and literature exams had just been revised. Before 1987, students were separated into two examination tracks: one for the university bound and the other for the nonuniversity bound. Beginning in 1987, all students took the same course and the same exams, the General Certificate of Secondary Education or GCSE. The revised examination allowed Gillian to teach mixed-ability exam classes.

In 1987, a further innovation of the GCSE was also implemented: schools were able to choose the option of coursework (a portfolio) as the only basis for evaluation. Before the coursework-only option, students were evaluated solely by their performance on a "terminal examination" at the end of the two-year course. The "terminal examination" consisted of impromptu essay questions and writing prompts, given in a testing setting. At the time of the exchange most British teachers, including Gillian, were pleased with the progressive direction that the GCSE examination was taking.[1]

When I was planning the exchange project with my British colleagues, Alex McLeod and Ellie O'Sullivan, we assumed it would be possible for the exchange writing and the exam portfolios to be merged. Ellie's experience in a writing exchange with Swedish students made her enthusiastic about its potential to stimulate strong examination writing: "My feeling is . . . that they [the exchange and examiner audiences] are compatible. It simply means planning quite carefully how you set about the whole thing, and having the communication with the teacher on the other side, because they don't have those conflicting expectations" (Interview, February 6, 1989).

Gillian began the exchange year by combining the exchange and examiner audiences. She sent the first two exchanges, school introductions and autobiographies, to the United States and kept the originals for possible inclusion in the students' examination portfolios. But after these first two exchanges, she stopped combining the two audiences. She felt constrained by the examination syllabus and those parts of the exam writing that included essays on literature and arguments relevant to topical issues, and she worried that such writing would bore U.S. students. Gillian decided to separate the two audiences and have her students write different pieces for their GCSE portfolios and for the exchange: "I thought it [the exchange] was like an opportunity, an opportunity for writing for an audience, and I thought at the time that the GCSEs were in fact—were probably far enough away for it not to matter at that stage" (Interview, February 6, 1989).

From mid-December through mid-February an ongoing teachers' strike at Manderley Grove kept Gillian from meeting with her exchange class for two months.[2] After the strike Gillian and her students faced reconnecting with Ann Powers's class in the United States and catching up with their GCSE writing. Gillian and her students felt that they had lost their stride. As Surge commented, "There was a bad moment . . . with the teachers' strike. We could have got a lot more work done, a lot more things accomplished, but carrying on with the teachers' strike spoilt it a lot" (Interview, July 21, 1988). Gillian explained her students' attitudes after the strike: "You know, when you pick up kids at the end of a strike like that, you don't pick up the same kids you had at the beginning . . . You pick them up and they're angry and they're disillusioned, and one bit of them is saying, 'We've missed out a lot of work, and I want to catch up.' But the other bit, you know, which is just kids, and they are out of all those habits, and all those routines, and they have done absolutely nothing for you for about six weeks—it was probably longer" (Interview, March 13, 1989).

By mid-February, with more than half the year over, Gillian found it burdensome to continue to have her students write for both the exchange and the GCSE. The GCSE, with its high stakes, took priority, and the exchange writing for the rest of the year was minimal. The final two exchange projects in Gillian's class consisted of an audiotape and photographs of the students' neighborhood with short, ironic commentary.

An Exchange of Responsibilities with Low-Tracked U.S. Students

Ann Powers's students had low scores on standardized reading and language tests and were grouped in a "remedial" class. Before entering Ann's class, these students had minimal reading or writing skills, and they had to work hard to produce any extended writing. Ann found the exchange to be a catalyst in motivating her students to write, even though the writing from England was slow in coming. Fortunately, unlike Gillian she was not pressured by an outside examiner audience and could focus as much of her writing curriculum as she wanted on the cross-national writing exchange.

Ann engaged her students by carrying out a U.S. version of exchanging responsibilities with them. She encouraged her students to take ownership of their writing and allowed them to compose in class, while they sat in small groups around tables (see Figure 3.6). The class was similar to a writing workshop, where feedback is freely given by the instructor and students' peers.

The class's enthusiasm for the writing exchange was not dampened by the limited amount of writing they received from Gillian's class, but to make up for the reduced flow, Ann initiated and developed a continuing classroom conversation about England with her students. She also helped them read and reflect on the British writing that did arrive. When the writing exchange was over, Ann, inspired by the British model, arranged with her principal to teach the same students for a second year.

Effects on Student Writing

For the first two writing exchanges, the school introductions and autobiographies, when the British students addressed a merged exchange and examiner audience, the contrasts between the two classes centered mostly on subtleties of depth in the students' writing. By the end of the year, however, as the exchange and examiner audiences diverged, for the British students the contrasts shifted and became more pronounced. The last piece Ann's students wrote for the cross-national exchange, interviews with twelfth-grade students, and the writing Gillian's students prepared for their examination portfolios illustrate the differences.[3]

School Introductions

Both Gillian's and Ann's students devoted the first month of school to writing school introductions. Figure 6.1 shows when these introductions were written and charts the writing across the year.

Gillian followed the usual British approach. Since her class was preparing for the British national examinations, she planned it so that these school introductions could be included in the students' coursework portfolios. She kept the original work and sent photocopies to Ann's students. As Comp explains in her response to the U.S. introductions, "The reason you did not receive our original letters is because we used it for our course work."

Meanwhile, Ann chronicled the evolution of her approach to teaching writing in a log. For the students' first piece of writing, she assigned the paper topic: the class would introduce their high school, Costa Mesa. But by mid-September, her ideas about assigning paper topics were changing, moving toward a more collaborative approach. Evidence of this change is found in Ann's log entry on September 16, when she first wrote "assigned topics" and then corrected herself by adding "negotiated actually."

In actuality, Ann was not negotiating topics but rather the focus within a topic. She recorded how this process worked. After a class discussion her students chose to focus on school issues such as "daily student life, student activities, athletics, lunchtime, classes, our class." Like the British teachers, Ann used this interaction with her students to encourage them to take responsibility for their writing and provided a structure that was flexible enough to offer choice within it.

Ann realized that it would be a challenge for her students to write the lengthy pieces she felt were necessary for the cross-national exchange. Her students had had little opportunity to write, let alone tackle difficult tasks such as writing to an unfamiliar audience. She contemplated various ways to decrease her students' stress while

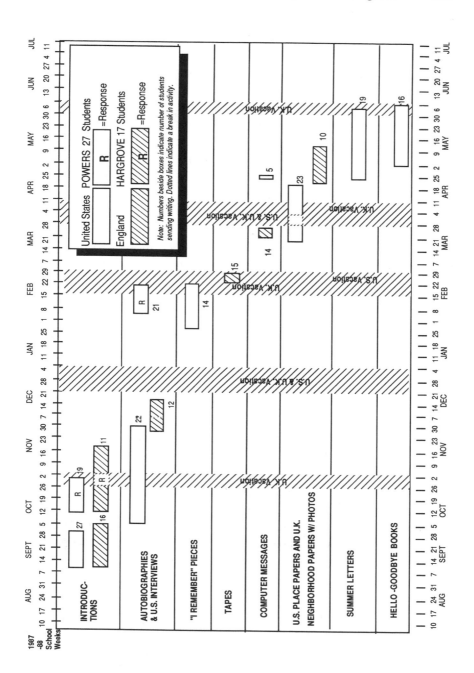

Figure 6.1 Timeline for the Ann Powers–Gillian Hargrove Exchange

making their writing challenging and meaningful, and appropriate to send to Britain in the exchange. Ann finally decided to use collaborative writing to ease the pressure. She reflected on this decision in her log: "I hope writing a letter from the whole group is best. I wonder if they should be able to write different parts. Maybe a choice—each table writes one or each student writes about *one* aspect of the topic. I like that. Somebody writes a summary statement. Each person chooses a subtopic." After considering several alternatives, Ann decided to have each student, in a table group of approximately four students each, write a section of the piece so that each of her eight tables would produce a single multi-authored offering.

Ann also appointed each student at the table to a leadership role: one was in charge of taking notes; another compiled the first draft; another revised the final draft. Ann used "note taking" to help her students brainstorm and begin the writing process. She recorded in her log on September 18 that her students had begun taking notes at their tables: "Each table compiled a list of ideas to go in their letters to London. Then we shared them with each other." Ann also explained how she supported her students' brainstorming: "I suggested that we could bring in others to discuss various topics—like a counselor to talk about classes. Maybe Mr. Storer [the principal] to talk about Costa Mesa."

Ann's "remedial" students were so enthusiastic about writing and creating for the exchange with London that they even stayed after class. She noted evidence of the class's excitement: "D.M. stayed after class to ask about taking photos. He wants to get different groups' pictures. Table 8 wants to send Amer. flags."

Ann was so delighted by her students' enthusiasm that she concluded her September 18 log entry with "What a terrific day." On September 24 the table groups revised their writing in class: "The sharing they did in their letters was remarkable. Many took theirs home to type. Each underwent substantial revision. I have never had success working with groups so early in the year with a stanine 3 [remedial] group."

By the end of September, Ann's class had completed their first project for the writing exchange and mailed it to Britain. The eight multi-authored pieces were bound as a single book. At the end of the process Ann concluded: "The spirit in the room is different from any of my previous English classes. The dynamics are not the same. It is definitely not a teacher-centered class. They think 'table.'"

From the start, Ann used the writing exchange to change her classroom structure to allow her to collaborate with her students. By focusing her curriculum on her own students' interests as writers, and the British students' interests as readers, she was able to excite her students about the writing exchange and about her exchange of responsibilities with them. On September 11 Mark wrote in his journal, "I hope it will be fun writing to these people. I think it will be fun." In her journal entry, Lisa wrote, "I think It is neat we will be communicating with other people out of our country. There are interesting things to find out." The writing exchange offered Ann a device for engaging her traditionally low-achieving students in more serious academic activities than they had experienced before.

Although Ann pushed her students to assume a great deal of responsibility, it was difficult for them to veer far from her directions. Her students are a part of an educational process that discourages student control and makes it difficult for students to make their own choices. Every group kept to the assigned topic, introducing Costa Mesa High School. D.M.'s group chose to focus on pep rallies:

> Dear Students of Manderley Grove,
> How are you? We are fine. I'm going to tell you a little about Costa Mesa High School . . . We have a big ceremony called a rally. At the rally we have dances. We also have competitions like hiting a pinata or who can scream the loudest. The cheerleaders come out and do great cheers for us. The rallies are always on the day of the football game.

Jessica's group wrote a similar piece about school life that focused on the prom:

> I guess I'm going to start by telling you about our special occassions at C. M. Its' special because it's fun to show off your new clothes and your date. Some people get rental cars, or some just have there on, but people that like to be the fanciest get limo's. The girls wear dresses and the guys wear tuxedos or suits. You and your date take pictures. They play music and you dance or walk around looking at other couples.

These samples are typical of the class's writing at the start of the year. Ann's students showed little variation in approach, style, or quality and were almost formulaic in their writing. Their prose had little personality, vitality, or strength. Some would assert that this type of writing represents the limits for "remedial" students, who have difficulty producing any writing, much less powerful writing. Delpit (1986, 1988), however, argues that basic writers are capable of interjecting their voices into their writing but need to be taught technical skills. Others might claim that the lack of voice is due to group rather than individual authorship, what is commonly called "committee prose." However, the students' subsequent individual writing also showed a similar lack of personal voice, indicating that the lack of voice in these pieces did not stem from "committee prose."

Unlike Ann's group, Gillian's mixed-ability students were accustomed to taking responsibility for their writing and were confident enough to personalize what they wrote. Gillian's students strayed from the assigned topic and wrote about everything from the dearth of English television channels to the rough neighborhood that surrounds Manderley Grove School. Their school introductions expressed each writer's unique personality. For example, De Mille's writing voice captivated his audience. He rejected the assigned topic, saying he "just cant be bothered to go through all that again." His casual opening establishes his tone:

> Dear Pupils in California,
> Sunny California I believe the saying is. And what a place to be in. The sun, the moonlight, the romance in the air and all the good looking girls. WOW. That's the place I'd like to be. And one day (by Gods Grace) I will go to Sunny California where all the nice business like people are at.

De Mille then introduces himself and reports that "Europe ain't much of a place to live in all your lives" and that "If you want to have fun and adventure, then England would be the last place to go. But if you want to die early, grow ugly and live like a pauper, then ENGLAND would be the best place to go." Keeping his readers' attention, De Mille continues:

> Anyway, lets not make the day dull. I know you've got to read a lot of letters and I appreciate that. So i'll just get straight to the point. Could you perhaps tell me approximately how many channels you have on your t.v.s?
> Another thing that has fascinated me is that in America there are plenty of good looking girls and women. Lovely legs, big *busts* and pretty features. Not like over here in ENGLAND. There are hardly any

decent looking, good figured and pleasant girls. They are all dry faced, rusty skinned and out of shaped things called girls/women.

De Mille ends his introduction by describing what he is wearing in the class photograph and asking for pictures of Ann's students. In an interview, De Mille discussed creating a written voice for the U.S. audience: "I tried to act as an American, acting like, uh, Texas. Using kind of slang of Texas. That was my introduction to, that's kind of how I stereotyped . . . perhaps something like J.R. [from the television show *Dallas,* which was popular in England at the time]" (Interview, May 26, 1988).

As soon as the British introductions arrived, Ann distributed them to her students. Word spread quickly that De Mille's was "phenomenal." In order to share his writing with the entire class, Ann asked D.M. to read it aloud. D.M. began reading but stopped because of his uncontrollable laughter over the word "bust." Ultimately, one of the girls completed the reading.

Within two weeks of receiving the British students' introductions, each of Ann's students sent a response letter to someone in Gillian's class. Ann wrote in her log on October 26 that her students voluntarily stayed in class late on a Friday afternoon when the rest of the school was at a large pep rally because they wanted to complete their responses: "What a miracle occurred on Friday . . . Special schedule— rally—parade and all. They wrote their letters willingly. Even Jack Harper who doesn't read or write worked all period on a response. One full page. Everybody worked! . . . They were delighted that Guillermina [vice principal] gave them pens too . . . I told them she did this because she was so impressed with what they were doing. She couldn't believe they did that work on Friday either."

Writing to the British students encouraged Ann's students' enthusiasm about writing and encouraged them to be meticulous about their work. Ann wrote on October 29 that her students were willing to proofread their letters twice and to help each other: "I'll remind them of how they snickered at the Manderley Grove students who misspelled some words." Even after the proofreading, Ann worried about her students' mechanics: "London is going to see a few boo boos."

In an attempt to establish a personal connection with a particular British student, the U.S. students mimicked the British introductions. Jessica's letter to De Mille echoes his style and even uses his words:

Dear De Mille,
Hi my name is Jessica Franklin I'm 14 years old and I attend Costa
Mesa High School. I'm in the 9th grade. I have black hair, brown eyes,
I'm light skin I weigh about 111 pounds. My height is 5'4.
   We had recieved your pictures today but I didn't get a chance to look
at them. Your school seems real fun cause you can have all kinds of
people come in and out of your school. California is not so sunny right
now it's rainy. In your letter you had asked about how many channels
we have we have many channels. You said that you guys only have 4
channls, but do you have channels called like HBO, MTV, Showtime.
It sound like London is so poor. You said that the girls over there looks
so ugly, dry faced, rusty skin. California seems to be a great place for
you, can see the sun, the moonlight and the romance in the air, but if
you do come down to see sunny California come down to Costa Mesa.
Now I had got the chance to see your picture today and you guys took
a good picture. I had seen you, you are wearing a black and grey jacket.
I think your real cute in that picture. Well I have to go now cause my
teacher is going to mail this letter now. See ya later and write back.
Yours Turly,
Jessica

Jessica has taken on so much of De Mille's voice she has obscured her
own.

   Ann's assessment of her class's responses was that they "did a
credible job of addressing individuals, answering questions about
Calif. girls, weather, TV channels, litter. Asking others . . . why they
put down their country." However, she continued to worry about
how her students' weak mechanical control would be viewed.

   Like Ann's class, Gillian's class was also excited to receive the
writing from abroad. In their replies Gillian's students again allowed
their lively voices to come through in their writing. De Mille begins:

Dear Folks,
How you down there, dear kids of California? Before I go any further,
I have to ask this one question. Do you have any girls in your form
class? The amount of girls I saw turned out to be boys. Now why
would I think of a horrid thing like that I wonder?

After complimenting the U.S. letters, De Mille continues:

Tell me. Have you got a programme over there in the states called
"Rod Serling's Night Gallery?" That is one series I would like to see.

He concludes with a few personal words:

> To tell you the truth I haven't really got much to say to you guys. I'm not one for going into great detail about school and activities. Although our teacher's head does look like a cabbage.
> Anyway folks. I've got to be saying goodbye so . . . goodbye
> From Master De Mille

With this first writing exchange, Gillian's and Ann's students initiated a written dialogue between the two countries. They wrote about themselves, keeping in mind how their foreign audience viewed them. They were forced to observe and reflect on the similarities and differences between their countries. They encouraged one another, relayed personal experiences, and responded to each other. The British students were practiced writers who had been encouraged throughout their schooling to show their personalities when they wrote, while the U.S. students struggled to produce the most extended writing many had ever attempted.

In both countries the students' control over the mechanics of writing was far from perfect. Ann helped her students with spelling, punctuation, and sentence structure, often correcting their prose for them when they had difficulty doing it on their own. But even with her help, Ann's students still had many residual errors. Gillian adhered to the strictures of the British examinations, which forbade her from correcting even her bilingual writers. She would correct a paragraph to model proper mechanics, but then her students were left alone to correct the rest.

Whereas Ann and her students worried about how the British students would react to mechanical flaws in their writing, Gillian and her students were concerned about something entirely different. They were bored by the sameness of the U.S. presentations and wondered where the individual personalities were. When Ellie O'Sullivan interviewed Gillian and Philippa Furlong, who taught the other British examination class, about their difficulties in managing the exchange and the examination, Gillian worried about the mismatch between her "mixed-ability" and Ann's "low-tracking" class and, for the first time, spoke candidly about her impressions of the U.S. students' writing:

> I do have a reservation about matching a mixed-ability class against a low-tracking class because one of the things I found about the low-tracking class, and I do know that Ann Powers at the other end didn't

feel this about her kids' writing, I found their writing very bland . . . because, um, there was a kind of chatty monotone about it. And it wasn't about ideas. It was almost as if everything I'd got from the students was like, you know, yet another chatty effusive introductory letter and nothing developed. As though, you know, nothing more was going to come. Now my worry about pupils at my end, and God knows and I worked not to, not to convey that way, was that they got bored. And indeed they did. I mean they were actually bored by these letters from America. And I've not been able to say this properly, you know. (Interview, July 18, 1989)

Autobiographies and Mini-biographies

As soon as Ann's students' responses to the British students' introductions were in the mail, Ann prepared her class for the next exchange. It would include two parts: personal autobiographies and an interview of another student, a kind of mini-biography.

To help her students begin their autobiographies, Ann first asked them to write eight impromptu "Who Am I" pieces. They wrote on notebook paper, which they placed in their writing portfolios. Ann provided a general topic: an "influence on your life"; "family"; "when I look in the mirror I see . . ."; "I collect . . ."

Ann was impressed that her students exhibited what for them was a long attention span. During one "Who Am I" session, she wrote in her log, "They have been working for 8 minutes and most are still going. Remarkable." About another session she wrote, "worked quietly for 10 minutes." For the "Who Am I" writing, Ann and her students did not negotiate. She decided how this writing would be done and what the focus would be.

As Ann's students prepared to start their autobiographies, she asked them to choose four of their "Who Am I" pieces to merge together into a piece of at least four paragraphs. In her December 1 log entry, Ann explained that she expected the move from the "Who Am I" impromptus to the autobiographies to be difficult:

> I anticipated some trouble. Usually, kids don't want to move one piece to a longer piece. My experience shows me that teachers see these layer structures but kids don't. Put an essay together in pieces, tell them to turn it into one and they say "What?" again and again. Also, I feared that the 4 paragraphs would remain just that: lumps. Separate and unconnected.

But she felt that she was mistaken:

> I was wrong. Because this class knows where their writing is going (+ who is going to read it). They all, without exception, gave their writing a context. Their beginnings have voice, they are conscious of audience. "Hi! My name is D.M. Gibbs." "My name is Nikki. I'll tell you first about what I look like." "I'm going to begin by telling you a story of myself."
>
> They also put the pieces together smoothly; most adding material not originally in drafts.

By December 4, the final autobiographies were ready for mailing to England. Jessica's is typical. She begins with an overview:

> I'm going to tell you about myself, about what I look like, what I like to do and where I'm going to be in five years. But now I'm going to tell you about my favorite sport and that is track in the springtime I'm going to sign-up for it. Track season starts in January. I enjoy running in the summer I would always go out and run.

She continues by describing her looks:

> Right now I'm going to tell you about how I look. I have black hair, brown, a light completion I'm 5'3 or 5'4 and my hair is the fair length.

After explaining her college plans and her desire to be a secretary, she embarks on her most elaborate section:

> The most funest place I'd like to go is Disneyland and Great America. If you don't know what they are I well tell you Disneyland is a fun entertainment place where people would go with there family or friends. Disneyland has many fun rides to get on and a show to see and going out to eat. At Great America they have the some thing to but different rides to get on. But at Disneyland they have this ride called Magic Mountain. And those are the fun place I'd to go.

Jessica then describes her hobby, collecting goldfish. In her last lines, she calls her autobiography a "letter" and closes with a letter form:

> Will I'm going to end this letter now so I hope to hear from you very soon.
> Yours Truly,
> Jessica Franklin

In her final interview Jessica reported: "I never did a autobiography of myself before" (Interview, June 2, 1988), and explained, "In my other English class, we just did reports and read books, but we never written things." Like most of her classmates, Jessica did not connect writing the autobiography with writing the "Who Am I" pieces. When asked how she got her ideas, she mentioned help from her table mate and friend, Traci, and also said that ideas just came to her. When asked how she decided to write about her hobby of collecting goldfish, for example, Jessica explained: "My mind just popped into my bedroom. And so then I just went in and started talking about my fish" (Interview, March 31, 1988). Although it was not the case, Jessica perceived that she completed her entire autobiography in one day, during one class session, and remarked, "I was kinda fast" (Interview, March 31, 1988).

When asked at the end of the year if she could improve her autobiography if she had a chance to revise, Jessica, like most of her classmates, said she would "put down more details": "I think the most interesting part of my life was when I was little. More little. And you know being put in this world . . . I think that's, that's what I should have mainly did. My autobiography of, of my childhood while I was growing up" (Interview, June 2, 1988). By the end of the year Jessica had begun to think about connecting herself to her writing, and, as the writing from Gillian's class will show, she modeled her ideas for improving on the writing she read from England.

When D.M. discussed his autobiography, he showed that he was able to provide details orally but had difficulty incorporating them into his writing. His written work describes his memory of his first home run:

> I'm going to tell you about my first homerun. It was April 12, 1983 I was a minor league baseball player for the Vallejo Twins. It was the bottom 9th inning and I was batting next after my best friend Chris Smith (shortstop). He struck out and that made it 2 out and one man on second base. It was my turn at bat. I swung at two pitches and they were both strikes. I walked away from the plate swung the bat a few times and walk back up there again. Everyone was cheering for me because it was the Little League World Series Championship. The pitcher threw a curveball across the plate. I swung and the ball connected with the bat. It was for sure a homerun. We won 11 to 10.

D.M. provides facts about the game and his home run but fails to convey its personal importance. In his interview, however, he easily and proudly described its significance for him and his reasons for writing about it for the British students:

> I thought, you know, pretty amazing, you know, this little shrimpy kid hitting a home run. I was ten. Yeah ten . . . I was real powerful. I could, you know, back then I think I could throw about forty miles per hour in baseball, and, you know, I was pretty good. Know, we won the championships, um, went to the World Series . . . Usually I would strike out, but I was a good pitcher, but I would usually strike out. Wouldn't really hit that much. And you know, so I thought I write about something, baseball, which they probably don't even play. Mostly they play is rugby and football, yeah. And I thought that was, you know, maybe I should write about it. It's pretty interesting. (Interview, March 25, 1988)

At the end of the year D.M. reread his autobiography and orally added even more detail about the game—how his team traveled from California to Pennsylvania and "played the Japanese Little League team" and that the game was televised. He went on to explain his role in his team's win and the significance of this game in building his confidence and improving his future performance: "I hit two home runs out of that season so, and after that minor league . . . that was three home runs of that year, and then that following year, I went and I hit all fifteen, out of 20 games we played. So that was a exciting year for me" (Interview, June 2, 1988).

D.M. said that if he had an opportunity to revise his autobiography, he would add more detail: "I should have told them . . . what I played. I mean, you know, what position I played, uh, should have told them, you know, what was this World Series Championship located at . . . what was the crowd like, you know. Hmm, hmm. That's about it. Because basically everything else was pretty good" (Interview, June 2, 1988). By the end of the year D.M. knew he needed detail in his writing, but even then, he did not realize that he could improve it by conveying the feelings he expresses so well orally.

As Ann's students wrote their autobiographies, they began their mini-biographies. The students first worked together to prepare incisive interview questions. On November 13 the class paired off and conducted fifteen-minute interviews for their biographies. On November 20, they handed drafts of the interviews in to Ann, and again she was pleased: "Everybody finished. They seemed to take more than usual pride in this writing since they called out to me that theirs was finished . . . This calling out seemed to be a self-congratulatory remark—look what I accomplished" (Log, November 20, 1988).

The biographies were remarkably similar to the autobiographies. In his biography of Henry, D.M. again has difficulty expressing himself in writing, but when he was interviewed about it on March 24, he again spoke with detail and voice. D.M. explained the process of interviewing Henry. Henry "wanted to talk about girls," and so D.M. followed Henry's lead and asked him questions about girls: "What kind of girls you like?" "How do you treat your girls?" "What's your secret to getting girls?" "What's the age?" "What kind of girls you talk to and and uh how many do you see usually a day?" Also, D.M. "asked him . . . where do he take, you know, his real girlfriends, the ones he be really going with. Where do take them, you know?" Henry's reply impressed D.M.: "He says he takes them on a cliff overlooking a shiny moon . . . He told me that he likes black, white, and Mexican. Um, then, um, I ask him did all his girls are they very good looking. And he said, you know, yes." Later in this same interview D.M. filled in more: "Nowadays he likes any girl that walks the streets. And, uh, so you never know who he likes. You know, one day he's with a Filipino. Next day he's with a black girl, you know."

D.M. writes:

> There a cool student in our 6th period English class named Henry Robbins. He's 5'7" and has black hair and Brown eyes. Henry is sixteen years old and drives a 1987 dropped Fiesta. His hobbies is girls, partin', having fun. Henry talks to all kinds of girls such as Black, White, and Mexican. All the girls he talk to are very good-lookin. Sometimes he talks to 10 to 15 girls a days. But sometimes he goes very serious with a girl once in a while. When he's with has a real girlfriends he takes her to a cliff over looking the shiny moon. Henry likes girls as much as they like him.

When he wrote this biographical piece, D.M. said, Henry helped him and Ann corrected his punctuation, but "everything else she [Ann] said was, you know, great" (Interview, March 25, 1988).

For this autobiography/biography exchange, Ann narrowed the scope of her negotiations with her students at some points in the teaching process and widened it at others. At times she controlled the decision making, and at other times she helped her students make decisions for themselves. At the end of this exchange, Ann's students assumed more responsibility for their writing than they did when they wrote the school introductions.

Meanwhile, Gillian continued to negotiate with her students in the usual British way. Her class wrote autobiographies but no biographies. Leabow explained how the process of negotiating with her teacher helped and motivated her but allowed her to decide what she would write: "We [the class] had a big long discussion about what we were going to put in, and I was one of the first to say what I was going to put in" (Interview, June 9, 1988).

As was the case for the introductions, Gillian conceptualized the audiences for the writing exchange and for the examination as one and the same. She made copies of her students' autobiographies to send to Ann's students, keeping the originals for possible inclusion in the examination portfolios. Gillian felt that autobiographical writing would be both appropriate for the examination and interesting to the students in Ann's class. In fact, at this point Gillian found the U.S. audience beneficial for the exam writing: "In some ways I felt that I got through to them because of the exchange . . . You really have to demand their cooperation in a way that you don't normally and that just brings you closer because you've got to be in it together. That's how I see it, so I think that's what made me able to know them better" (Interview, June 6, 1988).

The autobiographies from Gillian's class were more fully developed than those from Ann's class. Table 6.1 shows the length differences between the U.S. students' autobiographies and biographical interviews and the British students' autobiographies. Ann noted in her log that the British autobiographies were mostly autobiographical incidents or childhood memories. Gillian's students were able to achieve depth by focusing on relatively specific topics. Many wrote about an early traumatic experience, letting their voices come through. Deenie's opening in "My Early Memories" is typical:

> Lots of things have happened to me when I was little. I shall tell you some of them. I think the earliest thing I can remember was when I was about three. I had to go to the hospital for an operation on my navel. My mother said that when she felt my stomach once. She felt a hollowness near my navel. So she took me to the doctor and the doctor said that I would need an operation. I only spent a day in the hospital. I remember when I was wheeled to the operation room. and when the doctor was giving me gas to fall asleep. I was struggling not to smell

the gas! After that, I remember when my mom and dad came for me to go home. A few weeks after that. I remember when I came back to the hospital, so the nurse could take out my stitches.

Sly begins his piece, titled "In My Prime," with the following:

> When I was about 10 years old I shot a boy in the leg with an airgun because I did'nt like him and I was hideing behind a dustbin in the flat I lived in.

He continues to elaborate on the incident for two and a half pages, telling about how he fought with this boy, how he and a friend scared the boy with a dog, and then how a dog chased him and his friend until he fell. Sly then reports, "When I finished telling my mum what happened this is what she said, 'that fucking boy allway bring his damn dog around here.'" His mother then threatened to call the police on the boy and Sly concludes, "me and my friend began to laugh."

De Mille wrote about the traumas he experienced when he was about eight years old and working with other kids to produce films. The first chapter of his two-chapter autobiography begins:

> In 1981, a couple of mates of mine all grouped together in a meeting, deciding that we as kids should all start on a film production. I came

Table 6.1 Autobiography (including U.S. biographical interviews) and place: Focal students' word counts

	Autobiography	Place	Total words
Powers (US)			
D.M.	280	147	427
Lisa	470	304	774
Mark	353	141	494
Jessica	502	276	778
Total	1,605	868	2,473
Hargrove (GB)			
Deenie/Surge	610	292	902
Leabow	647	233	880
K.C.	1,251	452	1,703
DeMille	779	336	1,115
Total	3,287	1,313	4,600

up with the titles, plots, ideas and facilities. The rest were just a cast, production team, or pretence cameramen.

De Mille tells about a Kung Fu film the group tried to put together but which never saw production because of infighting among the kids. In De Mille's second chapter, he writes about his eventual success at a new school:

> When I left Crissmore School in March 1982, I was very relieved. The pressure that I got from there was terrible. I had to leave otherwise the important events that have happened in my life, wouldn't of happened.

About his adjustment to his new school, he writes, "Here I was more content. I made friends quickly and fitted into the school like a jigsaw puzzle." With these new friends, De Mille produced a film:

> This time it was successful. I had the right kind of people, perfect co-operation, and most of all I had the freedom and equipment to do what I wanted.
>
> I got a close friend called Suhara to design our own paper money which would be our wages. I asked Ahmed to write the scripts because he was a good storywriter. I got Steven to create the props.

He continues on, explaining the roles of four other peers, and then comments, "And our teacher, was the audience, the adviser, the one we got permission from and the one who gave use the freedom. And lots of it." De Mille next describes the elaborate projects he and his friends completed but concludes by explaining that he again had to change schools. At this point, his film career stopped. Recently, however, De Mille writes, he authored a forty-five-minute radio play, *Ride on the Orient Express*.

To write his autobiography, De Mille stayed up all night and wrote it essentially in one sitting, working alone. He said it was easy for him to write and that he did not draft; if he did not like a direction he was taking, he would just throw away what he had written and start again. De Mille assessed this writing: "I think it was an average piece of work. I'm glad that I wrote it and I think that its so forceful that you have to rush so that you forget if— so that when you write it on paper, you're rushing through to get it all" (Interview, July 21, 1988).

Gillian was pleased with her class' autobiography writing: "Those pieces that my class wrote for the autobiography, I found them . . . very touching pieces and there was a lot of trust in them" (Interview,

June 9, 1988). She did think that some of her students, De Mille for example, could have stretched themselves more: "His autobiography, for all that it's kind of lavish in appeal, is actually, I think, really quite thin compared, say, with his [subsequent writing about literature] . . . That was the worry about his work in the early days, that, you know, he would just write very quickly, um, almost off the top of his head, and he wasn't a crafter" (Interview, June 9, 1988).

But in an interview late in the year, De Mille put forth another view about his writing for the exchange. When asked what his best writing for the year was, he replied: "Some of the work I did from about September to November [introduction and autobiography]. Other people may not see it, but what I wrote there was kind of like what was inside me. I could read that and feel what I was actually feeling at the time. It was kind of like representing my life" (Interview, May 26, 1988).

The British autobiographies arrived in late January. Ann's students were excited to get the package but had trouble reading them, both because they were long and because the photocopies were light. Ann's solution was to read them aloud, selecting several each day: "We savour each one when we are fresh—at beginning of period. Then we write in our logs about what we notice" (Log, January 28, 1988). By February 4, Ann had completed the reading and wrote that her class had decided that "each of them would pick up a Manderley Grove autobiography and begin a thank you." In the end, Ann's class replied to each British student, so that several students received more than one thank-you. D.M.'s response to Deenie is typical:

> Dear Deenie,
> Hi! I just would like to thank you for writing about yourself it was very good and I like it. I liked it when you told us about when you were scared of big people and you used to run, cry, and scream back to your mother. I bet your mum has a migraine every once in a while. I had an operation once when I was 10 years old, for my foot. I know how it feels to have an operation. So never be very scared of any doctor because they can save your life.
> Your American friend
> D.M.
> Age: 15½ years.

Mark writes to Sly about shooting the boy with the airgun:

Dear Sly Gardiner

I thought your letter was funny. I think I would shoot that kid to if I didn't like him. So he brings his dog. Well I'd bring two big dogs to scare him. I would of went over to him and beat him up. He sounds like a punk. You should of went to his house or something and go egg and tp his house. That would be great. That's what me and my friend did when we didn't like this one kid. We were laughing for days.
Your friend,
Mark Masterson

Jessica once again chose to write to De Mille:

Dear De Mille,
Thank you very much for your letter. That's nice when you have your life already knowing what you want to be when you get older. You had said that you and some friends had made a movie called the Hauted House and the Stunts Are Here Again. That's real nice to have a acting career. We have a week off from school this week because of Valentine's Day. Do you get a week off from school too? Well sorry I didn't get to much. Will hear from you next time.
Sincerely yours,
Jessica Franklin

Jessica confided to the research team that she learned a great deal from reading De Mille's writing. As she reflected on the differences between her own autobiographical writing and De Mille's, she criticized what she considered her unexciting decision to focus on personal and immediate concerns: "My autobiography seems so, so little, because he wrote about the movies and stuff. That seems big . . . I had nothing big to write about, and the one thing that I really enjoy is to run track, and so I signed up for that in the spring time. But then I got cut, 'cause I just haven't come to only two track meets, and so he [the coach] took me and my friend off . . . I want something really exciting to write about" (Interview, June 2, 1988).

Jessica also speculated about the magnitude of the effort she imagined De Mille put into his writing: "His is more longer. Seemed like it would take a long time I bet. And, um, like he have to, if he had done that movie acting career stuff a long time ago, he would have to go back, think of the things, you know, that went on in making that movie. And so he just sat down, took his time. I think that thing probably took about a week to write" (Interview, June 2, 1988).

For Jessica, who perceived that she had written her autobiography in one class period, a week seemed a long time. She thought De Mille wrote about the movies because his teacher motivated him and gave him free rein: "I think that, um, teacher said, um, write something real interesting, something good, something that was very exciting in your life and something that you're doing now and still good at it. So he just wrote it in."

By the time Gillian's students received the U.S. autobiographies, the teachers' strike had made it impossible for them to keep up the momentum of the writing exchange. Although Gillian's students appreciated Ann's students' efforts and their response to their writing, they did not know how to respond to the U.S. autobiographies and biographies. Also, as Gillian commented, even though the U.S. students responded generously to the British writing, the exchange still felt lopsided when the U.S. students didn't give as much of themselves in their writing: "I certainly got back from them, you know, generous statements like it, you know, was good of you, it was brave of you, it was, you know, to write like this, without my feeling I got the same kind of stuff back, you know, the same kind of stuff back" (Interview, July 18, 1989).

When she had read quotations from the U.S. students' interviews and heard about Gillian's desire for something more from the U.S. writing, Ellie O'Sullivan lamented: "If they had put anything of that [the substance from their interviews] down on paper, it would have been really exciting. Somewhere along the line either that wasn't asked of them or I, I, I mean, I don't know what it is that happened. But certainly the issues raised, the way in which they expressed them, is really touching . . . the potential was there, the kids were there." Speaking to Gillian, Ellie identified one of the essential differences between what is expected of writers in U.S. schools and in British schools: "I do feel, she didn't feel that she could ask that [more substance] of her students. And in a way in America that isn't recognized as the possibility of what might happen in schools . . . The kids in America benefited. But I mean in a way I think Ann, given her time over, would, would work it very very differently now. She is more confident about what she could expect from them. She wasn't then. She was trying something that everyone else would have said to her she was stupid to do" (Interview, July 18, 1989).

Later Writing

In Ann's class, the later exchange projects consisted of a book about favorite places and another about the academic experiences and life plans of older students at their school. Throughout the year of the cross-national writing exchanges, Ann mainly tried to help her students get used to producing work in writing. She was building a base for future academic work. She reported that in her second year with this same class, their progress was remarkable (Reed, 1990). Unlike Ann's class, the story for the remainder of the year for Gillian's class is complicated because of the burdens of the national examination. The exam required a great deal of writing in varied genres and left Gillian and her students little time to exchange ideas with one another. In addition, the examiner audience proved a complex one, which often inhibited her students' writing and preempted her ability to share responsibilities with her students. The outside examiner took on the position of the highest authority, to which both teacher and students must answer.

The GCSE Exam in Britain

To understand the difficulties the examination posed to the British students, one first must understand what it required. By 1987, the continuous pressure for change in the examination system had resulted in major reforms, but the best of these were short-lived, and the exam requirements have been in flux since that time. The one constant in the exam courses has been that they consist of a two-year program of study. In Gillian's 1987–1989 exam course, the exchange students were required to submit ten pieces of writing for the language exam and ten for the literature exam. For each exam, students designated five of the ten pieces for grading. Both teachers and students felt constrained by the amount of required writing.

For the 1991 exam, the requirements changed yet again. The Northern Examining Association (NEA) recognized that the 1989 requirements were too stringent and cut the amount of required writing.[4] In 1991, students submitted only eight pieces for their exam portfolio, and if the eight pieces were appropriately diverse, students would receive two grades, one for language and one for literature.

The NEA required that an exam portfolio include personal writing, original fiction, and essays, as well as analyses of poetry, drama, and prose.

In order to guide teachers, the NEA board provided a list of suggested books to be read in the exam course. In 1989, that list for the literature exam contained "suggestions of material which could appropriately be used as a basis for assignments. It is not prescriptive, nor is it intended to be exhaustive. Other texts by the authors listed and other texts of comparable literary quality may be equally acceptable as a basis for study" (p. 12). Using the list as a guide during her 1989–1991 exam course, Gillian assigned sixteen pieces of writing, from which students could choose the eight required for their portfolios.

A further requirement of the examining board was that at least one of the pieces of writing be completed under "controlled" conditions, that is, all students in the school were to write on the same topic under testing conditions. At each school, teachers devised their own "controlled" writing topics. According to the NEA guidelines, the "controlled" writing must "represent the candidate's own unaided response to given material and must be done wholly in class. Such assignments should not be preceded by a directed discussion and the material concerned should not be made available, or indicated, to the candidates beforehand" (1989, p. 6). At Manderley Grove, Gillian's students had two hours to complete the "controlled" writing. Gillian described the process: "The school, as always in 100% coursework, chooses the material and the questions. Then the students are put in what we call examination conditions. So they sit as if they're doing a public examination. And they're not allowed to talk to each other or to the teachers or, indeed, to anybody. And they have to sit and work in total silence" (Telephone interview, August 4, 1992). During the two-year examination course, Gillian's students wrote several "controlled" pieces, from which they selected one or more for their portfolios.

Types of Writing Students Submit

Gillian allowed the research team to consider six examination portfolios from the 1991 language and literature examinations, which showed the range in the quality of students' writing.[5] The six portfolios had only two pieces of writing in common. The first of these, a "controlled" piece that focused on World War I, required students to complete three sections: the first asked for answers to five questions on an extract from Robert Graves's poem "Lance Corporal Baxter Wins the DCM, Western Front, September, 1915," the second required answers to four questions about a Siegfried Sassoon poem, "A Working Party," and the third required "imaginative work" in the form of a letter home from a World War I soldier describing the conditions in the trenches.

The second piece of writing common to all six portfolios was a "noncontrolled" expository essay on Arthur Miller's play *A View from the Bridge*. The students were asked to discuss the conflicts between the protagonist, Eddie, and four other characters. They were encouraged to write the piece in four sections, each explaining Eddie's conflicts with a different character: "Eddie and Catherine," "Eddie and Beatrice," "Eddie and Rodolpho," "Eddie and Marco."

Aside from the two common pieces, the portfolios sometimes included answers to questions about other works of literature, imaginative writing related to other literature, expository essays about literature and/or current events, original fiction, and personal writing.[6]

Grading the Portfolios

Completed portfolios were graded by a committee of teachers at the school and then sent to the NEA to be spot-checked for consistency with national standards. Every student portfolio is graded as a whole; no grades are given for individual pieces. Portfolios are graded from A to G, with A for the best work and G for the worst. Students who receive As and Bs generally continue on in secondary school with the two-year A-level courses required for university. Students who receive solid Cs sometimes continue in the A-level course. Approximately 65 percent of the students at Gillian's school receive Ds, Es, Fs, and Gs; Ds and Es are considered to be average grades, and Fs and Gs are considered below average. In Britain, E, F, and G are not failing grades.

In the NEA's 1989 *English Literature Syllabus*, the criteria for grade F and grade C in literature are as follows:

Grade F
The candidate can be expected to have demonstrated competence in:

(i) giving a straightforward account of the content of literary texts in terms of narrative and situation;

(ii)   understanding the surface meaning of literary texts;

(iii) recognising obvious differences in the way authors write;

(iv)   recognising other obvious aspects of the texts studied, such as characterisation;

(v)   communicating a straightforward personal response to the texts studied.

Grade C

The candidate can be expected to have demonstrated competence in:

(i)   giving an account of the content of literary texts, with detailed reference, where appropriate, to narrative and situation;

(ii)   understanding literary texts at a deeper level and showing some awareness of their themes, implications and attitudes;

(iii) recognising and appreciating specific ways in which writers have used language in the texts studied;

(iv)   recognising and appreciating the significance of other ways (for example, structure, characterisation) in which the writers studied have achieved their effects;

(v)   communicating an informed personal response to the texts studied. (p. 7)

Since the examiners attempt to assess the folder on its overall merit, they realize that certain pieces can be stronger than others. They note that the grade

> will depend upon the extent to which the candidate has met the assessment objectives overall and it might conceal weakness in one aspect of the examination which is balanced by above average performance in some other. For instance, candidates awarded Grade F might have performed at a relatively high level for some objectives, but on the whole will have satisfied most objectives at a simple level, demonstrating basic knowledge, understanding and skills. In contrast candidates awarded Grade C, while presenting weak responses to the testing of some objectives, might be expected to have performed most tasks more skillfully and to have demonstrated some ability to think in more abstract terms. (pp. 6–7)

Gillian's focal students received the following grades on their examinations: C for De Mille for both language and literature, and E for both Surge and Comp for language (neither took literature). Leabow moved to another school, and her exam results are unknown.

Time Pressures

The exam requirements exerted significant time pressures on Gillian and her students. In 1989, when twenty pieces of writing were required, most students in Gillian's exchange class were unable to complete both language and literature examinations. Like Surge and Comp, when Gillian's students could not complete both exams, they submitted work for the language examination only.

Although twenty pieces of writing during a two-year course may seem like a reasonable amount, it turns out that students have to complete one piece on average per month. In fact, in a nonexamination setting, British teachers often spend more than a month on one piece of writing. This type of extended writing is illustrated in Chapter 4 in Fiona Rodgers's nonexam class and in Chapter 5 in Peter Ross's.

In 1991, with the new reduced requirements, Gillian's students were generally able to complete work for both language and literature examinations. However, as Gillian acknowledged, even with the decrease in the number of required pieces, time pressures remained. Given that Gillian's 1991 class chose their eight pieces from a set of sixteen, most students probably did complete close to sixteen finished pieces.

Surge explained the pressure that the GCSE created for him during the exchange year: "With America it's not as much as important as the GCSE because writing to America, I enjoy it very much, but my GCSE is what's going to get me to going" (Interview, June 9, 1988). Surge elaborated on his frustrations with GCSE writing: "Everything has to be perfect, and you get so much course work on top of [unclear]. It's just so confusing, you don't know what to do, and you get really frustrated sometimes, and like the teachers will either end up getting in arguments with the class or the class will end up getting in an argument with the teacher, but it's only because, I think what some teachers don't understand is that we get so much course work, like from English, maths, history, and all that, and it's got to be in on a certain date, and it's just hard to bring it all in at once" (Interview, June 9, 1988). The demands on the students are enormous, since each is enrolled in an average of six or seven exam courses in subjects as diverse as music, art, geography, foreign languages, biology, physics, chemistry, and mathematics.

Complications in the Exchange of Responsibilities

Exchanges between Gillian and her students within their classroom were complicated because of the time constraints of the exam and the somewhat fixed requirements of the exam writing. During the autobiographical writing for the cross-national exchange, Gillian was able to exchange responsibilities with her students, but for the exam audience, she began to take away her students' power over and responsibility for their subject matter. Gillian prepared specific topics for her students to address without class decision making. The following handout contrasts an assignment for the examiner and an assignment for the writing exchange:

4th Year English
Assignments for November 1987

[For the Examination]
Follow up to Basket Ball Game TO BE READY BY NOV 17
Choose one of these:
1. Allen and Rebecca meet up in 10 years, or 5 years time. Remember they won't be able to meet just anywhere. Maybe you can change the balance of power between the two of them and make them meet on Allen's territory.
   What are they doing now? How do they remember that short summer of the Basket Ball Game? Does Rebecca feel guilty about cutting Allen? Does Allen feel hurt or angry? How do they feel about segregation? What about human rights? How have they changed and developed as people?
2. An alternative ending to the one in the book, or a further chapter. Maybe Allen rejects Rebecca, maybe the parents try to intervene and Allen and Rebecca try to resist them.
   Whatever you choose, your new ending has to be consistent with the characters as they are in the book.

[For the Writing Exchange]
Autobiography HAVE IT READY BY THURS. NOV 26
This is to send to our colleagues in California.
These are the ideas we discussed:
a. Key events in your life/or major influential people

b. An important year or few months when your life changed dramatically

c. Selected highlights from your entire life

d. Early memories—harder than it seems to get back to how you thought and felt

Gillian determined the focus for the writing on *The Basketball Game,* but for the autobiography she and the students "discussed" which ideas to include.

Leabow commented on the difference in classroom spirit when the class wrote for the U.S. students and when they wrote for the examiner. In writing for the U.S. students, Leabow shared her work: "Sometimes we might nick ideas from each other." But the sharing atmosphere of the exchange writing disappeared with the GCSE writing. Leabow was in control when she wrote for the U.S. students but constrained and rushed when she wrote on "set topics" for the exam: "I would really like to write what I want to write, not get set assignments although . . . that is the most important, but I'd like to put some of my own stuff and have my own time to do it and not be rushed" (Interview, June 9, 1988).

Conflicting Audiences

Combining the writing exchange and the examiner audiences, Gillian found, "became tougher as we went along" (Interview, June 6, 1988). Time pressures aside, the exchange and the examiner audiences proved to be difficult to merge. At the start of the examination course, Gillian's students' school introductions and autobiographies fulfilled the examination requirement for personal writing and worked well for the exchange. During the year, however, Gillian could not figure out how to integrate the less personal writing required for the examination into the exchange format. She worried that the expository writing would not interest Ann's students. Yet when she reflected on the year, she thought that if she'd had more time to work closely with Ann, they could have created a program in which both groups of students could have exchanged writing about literature: "What would be nice . . . if in each country, for instance, people studied the same book or something like that . . . And if I was doing the exchange again, I'd probably like to set up something like that, just something to get away from pieces of writing in a very much letter-writing form" (Interview, June 6, 1988). Gillian also felt that she could have merged the two audiences better had the teacher's strike not occurred: "I don't think they [the exchange and examiner audiences] would have become two separate things had it not been for the strike" (Interview, March 13, 1989).

Furthermore, Gillian's students claimed that the U.S. audience would have helped with their exam writing. For Surge, writing in school but not for the writing exchange had only one value: it might "help you out in your GCSE." By contrast, the U.S. audience was real and important to him: "It makes a lot of difference to me that someone in America is reading my work, to think that it come all the way from England" (Interview, June 9, 1988). Leabow explained how hard she worked to connect with the U.S. students, something she did not do for the examiner: "You had to . . . sort of build up a personality for themselves so they could imagine what you were like through your personality . . . you've really got to build up an image for yourself to make them see . . . who you are" (Interview, June 9, 1988). Leabow felt that her exchange writing had to be as "interesting" as she could make it. Her goal was to "really impress them." As she noted, "You got to make it slightly longer."

Examples of Examination Writing

To give a sense of the examination writing, I will compare samples from an *A,* a *D+,* and an *F* student portfolio. The *D+* writer is a bilingual student whose native language is Chinese. All three students wrote about Arthur Miller's *A View from the Bridge.* All begin by explaining the conflicts between the protagonist, Eddie, and Eddie's wife's niece, Catherine. The *A* writer begins:

> *Eddie and Catherine:*
> Eddie is Catherine's uncle and guardian, having promised her mother on her deathbed that he would look after her. Eddie is very overprotective and possesive towards Catherine and he restricts her in what she does, essentially trying to stop her from growing up. His reasons for restricting Catherine are partly due to his feelings of responsibility for her (Eddie brought her up as a child), but also as Act One progresses, it becomes apparent that he has a growing sexual desire for Catherine (apparent, that is, in the way he acts towards her).

The first conflict detailed in Act One concerns Eddie coming to terms with Catherine's sexuality now that she is growing up: Eddie disapproves of Catherines new short skirt, and the way she is "walkin' wavy". He feels that the boys in the area have been looking at her, their heads "turnin' like windmills."

The *A* writer continues on for three more paragraphs, each providing another example of how Eddie tries to keep Catherine from growing up. She explores the conflicts between Eddie and three of the other characters in a similar manner. Her writing is competent; she understands the play, presents her ideas clearly, and supports them with well-chosen references from the text. Her piece is well organized and relatively free of mechanical errors.

The *D+* bilingual writer runs into more difficulty. He begins:

> *Conflicts between Eddie and Catherine:* Catherine was a girl whose life was controlled by Eddie and was confused and innocent through Act One. Catherine is Eddie's niece. Eddie was the main character in the play. He seem to be the most important charactor of all as he was the one who always started the arguments and had conflicts with all the main charactors in the play, for example, Catherine, Beatrice (his wife) and the two brothers Rodolpho and Marco.
>
> There were many conflicts in act one between Eddie and Catherine. The very first conflict was how Eddie dissapproved of the way Cathcrine dressed in a fashion and attractive way and walking in a wavy manner. Eddie felt discomfort if he walked with Catherine down the street. As Eddie once said, "Listen, you been givin' me the willies the way you walk down the street, I mean it". Catherine could not help from seeing herself as a very attractive woman.

This writer continues to describe this conflict and then concludes:

> It seem that Eddie want Catherine as his procession and nobody else apart from Eddie can order Catherine around.

Without a paragraph break the writer then moves to the next conflict over Catherine's new job: "Eddie was shocked and he did not except it." After describing the job and what Eddie wanted for Catherine, the writer again concludes with an opinion:

> I think he was trying to prevent Catherine being taken away from Eddie by any other men working by the shore since Catherine was an attractive girl. Eddie did not want to loose her.

In the same paragraph, the writer describes a third conflict between Eddie and Catherine over her love for Rodolpho. Finally, he moves on to describe the conflicts between Eddie and three other characters.

Besides his difficulties with form, this writer does not completely portray the sexual attraction Eddie felt for Catherine, although he alludes to it when he realizes that "Eddie did not want to loose her." And he has difficulty thematizing his main ideas, paragraphing, and dealing with the mechanics of the language.

The final writer received an *F* grade. This writer presents a dialogue and then comments:

> *Section A Eddie and Cathrine*
> Eddie: Now dont get mad kid.
> Eddie: I think it's two short anit it.
> Cathrine: (Standing) Not when I stand up.
> Eddie: Yeh but you gotta sit down sometime.
> Cathrine: eddie its the style now (she walks to show him) I mean if you see me walkin down the street.
> Eddie: Listen you been givin me the willies the way you walk down the street I mean it
> In this section eddie dont like what shes wearing because she is growing up to fast.

This writer portrays additional conflicts between Eddie and Catherine by presenting two other bits of dialogue with similar commentary. Then she moves on to the conflicts between Eddie and the other characters using the same technique. She needs to go beyond finding and repeating examples; she needs help in writing extended prose as well as in gaining control over mechanics.

None of these writers demonstrated any personal connection to what they were writing. Even the *A* writer, who understood the tensions between the characters, did not comment on them. Unfortunately, Gillian was not able to help her writers make such connections. In addition, she could not give sufficient time to the writers at the lower end of the continuum. The *D+* writer could be taught to organize his ideas and helped to make explicit inferences from what he is reading and then to support those inferences. The seeds of an excellent paper are present in his text. However, he needs time and guidance to progress as a writer. The *F* writer needs even more time. In an ideal instructional setting, neither writer would be pushed to submit this writing. Both students need much more time and support to do a better job. Ironically, the examination not only presented time pressures, it also prevented the teachers from helping the students too much. As was the case in 1987 and 1991, the 1994 exam syllabus is explicit about how much help the teacher may give when students submit coursework:

> Where work is drafted and redrafted the ideal role of the teacher is to discuss with the candidate and advise on a wide variety of issues including structure, content, plot, style, tone, character, spelling, punctuation, vocabulary and syntax. The emphasis, therefore, is on reconsideration by the candidate of the whole piece and its effect on, and clarity for, the reader and not solely on the correction of surface features. In this circumstance, advice remains on a general level, only becoming specific to exemplify general comments, and the onus is left on the candidate to incorporate the teacher's general advice by making specific alterations and thus submitting a final draft. This level of advice is acceptable whereas proof reading, where the teacher points out a detailed series of errors, omissions and amendments for the candidate to correct in the subsequent draft is inadmissible. (Northern Examinations and Assessment Board, p. 5)

Such policies inhibited British teachers from offering the kind of explicit teaching needed to reach the most needy students. As Gillian noted, these requirements were especially problematic in teaching bilingual writers. It is also crucial to remember that the lower-scoring students make up some 65 percent of those taking the exams.

Conflicts between Community Building and Individualization in the United States

Ann Powers showed that it was possible to structure a U.S. classroom to allow teachers and students to share responsibilities. Ann charted her own way, in the end following theories espoused by Nancie Atwell (1987), who advocated an individualized workshop approach. As Ann noted, "I would make changes in the classroom first, changes to help them become more independent. I would give them responsibility for many of the decisions I had made for them the year before. As Nancie Atwell puts it, I needed to come out from behind the 'big desk' . . . I would set up a supportive workshop, similar to the model Atwell describes in her book, *In the Middle,* structured according to the needs of writers" (Reed, 1990, p. 183). Like her British counterparts

Fiona and Peter, Ann gradually handed responsibility for their writing to her students. By the end of the two-year period, she hoped they would be independent writers. Ann's ideas about responsibility evolved throughout the writing exchange and over the following year. Her techniques worked effectively for the audience exchange class. Now, however, Ann has moved to a new school where she teaches her classes for only one year. In this context she finds that to follow Atwell's ideas about individualization she must share responsibility with students relatively abruptly, and she has had difficulty building the kind of trusting learning community she established with the exchange class. At the same time, during the exchange year she was able to get just so far with her student writers. She helped them learn to write more extended prose than they had before, but she did not push them beyond the complacent writing that Gillian and her students often found "monotonous."

Exams as Agents of Reform: A Word of Caution

Gillian's situation demonstrates the pitfalls of the British national exams. The 1987–1989 reformed examination course offered great hope to British teachers. However, Gillian's experience shows how even the best-intentioned national examinations can get in the way of crucial classroom structures for teaching writing. In the early grades, the British teachers see it as their responsibility to work together with their students to agree on activities that will encourage them to write. This process insures that the students feel committed to their writing. The exams change that dynamic. They become the primary motivator for writing. Students' personal investment in their writing takes a back seat. The exams also restrict teachers' pedagogy. They can only give general advice on student writing, which proves especially problematic for the 65 percent of student writers whose portfolios demonstrate their difficulty with written language. These writers need specific guidance and special attention from their teachers.

More recently, the British examination system has become more conservative, and many teachers feel that it is deteriorating. The instructionally sensitive exams of the late 1980s have now been eliminated. The exam courses beginning in 1992 will lead to exams in 1994 in which most of the score will be determined by "terminal" exams because government officials feared that the coursework-only option would erode national standards.

Using a national examination system as a path to curriculum reform is tempting but its benefits are elusive. An exam system is popular among policymakers because it is one of the few curricular levers they can control. Yet as Gillian's experience shows, when an exam system takes control of something as personal as writing, it affects curriculum negatively. The teacher and students no longer work together to own their writing; the writing is owned by a distant examining board. Human beings with unique talents become puppets to the exam. Educational leaders in the United States advocate introducing national examinations as a way of improving curriculum and raising standards (for example, Simmons and Resnick, 1993; Tucker, 1992), but it seems prudent that they first look critically at the ways even instructionally sensitive exams can inadvertently diminish instructional opportunities.

Chapter 7

ᥣ Elevating Expectations, Facing Constraints

Bridget Franklin, Philippa Furlong

Like the classes of Ann Powers and Gillian Hargrove, Bridget Franklin's students at Los Padres High School were in grade 9 and Philippa Furlong's at Hampden Jones in its British equivalent, Form 4. Philippa had taught these students since they began secondary school in Form 1 (grade 6 equivalent) and would continue with them through the end of their examination course in Form 5 (grade 10 equivalent). Her students were in the first year of their GCSE examination course, and this would cause them some difficulty during the writing exchange. But Bridget's U.S. students, who were placed in the lowest track in their school, flourished with their participation in the exchange.

Examiner versus Exchange Audience

For the British students, the exam and the exchange functioned at cross purposes. Philippa began the year expecting that her students would write for both the examiner and the exchange audiences, but as the year progressed, she found that combining these two audiences became increasingly difficult: "I was very worried that at the end of the fifth year if I stuck to our program [the exchange], I was going to end up with insufficient work for the [examination] folders and that was a major cause of panic" (Interview, April 20, 1989). By the end of the year, Philippa had completely separated the exchange and the exam and was focusing most of her attention on the exam. As Philippa's attention shifted away from the exchange, she was less able to coordinate her efforts with Bridget's.

Focusing on the exam created additional problems for Philippa. During the second semester, her students wrote less regularly for the exchange than they had at the start of the year (Figure 7.1). And she felt that their writing was inhibited when they wrote for the examiner: "The kids didn't feel that confident about really baring their souls in an assignment that was going to go off to an examiner even though they knew that I was one of the examiners. They knew that beyond me there was an unknown quantity" (Interview, April 20, 1989). Philippa's students confirmed her assessment. Like the other students we interviewed, Andi claimed that she censored her content because "they [the examiners] are not people at all" (Interview, May 1988). For Joshua this audience was equally problematic: "I have this picture of the examiner sitting down there reading them [the exam papers] and putting marks on them" (Interview, May 1988).

Throughout the year the students sometimes emphasized the exchange class, sometimes the examiners. Andi, for example, concentrated on the exchange audience at the beginning of the year, expecting that her writing would be appropriate for both the U.S. students and the examiners. But by the end of the year she found herself concerned primarily with the examiners: "When you are marking a GCSE paper," she concluded, "then it's your future, which is serious" (Interview, May 1988).

By contrast, Marisa never attempted to combine the two audiences. The writing Marisa sent to the United States was for "kids of your own age," while the writing for her exam folder would be judged by "an old person" (Interview, May 1988). She felt that whatever she wrote for the exchange would be inappropriate for the examiner, and vice versa.

Joshua did just the opposite of Andi. The audience he wrote for was simply the exchange class: "I just forget about the examiner. It makes me feel easier if I just, you know, it's kind of like a letter. Makes it more easier and I can write a bit more" (Interview, May 1988).

Mismatches across the Exchanges

Two mismatches between Bridget's and Philippa's classes had a marked effect on the progress of the exchange. One involved a disparity in the ethnic composition of the two classes, the other a disparity in the ability-level placement practices in the two countries. In Bridget's U.S. classroom 68 percent of the students were black, while

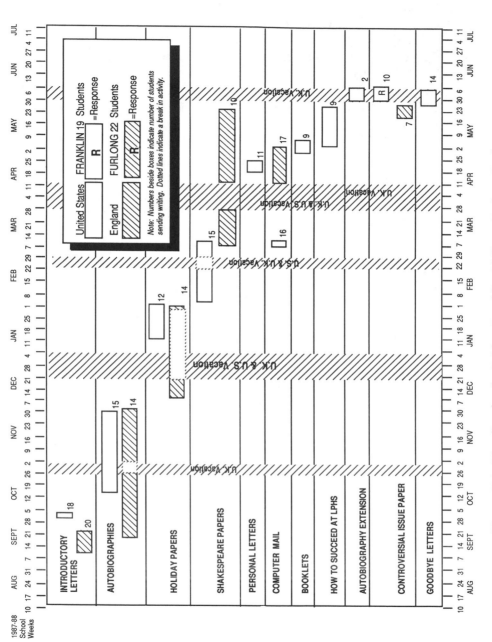

Figure 7.1 Timeline for the Bridget Franklin–Philippa Furlong Exchange

in Philippa's British classroom only 38 percent of the students were black. In Bridget's classroom all of the students were labeled low ability; Philippa's students were labeled mixed ability.

These mismatches affected the writing in Philippa's classroom but not in Bridget's. Philippa's nonblack students felt alienated from the project, an alienation that resulted from the social relationships the black students created among themselves. Philippa's nonblack students were not included in this social circle, which made them resent their black peers. As a result, Philippa's black students took over while the nonblack students retreated from the exchange and turned their attention to the traditional examiner-only audience. Philippa, whose own feelings about combining the two audiences were mixed, had difficulty handling the situation.

Adding to the complexity was the fact that Philippa's group was considered mixed ability while Bridget's was considered the most "remedial" ninth-grade group in her school. Philippa feared that her best writers would have few peers in the U.S. class and might not benefit from the exchange. She also worried about taking advantage of the closeness she had built up with her students over the years to push them into participating in writing activities when they felt reluctant and when she feared the activities might not help them meet their immediate goal: high marks on their exams. In the end, a number of Philippa's top students withdrew from the exchange. Philippa had hoped that her students would work as a well-functioning community of learners, but the exchange seemed to open some uncomfortable cracks along what appeared to be already extant fault lines.

Building Community in the United States

Bridget's approach to teaching was to meld the diverse students in her classroom into a cohesive community. She encouraged a community feeling by organizing a supportive classroom network and by involving students' families. She used the ties of this community to promote individual academic growth. Community-building provided a solid foundation for her sharing of responsibilities with her students.

Providing Emotional Support

When we got in, she [Bridget] just established this was going to be our little family . . . We would work together, and we would share all types of things, and you know, she made it very clear that . . . she didn't want us teasing each other or nothing like that bad . . . Everybody's her kid and . . . she takes time and . . . she just really cares for all the students. And you know, she wants everybody to . . . help everybody . . . And so once everybody . . . recognized what she was doing, everybody cooperated . . . I never been that close with many of my friends like I have now . . . My friends come over, spend the night, we go to the movies, and it's just like, some of them are my brothers and stuff you know. We see each other every day at school and it's not like, you know, I go home and then I hang around with my friends at home and stuff here. We spend a lot of time together. (Easy E., Interview, March 21, 1988)

As Easy E.'s remarks suggest, Bridget cared about her students the way a mother cares about her children. In turn, her students treated their classmates like family members. The nurturing atmosphere in Bridget's classroom created an environment in which students worked together and supported one another's efforts.

Bridget's classroom was so inviting that her students felt comfortable asking their friends to visit during their free time. Students congregated in Bridget's room before school, during lunch, and after school. They knew that during free time the classroom was a place where they could talk to friends, meet one another, talk to Bridget, or do schoolwork. Bridget was so accommodating that she even gave her students rides home so that they could stay for after-school activities.

During class Bridget's students were free to move around the room and work with their friends. In fact, movement was essential because the students did much of their writing in class at the computers that ringed the room (see Figure 3.8). As the students shared the computers, they were free to talk to their friends about their writing (see Greenleaf [1994] for a full explanation of how the computers helped Bridget increase the quantity and quality of student talk in her classroom).

Bridget's nurturing was not without a strong academic edge. She demanded a great deal of her students, and they came through for her. Easy E. contrasts Bridget's way of pushing students to do their best with the more punitive approach of his past teachers: "Like if, uh, I missed a assignment, you know, a teacher would just say, 'Okay, you have a detention . . . and you got a make it up,' or something. She

[Bridget] will really stick to you and make you do it. I mean it's like she's your mother . . . She really pressures you because she wants you to do good, and you know, most teachers it's just like they give you the grade. But she really wants you to . . . make an effort and try harder" (Interview, March 21, 1988).

The close community in Bridget's classroom ultimately inspired the students to develop new attitudes toward literacy activities:

> The first week [of the exchange] we were like, "I don't, we don't really know about all this." And so then, um, after, um, a couple of days we got in the habit of doing the same things, and . . . wow, I haven't never did nothing like that. I mean, you know, I was enjoying it, and, like, when something was wrong, like, she would come to me and ask me to help and . . . I was happy for her to come to me, and ask me to help somebody. (Easy E., Interview, March 21, 1988).

Thus, Bridget built community in a number of emotionally supportive ways: through her explicit actions (for example, opening her classroom during students' free time, giving students rides home), her subtle interactions with her students (which showed both firmness and caring), and the tone she set for appropriate student interactions (cooperation, sharing, and helping one another).

Involving Families

To build a supportive community, Bridget also took advantage of structures external to her classroom. Of these, the most important were students' families, whom she involved in the intellectual life of the classroom. Bridget routinely telephoned parents to let them know about their children's progress; by the end of September she had called every child's parent or guardian. Her initial call served to establish a partnership with each family. Then, Bridget explained, if she needed to call a student's parents about a problem later in the year, they would already know her as a caring teacher. During the year Bridget talked in this way with every family a minimum of two or three times, to compliment the student and/or to enlist the family's help with problems. Through these phone calls, her open sharing with her students, and her long-term relationship with the community around Los Padres High School, Bridget kept informed about the students' out-of-school environment and integrated their experiences at home and in the community into the life of the classroom.

Bridget also produced a newsletter for parents and guardians twice each quarter. The newsletter served to keep parents, who were often uncomfortable visiting the school, connected to what was happening in her class. Many parents even wrote pieces for the newsletter. Parental writing thus became a part of the classroom culture. The newsletter also stimulated the students' thinking and became a basis for ongoing classroom conversations.

Although Los Padres was not a "community school" in the British sense of the term and offered no support structures of the sort the British community schools did (see Chapter 3), Bridget aimed to create similar community structures. In the end, because she established a safe, caring, and inclusive community, she was able to work out a demanding curriculum with her students. Her ways of sharing responsibility with her students were similar to those of British teachers Fiona Rodgers and Peter Ross (see Chapters 4 and 5). As the unfolding story of the writing exchange will show, Bridget was able to frame activities for the writing exchange in ways that drew on the community and thereby integrated the sociocultural with the academic aspects of her students' lives.

Effects on Student Writing

Three exchanges between Bridget's and Philippa's students show how the students' writing changed during the year: the introductory letters, the autobiographies, and then, later in the year, the Shakespeare papers.

Introductory Letters

Philippa and Bridget began the exchange with informal introductory letters. Their purpose was twofold: to get the students acquainted with one another and to form a social foundation for future academic work. Through these letters the students began to make personal connections with each other and to enter distant and unfamiliar classroom communities.

Like many of Bridget's students, Easy E. felt inhibited when he wrote his first letter. His writing is controlled and restrained, although his personal voice is present:

Dear Girls and Boys in England,

My name is Easy E. and I am 14 years old and I love to play sports like football, basketball, and track.

I've played football and run track for a team but I've never played basketball for a team.

At Los Padres High School we have a football team, swim team, and a track team.

I would like for you to tell me something about your school. I would like to know if you have any hobbies like buliding model cars and airplanes.

Here at Los Padres High School we've got to have a 2.0 grade average to play any kind of sports in high school.

I would like to know if any of you girls or guys have any plans to come to America and visited.

I would like to know something you think that makes your school special. Here at Los Padres High School we have our own radiostation. Your friend. . .
Easy E.

Many of the U.S. students indicated their interest and curiosity about the British students through the questions they asked. Easy E. embeds indirect questions in his letter ("I would like to know . . ."), but Ice T. provides a long list of direct questions for his British counterparts:

I have told you a few things about myself now I would like to know a few thing about you and England.
1. Do you have a McDonalds?
2. Do you listion to rap music?
3. What kind of sports do you play?
4. Do you play football?
5. What kind of classes do you have?
6. What is your name?
7. How old are you?
8. What are your hobbies?
9. What kind of T.V. shows do you like to watch?
10. What city do you live in?
11. Do you play an instrument?

12. What are your goals in life?
Those are some thing I would like to know.
Your truly
Ice T.

Ice T.'s questions show his awareness of potential areas of similarity and difference in the two countries.

Geya's letter is slightly more adventurous and less constrained than those of the other students:

> September 29, 1987
>
> Hi, My name is Geya Anderson but mostly everyone at home and school calls me Gey. I am a black afro American and I am 5 ft. 2½. I have black hair that goes down to my neck. When I was small I had very long hair but as I grew up it kind of broke off. Most of the time I still wish I had long hair but I know that if I keep it up my wish just might come true. I am fourteen and I was born August 1, 1973.
>
> I have one brother and he is nine year old, He name is Shawnell. He was born july 21, 1978. My Mother's Name is the best that my brother and I could ever have because she get on us when we are wrong and compliment us when we are doing good. My Mom wants to see my brother and me with a beautiful education and terrific jobs that we can ever have. She wants us with the best in the world. You know I would like to ask you something now if I am kind of making you angry then I apologize but I would like to know if you have any black people out there. The reason I am asking is because I only see the other color on T.V. and I was just curious.
>
> I hope to talk to us soon. Well by, Nice talking to you
> Sincerely yours,
> Geya Anderson

The British research team noted that Geya's question about whether or not there were blacks in England and her comment about the absence of black people on British television provoked a profound discussion in Philippa's class. The students returned to this theme many times during the year. Geya's question was an important step toward friendship and understanding between the black students in the two classes.

Geya was one of Bridget's stronger writers and consistently let her voice speak, but Bridget still characterized her letter to the British students as less open than usual. Although Bridget's students wrote letters that revealed their own personality and voice, they showed restraint at first because of their unfamiliarity with their British audience. As Easy E. commented, "I mean people were, we were at first, um, we were, like, tightened, tightened up, you know" (Interview, March 21, 1988). Cool J. summed up his class's initial sense of their British audience: "They're so far away, I was thinking of them of like aliens" (Interview, March 10, 1988).

The British students were less restrained. They wrote with a casual tone that inspired enormous enthusiasm in Bridget's students. Especially engaging was the letter from Titch in calligraphy-style handwriting (see Figure 7.2). Titch established common interests with Bridget's students through her language, her musical tastes, her love of parties, and even her love of the United States. She was so likable and real that many of the ninth-grade boys in Bridget's class fell in love with her, and several of the girls became jealous. When Bridget introduced the exchange, her students agreed to go along with the plan, but Titch's endorsement—"I suppose it's quite good fun, doing our project and finding things out for your self," and her plea, "You must write me, who ever I am speaking to?!?"—proved the strongest motivators of all.

Although several other British students wrote letters like Titch's, Marisa's provides a more typical example. Like most of her classmates she includes her return school address (many gave their own home address rather than the school address), and then begins:

Hey 9th Grade,
  'Take a Walk on the Wild Side?' I don't really want to write but I have to since it is a assignment from Mrs Furlong, our English teacher. Well I don't know what I can write but I'll know when I start, I'll write a lot.

She continues for six pages, describing her family and then each of her classmates beginning with the girls and moving on to the boys. About Andi she writes, "I would say she's one of the brainest girl in our class but the way she carried on she got her enemies." And about Titch: "she's alright now, but in her days she was twofaced. First she said she was your friend but when you said a word against her, she would ignore you, and may make thing different." Most of Philippa's confident, mixed-ability students produced longer letters than Bridget's students, who had written little before entering her class (see Table 7.1).

Figure 7.2 Titch's Introductory Letter

Hi to all you funky clef people, In 9th grade,

L will start by telling you a bit about my self, I am 14 years old and will be 15 years on January 2nd.

L go to an School called Burlington Danes, I am in the fifth year [will just started].

L suppose its quite good fun, doing our project and finding things out for your self.

At the moment we are doing course work for one New exam, GCSE.

In England our years are different from the ones In America, we have years and you have grades.

Well enough about school, ill talke about the things I do!!!

L love goingout with friends especcially travlling.

L Also Love raving at Jams [parties]. That brings me on to anbother point, L am one person who canot do with out music.

Especcilly, Hip Hop, Soul, Reggave. L hate heavey metal and all of that pop.

You must write me, who ever I am speaking to?!?

L have been to America, New Jears. It was beautiful.

When I grow up I would Love to come over and live. [Hopefully]

England is not bad, I suppose most of
the time its pretty cold,
Apart from that Its okay
        Oh before I forget I am also
an freaky person, well me and my
cousin   she is in the same class
and is also writing a letter to you all.
We wear really freaky outfits,
As for the hair, our hair, well thats
freaky too.
    I do suppose your freaky too who ever
you are ?
    I have got an Tag, It is Pride
        thats what I am know as

                    Anyway, I will hope
                        ill here from you.
                    Here my address
                    again.
                    Lov ya

                                        xx

PRIDE!

With her help, Bridget's students found much to connect with as they heard the voices of kids from England who shared their interests and whom they began to think of as potential friends. Easy E. stressed the importance of the British letters to his class's attitudes and to their immediate ease and identification with this new audience:

> At first . . . I wasn't really interested . . . I guess everybody, you know, we just took it like an assignment . . . We gotta do this for a grade . . . She [Bridget] explained it, but I guess we didn't really catch on until after, you know, we got letters from England, and everybody was, like, wow! . . . So we really, like, got into it, and we started telling them about, like, what we do out here, and it was really fun . . .
>
> The way they wrote their letters, it was really like, I mean, they were our friends, and we didn't even really meet them. I mean, it was, you know, they were talking to us, and I was like, I mean, you know, I never expected nothing like it . . .
>
> They did basically what, what we did but it was just, you know, they were in a different country and stuff. And it was just like, you know, it was another me over there. (Interview, March 21, 1988)

Cool J. and Ice T. also mentioned that they felt an immediate closeness to the students in England once these letters arrived. Cool J. went a step further to emphasize the exchange's effects on his writing: "Now I feel like I know some of the people over there—you just open

Table 7.1 Autobiography and Shakespeare: Focal students' word counts

	Autobiography	Shakespeare	Total words
Franklin (US)			
Easy E.	565	659	1,224
Ice T.	410	480	890
Cool J.	1,171	450	1,621
Geya	886	2,601	3,487
Total	3,032	4,190	7,222
Furlong (GB)			
Andi/Garney	1,860	901	2,761
Joshua	2,352	1,136	3,488
Tootsie	2,525	2,706	5,231
Garney/Marisa	2,677	763	3,440
Total	9,414	5,506	14,920

up and write to them" (Interview, March 10, 1988). Geya's and Rose's initial responses were positive, but they were more cautious than the boys.

In England, the U.S. letters created some difficulties, which Philippa at this point attributed primarily to the fact that Bridget's was a low-tracked class while hers was a mixed-ability group. Although the U.S. letters were carefully written on standard notebook paper, Philippa reported that many of her students reacted negatively:

> We got letters on very thin paper like toilet paper with what, and this is quoting one of my children, "They sent us work on toilet paper in lead pencil." Now this was, as far as my kids were concerned, a total insult. It wasn't, it wasn't a disaster. It was an insult. You know, "What the hell are they playing that?" You know, and my kids turned around and said to me, "You would never let us send that off." And, I mean, it wasn't just that the paper was thin. You know how when paper gets creased up it probably, and a lot of it was illegible because the lead pencil had been rubbed off either in the folding or the transit . . . I remember [the] day we opened those letters. There was Alex . . . And I can remember being appalled at the behavior of my class, who started to go through looking for full stops, capital letters. And I thought, what are you doing? They started making terrible statements about, "These kids are thick. Why did they match us with these really thick kids?" (Interview, July 18, 1989)

As Ellie O'Sullivan pointed out to Philippa during this interview, the students' reactions may have reflected their own insecurities about how their writing would be received in the United States. Philippa agreed but argued that she would not have let her students send letters in pencil on thin paper. In their own interviews several months after they received the U.S. letters, however, Philippa's students did not mention any negative responses.

Beyond issues of presentation, many of Philippa's students, especially those she labeled her "high flyers," felt alienated because they did not think they could find intellectual equals in Bridget's "low tracking" class. Their alienation, however, may have had more to do with the exclusivity of the black students in their own class than to the ability level of the U.S. students. Andi, one of Philippa's "high flying" white girls, recalled that when the U.S. letters arrived "It was just Titch and Louise and that lot. They all sort of snatched them [the letters] up . . . I felt a bit hostile to Titch after that because I thought, well, she had more in common with them anyway, you know. She liked the same music. She did the same things, you know, went out to parties all night or something" (Interview, May 1988). Regardless of their own ability level, most of Philippa's black students found something to connect with in the U.S. students' letters.

Autobiographies

If the introductory letters initiated a social dialogue between Bridget's and Philippa's students, the autobiographies allowed the social dialogue to continue—but in a more academic form.

Having seen the relaxed and open style of the British letters, Bridget's students began to reveal their voices in writing their autobiographies. Some created authorial personas, presenting themselves to the British students in appealing and partially fictionalized ways. Bridget's class seemed to be seeking respect from the British group in the same way they looked for respect from their classmates.

Some of Bridget's students composed more elaborate autobiographies than others (see Table 7.1), but all felt successful and were proud of their work. Each autobiography bore the unique stamp of its author. Ice T., for example, opens with a rap:

ENGLAND
THE ICE
AUTO
BY:
ICE T
THE ENGLISH RAP
I was born son of Thomas, brother of Tom,
Anna's my mom and Easy E.'s my pal.
It's mac T's not Mac Tony,
these rhymes are Willies and they'll last forever.

After this opening rap, Ice T. divided the rest of his autobiography into three sections, each serving a different function. He called the sections "THE FIRST SIDE," "THE FRESH SIDE," and "THE LAST SIDE." Ice T. probably copied this organizational format from a rap record by the group NWA (Niggers with Attitude).[1] The two sides of their recording are "Radio Side," which is formal and proper, and "Street Side," which is more informal and familiar.

Ice T.'s autobiography also has a factual and a familiar side. He begins his factual "FIRST SIDE": "I was born on July 21st, 1973, in Casey Hospital in Oakland, California. I am the third child in my family. I have one brother and one sister."

After giving a few additional facts, he turns to his more familiar "FRESH SIDE," which both mimics and serves as a response to Titch's introductory letter:

> Well, that's all I can say about my family so now I'm going to tell about me. Hi, all you def homeboys in England this is ICE T and I'm going to tell you all about me. I am fourteen years old. I like to listion to rap music and play football. I am not an all-star but I think I'm pretty good for a freshmen free safety. I hope to get a letter from Titch because she is freaky. My friend Easy E. and all the boys in the class really like Titch but someone should tell her that freak means a whole different meaning in America than it does in England. It does not mean what you think it means—out here it means that you like to have sex a lot. I hope you are not mad at me for telling you this.

When Ice T. begins addressing Titch individually ("I hope to get a letter from Titch"), he gradually moves away from his group audience. He continues to address the group, as he had when he discussed sports and excludes her as an outsider ("but someone should tell her"). But then he uses an indefinite "you" that could refer to either the group or Titch ("It does not mean what you think it means") and finally addresses her with a "you" that could only be for Titch herself ("I hope you are not mad at me").

Ice T.'s "THE LAST SIDE" contains only one line: "I have told all I can tell about me and what I like to do so this is so long. Your friend, Ice T."

Ice T. explained how much care he took with his autobiography: "I erased about a million words that I didn't like" (Interview, March 21, 1988). When asked why he erased, he continued, "'Cause you—I had to make sure that it sounded right to them, it was interesting not boring." When asked how he made his writing interesting, he replied, "You just have to have a imagination . . . You have to think in your head just what is interesting to you, it might be interesting to them."

Ice T.'s friend Easy E. used a number of the same techniques, making evident their sharing at the computers. Easy E. opens by writing about himself and then about Ice T.:

One of my best friend's name is Ice T. and he is real cool or he thinks he is real cool anyway. We have three classes together so we have a lot of fun and spend a lot of time together. Sometimes he acts like a real big baby. I mean he plays like a little kid, but like I said before he's cool or at least he thinks he is.

Like Ice T., Easy E. uses pieces of his autobiography to respond to the letters from England. To Titch, Louise, and Marisa he writes:

Ice T. and all the other boys in my English class like Titch and her cousin Louise because Titch said she and Louise dress like freaks. I am not going to say that I don't like you two young ladies because I know I do a little bit, but I think I like Marisa a little bit more because of what whe wrote in her letter. You see I like a young lady who's not scared to say what she wants to.

Our whole class is going to send picture of ourselves and our families and I hope your class will do the same especialy Titch, Louise, and Marisa because all the boys in our class want to see how you three young ladies look and so do I, so please send pictures.

Easy E. also keeps his British audience in mind as he writes. He reports that his goal in writing his autobiography is to move beyond the introductory letter "so they can get to know me a little bit better" (Interview, March 21, 1988). Because he had shared ideas with Ice T., Easy E. chooses a similar format and similar content. Both writers felt full ownership of their writing, and when asked how they decided what to write, said they made their own decisions. As Ice T. explained, "[The] first thing I did is I thought in my mind . . . what am I gonna write, what am I gonna say?" (March 21, 1988). With similar independence, Easy E. asked himself, "What should I tell them [the British students] about?" (March 21, 1988). As a result, the voices and personalities of both writers are prominent. Both show their serious side and use the autobiographies to continue the informal dialogues they initiated in the letters.

Geya, the self-proclaimed loner, also had her own distinctive style. She used writing to reveal and work through feelings and reactions to events in her life that she could not express orally, especially to peers in her own class. Otherwise alone, Geya needed writing to communicate. She tells the British students, for example, about her reactions to her new school, Los Padres:

So far it is o.k. but I don't like some of the people that go here. I like all of my teachers except for my art teacher because she thinks that the beginners are supposed to be perfect. What she don't know is that there is not one person on this living earth that is perfect. Some people could be born with talent but can't no one on the planet earth be perfect but one MAN and his name is JESUS CHRIST.

Geya's audience is not the same as Easy E.'s and Ice T.'s. She never addresses her autobiography to particular individuals, although she clearly tries to connect with the British students. Her most explicit attempt to appeal to them comes in her concluding paragraph about her yearning to visit England:

> I am so anxious to go to England. Ever since I was small I couldn't wait to go out there. I would like to visit the schools and the stores. I also would love to see the sights because in England I heard that they have so many beautiful sights. When I get bigger I am planning to go there.

Whereas Ice T. and Easy E. were seeking romance, something they were not ready for in their home environment, Geya looked for friendship, something she could not manage in her home environment either. Like Bridget's other students, Geya too felt that she fully controlled what went into her writing. When asked how she decided what to write, Geya explained how she began: "I started to put my ideas to work" (March 21, 1988).

Cool J.'s autobiography was the longest of any of those written by Bridget's focal students. He wrote with more formality than most of his classmates. He tackled serious social issues that intersected with his life and was reflective in ways the others were not. He recounts, for example, the places he has lived, dwelling on his first neighborhood because he is concerned about it. As he observes, "Now there is a lot of dope there." He also worries about his classmates who now live there:

> You will also hear Rio talk about John F. Kennedy Manor. I was real young when I live there, but my mother told me that it was real nice in there. Now if the people who live in there don't know you, you take a big chance of getting mugged when you go there.

Like Geya, Cool J. opens himself up and does not attempt to create or project the "cool" personas of Easy E. and Ice T. In explaining his interests, he even reveals that he likes to cook:

> Cooking is something I took up about 2 years ago. I always liked to cook, but never really could. I watched my mother and grandmother while they cooked and kind of took notes. My mother gets home from work about 6 o'clock and sometimes she is real tired. That's when I cook or we eat out. What I don't understand is why my sister doesn't cook. She says it's because she doesn't feel like it.

Cool J. then shows himself to be the teenage boy he is as he moves on to what he says is one of his favorite topics, girls:

> Girls are something "I MASTER". Right now I don't have a girlfriend, but there are hell of girls that like me. I don't mean to brag, but if you got it then you've got it.

In their autobiographies, Bridget's students freely reveal who they are and what their world is like, and even present imagined selves. They openly criticize the art teacher, flirt with the opposite sex, and recount the dangers of their neighborhoods.

Bridget's students wrote their autobiographies mostly in class on the computers. Bridget helped them as she circulated around the room. In her journal she explained that she enjoys the one-to-one interactions that writing at the computers affords. The computers also open opportunities for Bridget's students to collaborate informally with one another. Easy E. described how he and his friends help each other: "She [Bridget] wanted, uh, it [the autobiography] to be perfect, I guess. And so everybody was, 'Okay. Okay. I'll change this.' And, you know, so it, it was, I mean everybody helped each other out and stuff. And so then we got on the computers. And you know, we were thinking about, 'Oh, I think I should change this.' And, you know, we were asking each other for help, and everybody was helping each other . . . I think I stopped and I helped, um, somebody out, and then I finished up mine, the next couple of days, or something like that . . . We were just having fun" (Interview, March 21, 1988). Cool J. confirmed this collaborative spirit: "In my class, Run helped me. You know me and him we'd, we would always work next to each other cause we both sports fans, so we talk about the hoop game or—and you know I'd ask him—you know we'd—we'd just helped each other out. I'd ask him how you spell this and, you know, how should I put this, and it went the same for him. We helped each other a lot" (Interview, March 10, 1988).

But some students found it difficult to have their writing displayed on the computer monitor for all to see. They did not like the public aspect of composing in class at the computers. As Geya explained: "Every time I get ready to write, or to type or something, everybody would try to come over my shoulder and look, and I don't like that . . . They just come and watch and try to peek at my stuff. Say 'Don't look, get away!' And I'll be hiding with my hands. They just trying to steal my stuff . . . They nosy. They want to know what I do. 'Cause I'm a loner and, you know, I like to, I like being by myself. And they just want to know what my business is, 'Yeah that's my business, get away!'" (Interview, March 21, 1988). Bridget understood the discomfort of students like Geya and worked to help them gain privacy. She discouraged other students from bothering Geya and offered herself as audience. When Geya was asked in the same interview, "Is there anybody . . . that you, you let share it with?" she quickly replied, "Ms. Franklin." Ultimately, despite the challenges writing publicly posed for students like Geya, Bridget tried to help each student find a comfortable way of writing.

Philippa assumed that her students would write autobiographies appropriate for both their exchange audience and the British examiners. However, even in this first formal exchange, Philippa's students found it taxing to write for two audiences, and most selected one of the two. When the examiner was not the only audience, Philippa's students wrote more freely and openly. However, because this writing was autobiographical, it functioned well enough for the exchange, even when the examiner took precedence.

Garney kept the U.S. audience in mind when she wrote, but she also recorded her experiences in ways that were formal enough for the examiners. Her writing worked well for both audiences. Her autobiography, the most fully developed of the British pieces, consists of five sections (Myself, my family, and where I live; My Religion; My School life; My Travels; and My life, past and present). In the section on religion Garney provides fascinating descriptions of Diwali and a Hindu wedding, including her thoughts on arranged marriages:

Hindu's also celebrate Diwali. Diwali is like an Indian Christmas. During Diwali fireworks are let off. Special food is made, (indian sweets) presents are given and recieved, and people go to the temple to prayer. Diwali celebrates the birth of an Indian God called Rama. Hindu's celebrate Diwali just like Christians celebrate Christmas.

During a Hindu wedding, lots of unusual things are done, between the couple getting married and the priest. A Hindu wedding is not necessarily held in a Temple it can be held anywhere, as long as there's enough room for the guests. The weddings I've been to are mostly held in a school hall. A the end of the wedding, the Bride and Bridegroom are driven off, to the Grooms house. Before they are driven off the Bride cries, and says godbye to her family, by embracing them, before she goes. All the weddings I've been to I've seen the bride cry. I think its a custom, but I could be wrong, because I would be sad to leave my family too! I was a Bride in my Uncles wedding.

My mum had an arranged Marriage, which I think is Absolutely pathetic. I repeat Pathetic. Because my mum had'nt met my dad. Although when she did meet him, my dad fancied her, but I don't think my mum did, but my mums dad thought my dad was good enough to marry my mum, so my mum could'nt argue. That's life. Sometimes she jokes with me saying that she wished she could have married another man. But I don't know about that one. After all he is my dad!

Anyway enough about the Wedding business, you're probably bored already.

Later in the year, Garney would again write about Diwali and arranged marriages.

Unlike Garney, Andi wrote her autobiography with mainly the examiner audience in mind, although she hoped "somebody might actually be interested in it" (Interview, May 1988). Because she had the examiner in mind, she left out "stuff like boyfriends," which her peers abroad might have found interesting. She commented, "If I was writing a letter specifically to the Americans then it would be all right to put it [the stuff about boyfriends] in there."

Andi's autobiography is clearly organized and well developed, but it lacks the exotic appeal of Garney's. She begins:

My Life is really in three parts, my life out of London, the move back to London and my time at secondary school. First of all before I start my autobiography let me tell you about myself. I'm 14 years old, I'm relatively tall, I have blondish hair and blue eyes. I live in London near Hammersmith. I also go to Hampden Jones School and I'm in the fourth year. I have a little brother in the school also, he's in the first year. My Dad is managing director of his own company, B's Estate Agents. Mum also works for Dad as his assitant manager. I have three brothers in all, my oldest, Ian, is 18 and is already married with a little son, my nephew, he's called Brandon and he's three months old.

Andi's most developed section tells about her idyllic life as a child in the country and the wrenching move to London. In a moving passage she reflects on her friend Charlotte, whom she hasn't seen since she moved:

> I often dream of going back and seeing how Charlotte's life has progressed. It's funny how your memory freezes pictures of people when you don't see them for a long period of time, that is why I would like to go back to see how she has progressed from the picture I have of her in my mind.

Andi recalls what it was like to leave her friend:

> I promised to write every week and that Charlotte and her sister, Rachel, could come up and visit me every other weekend, and I meant it. But every thing changed when I got to London, and well the friendship just faded.

Like her classmates, Andi enjoyed this writing: "I sort of feel very strongly about my past . . . [the autobiography] gave me a chance to write it down." She wanted to focus on her life before moving to London because "it was one of the best times of my life . . . so I sort of recorded it in much more detail . . . I sort of left everything behind, and it was a great mystery what happened to everybody and everything. So now I've actually made contact again but . . . everything sort of stayed the way it was. Really nice. When I moved to London everything changed, so everybody changed, my attitude and everything, for the worse actually" (Interview, May 1988).

When the British autobiographies arrived, Bridget's students received the news of the package from abroad with great enthusiasm, but their initial reactions were negative. In her journal Bridget explains how she analyzed and dealt with the problem:

> I was a bit upset about the negative reaction to the autobiogs. Most students very reluctant to settle down to reading. Most said autobiogs were "boring."
> When I got over my irritation I began to analyze what went wrong. Reading *is* a [unclear] to most of these kids. Add to that hard-to-read penmanship and guess what? Negative reaction.
> About the "boring" angle. These kids often label difficult tasks "boring." So my first rush to protect the Brit. kids' egos wasn't addressing the real problem.

I decided to back off the autobiogs and use this week before Xmas to finish rdg the book we're on. When we get back from vacation I'll approach the autobiogs differently—perhaps reading each one aloud and having kids take notes. I'll approach the papers as if I'm reading an essay or s. story—scaffolding meaning and making sure the kids understand. That should take care of the "boring" bit. (December 11, 1987)

After vacation, Bridget organized time for each British autobiography to be read aloud and discussed by the class. As her students talked about the British students' work, they discussed the qualities that made the British autobiographies interesting and made them as readers feel that they actually knew particular students. Bridget wrote in her journal:

I noticed that as I went along it was easy to point out things about effective writing to the kids. The British kids who write the most interesting autobiographies were those who showed not told and who gave enough background information to make themselves clear. Those whose stories were mere lists of places and events received the poorest ratings by my students. We talked a lot about the students that we liked best from what they wrote and the students we felt we knew best (usually one and the same) and we discussed why we had those feelings. The kids clearly got the point that they need to "jump off the page" in order to engage their reader. (February 1988)

No longer were the British autobiographies dismissed as boring. In fact, most helpful to Bridget's students was Garney's writing. Her experiences as a Hindu were particularly interesting to Bridget's mostly Christian audience.

If the introductory letters were a key factor in initiating a social relationship with Philippa's students, the autobiographies sealed it. Bridget's students' sense of social and cultural links to their audience in England was reinforced by this exchange, which allowed Bridget to engage her students with her academic agenda. As they read the British autobiographies together, she and her students discovered the characteristics of writing that appealed to a distant peer audience. These discoveries helped her students anticipate and respond to the needs of their British readers. In addition to encouraging their attempts to use writing to gain entry into the social lives of the British students, Bridget worked with them to take the academic steps necessary to write to a general rather than an individual audience. "Show not tell" became a useful strategy to help them "jump off the page" and reach their new readers.

In Philippa's classroom, however, the situation remained complex and became increasingly difficult to handle. Whereas the introductory letters came on what appeared to the British students to be "toilet paper," the U.S. students, oblivious to their first faux pas, inadvertently created another problem for Philippa with their autobiographies. Because the U.S. autobiographies had been typed on computers, Philippa's students now worried that they could not match the professional U.S. look:

> When we got the autobiographies from the American class, the American class had obviously, um, recognized the problem [with the presentation of the letter]. They switched from very thin toilet paper, lead pencils, to computers. My class hadn't got a computer. So their beautifully painstakingly handwritten autobiographies, which had taken them bloody forever, had taken an enormous chunk out of their GCSE, looked pathetic in comparison. And they didn't want to send them off. "Why can't we have a computer? Oh well." Because, you see what I mean, the mismatch exacerbated, and I actually felt myself in a situation which I personally couldn't handle. And they kept saying, and my kids were right, they kept saying, "We want to meet these kids. Forget the computers, forget the handwriting . . . We want to meet these kids. We want to talk to these kids." And the whole thing for my class came down to talk. "We want to talk with these kids." (Interview, July 18, 1989)

In Philippa's mind, the autobiographies were already taking time away from the GCSE course. Now the students thought they could best appeal to the U.S. audience by writing as they talked. As Marisa explained, "I wrote it [my autobiography] actually how I would actually speak it if I was, like, out on the street or in the playground" (Interview, May 1988). But this increasing desire for talk was inconsistent with Philippa's goals for her students' more formal GCSE writing, which she saw as necessarily distinct from talk.

On a related note, Philippa worried about how Titch's sense of appropriate writing for the exams would be affected by the positive response to her informal, talklike writing for her U.S. peers:

> Titch was one of the least able academically in the class, so I had to be very careful that I wasn't so pleased that she had got this recognition

that everything else went by the board . . . Her own sense of where she was at was being threatened and becoming unrealistic. She was getting a lot of response to what for her was a very good piece of work, but that wasn't saying that this was a piece of work that was going to, back in the exam situation, give her a C or above . . . I was saying to the kids, "There are two audiences. What was giving you an overwhelming response from your audience in America is not going to gain favor . . . from the examiners." (Interview, April 20, 1989)

Finally, the split between some of the black students in Philippa's class and many of the others intensified as the exchange became increasingly special for Titch and her black friends. Although Titch had received little confirmation as a writer in the past, Philippa explained how some of the other students felt: "The response that Titch's piece [introductory letter] gained was so total that a lot of the other kids felt negated and particularly, um, the white girls, Reg and Andi . . . They felt that there really wasn't a place for them in this exchange, that there wasn't someone at the other end of the computer that they really, um, had an affinity with, so they did to a large extent opt out" (Interview, April 20, 1989).

Although Andi enjoyed writing her autobiography, she didn't expect any response from the U.S. students because as she explained, "I suppose I'd got it into my mind that this exchange wasn't for me." Ream, a white male, reached out by working with a few friends to write "a rap back" but reported losing interest because of a lack of response to his work. Marisa, who was black but not part of the in-group, also resented what she saw as the lopsided nature of the responses from the U.S. students. She suggested a remedy: "I think it's not fair because like, some people like Jetty, Garney, like some of them don't get feedback. Like people like Martin and John, they're not interested because they're not getting any feedback. I think they should be assigned to someone." Ironically, Bridget's class had especially appreciated Garney's autobiography, but this fact had not yet been communicated to Philippa's students.

Shakespeare Papers

Toward the end of the year, Bridget was able to stretch her "remedial" students so that they could tackle increasingly serious academic projects. Their growth is evident in the Shakespeare papers, the last coordinated exchange between the U.S. and British students. They took risks, were comfortable about revealing themselves, and were confident about and involved in their writing. By this point they felt fully connected to Philippa's students.

Bridget explained in her journal how her class began the *Romeo and Juliet* unit: "I combined classes with the teacher next door who has only 8–10 students. We started out by telling the story of R and J and having the kids write summaries. They're completely engrossed. I'm amazed at how much they know already or how good they are at predicting what will happen next. Elaine is upset that we're showing the Zeffirelli film before we read the book. She says, 'Then we'll know how it ends'" (February 1988).

To support the group in their first reading of Shakespeare, Bridget and the other teacher got their students involved by having them act out an abridged version of the play, with different students taking different roles. In her journal, Bridget noted that Elaine "has already staked out the main part" of Juliet. In an interview she revealed how Cool J. had managed to get the coveted part of Romeo: "He's Romeo in our play. We didn't assign him to be. I think I assigned him to be Mercutio, I don't know, somebody like that. And the kid who was Romeo, who was from the other class, doesn't read as well as Cool J., and I don't know what happened, but the switch was made by the other teacher. And Cool J. loves the role. I mean, he kisses Juliet, who's this very shy girl, and you know, things like. So, but he's not an actor-out. He's very aware of classroom decorum" (Interview, February 24, 1988).

Bridget's curriculum building evolved, so that students assumed increasing levels of responsibility as the year went on. Her students now worked actively with her to choose writing topics. In a February letter to Philippa, Bridget explained the topic selection process:

We are going to begin two writing assignments, one my idea and one theirs [the students']. So far during our study of the play we have had our students write two personal narratives for homework assignments, one about a time they did something rash and another about a time their mother or father did something rash (if their parents refuse to tell them a story, the kids are writing another one about themselves). When we finish reading the play, they will choose to revise and rewrite the personal narrative they think you will enjoy most and they will type it on the computer. The next thing they will do came as an idea from

Elaine. She suggested—and the other kids agreed—that they rewrite some scenes and act them out for you on video.

Bridget justified her enthusiasm for personal narratives related to literature: "I have this thing about asking kids to write, like, a personal narrative or an essay connected to the theme of every piece of literature, so they really internalize it. There's always some kind of connection so that they really get into, you know, the main character's plight or the writer's theory" (Interview, April 27, 1988).

Ultimately, because of the incompatibility of British and American video equipment, Elaine's idea had to be modified. Instead of producing a video, some students rewrote various scenes from the play using modern language and street talk and sent their scripts to England.

Geya's modern version, *Oscar and Romance,* shows the depth of her understanding of *Romeo and Juliet.* Her play consisted of three scenes. The first two paralleled much of the action of the first two scenes of act 3 of the original, and the third summarized the rest of the plot.

Geya's first scene opens on the streets of San Francisco where her equivalent of the Montagues and Capulets are feuding:

> In San Fransico Jose [Mercutio], Alejandro his page, Jesus [Benvolio] and friends come out on the streets on a very hot an sullaty day.

> JESUS   Come on Jose let's go home. Man it's hot and I want some Ice Creame. and you know that I don't feel like fighting right now. It is so hot I just want to pretend that our greatest enemies aren't even there.

The resemblance to the opening of act 3, scene 1, is close:

> BEN.   I pray thee, good Mercutio, let's retire.
> The day is hot, the Capulets abroad,
> And, if we meet, we shall not scape a brawl,
> For now, these hot days, is the mad blood stirring.
> (3.1.1–4)

Geya captures the heat of the day, in terms of both the weather and the tension between the Montagues and Capulets. She embellishes the mood with Jesus' desire for ice cream to cool himself down.

As the original act 3, scene 1 continues, Romeo's best friend,

Mercutio accuses Benvolio of being too moody and too eager for a fight:

MER.   Thou art like one of these fellows that, when he enters the confines of a tavern, claps me his sword upon the table and says, "God send me no need of thee!" and by the operation of the second cup draws him on the drawer, when indeed there is no need.

BEN.   Am I like such a fellow?

MER.   Come, come, thou art as hot a Jack in thy mood as any in Italy, and as soon moved to be moody, and as soon moody to be moved.

BEN.   And what to?

MER.   Nay, an there were two such, we should have none shortly, for one would kill the other. Thou! why, thou wilt quarrel with a man that hath a hair more or a hair less in his beard than thou hast. Thou wilt quarrel with a man for cracking nuts, having no other reason but because thou hast hazel eyes. What eye but such an eye would spy out such a quarrel? Thy head is as full of quarrels as an egg is full of meat, and yet thy head hath been beaten as addle as an egg for quarreling. (3.1.5–25)

In her rendition, Geya maintains much of the gist of the story but adds her own interpretation. She captures Mercutio's accusation that Benvolio is looking for a fight, but Geya's Jose, who is Mercutio, also accuses her Jesus, who is Benvolio, of being a coward. Furthermore, Jose accuses Jesus of getting angry at the wrong things. Geya gives Jose an especially realistic, colloquial voice:

JOSE   You're a *coward* man that's what you are.

JESUS   Oh! I am, am I. Just see what kind of coward I am when you fight alone.

JOSE   Come on bro you know it's just hot and everyone is angry so how about if we just start on our way to get some Ice Creame.

JESUS   What?

JOSE   Jesus you know that you get angry at everything but the most important things that you are supposed to get mad at and you're telling me that it is wrong to get angry and yell.

Following the plotline closely, Geya next introduces Rogelio (Tybalt, Juliet's cousin) who comes to start a fight with the Montagues. Like Mercutio, Jose goads Rogelio, while Jesus, like Benvolio, continues to try to keep the peace:

ROGELIO   (talking to his men) Stay close behind I'm going to start something. (to Jose) Could I talk to one of you?

JOSE   I know you're up to something perhaps a word, then a swing at the head or below the belt.

ROGELIO   Give me a reason why? You think that way Jose.

JOSE   Think of one yourself. I don't feel like wasting my breath giving you a reason. Understand?

ROGELIO   Jose you are one of Oscar's men.

JOSE   Men and what do you mean by (men) tell me.

JESUS   Let's go where no one can hear our business or argue calmly about yourself's or just stop! People are staring at us. Man You're Dumbies.

JOSE   So let them stare Who cares I'm not moving for NO ONE. Understand ME NO ONE!

In several more pages of dialogue, Rogelio kills Jose, and Oscar jumps into the fray and kills Rogelio. After some deliberation, Joe (Prince of Verona) decides to exile Oscar, just as the Prince exiles Romeo.

As in act 3, scene 2, of the original play, Geya's second scene opens with a speech by Romance in which she declares her impatience to lose her virginity to Oscar:

ROMANCE   I wish night would hurry up and come because I am so impatient. I want to have Oscar now. We can make love all night and it would be so wonderful. After this night I will no longer be a virgin.

Geya's second scene continues to follow the original closely as Romance learns about the murders and about Oscar's banishment from her Nurse, whom Geya names Tiffany.

In her third scene, Geya incorporates the action of the remaining three scenes of act 3 as well as all of acts 4 and 5. Here she relies mostly on plot summary rather than dialogue, a technique that allows her to move the plot forward quickly:

Oscar and Romance hit it off that night and the next morning she was notified that she was scheuled to be married on Thursday and

Romance refused. Her and Her father got into a terrible fight and He said that she would marry him or she will be left with nothing in His will. It seems to me that, that got to her heart because then she went to Stephanie [Friar Lawrence] and she needed help and so Stephanie gave her a sleeping potion so she would not have to get married.

Aside from the fact that Friar Lawrence becomes the female Stephanie, Geya presents a fairly accurate interpretation of the Shakespearean characters' motivations, actions, and emotions, especially in the dialogue of her first two scenes, but even in the plot summary of the last scene.

Besides *Oscar and Romance,* Geya sent two narratives to Philippa's students, one about a rash deed of her mother's and the other about a rash deed of her own. Her own "rash deed" narrative shows that she had become as comfortable with her British audience as she had been throughout the year with Bridget. She tells how she cut school when she was twelve to go off with a twenty-one-year-old man. Apparently entirely truthful, she writes vividly and personally:

When I was in the 7th grade I was in love, at least that is what I thought anyway. I called myself madly in love with this guy and he was 21 years old then. His name was Roberto but I don't want to tell you his last name. Anyway one day I went to the bus stop and I was with a girl named Vanessa. After a while her uncle came and gave her a ride and they asked me if I wanted a ride. but I said no thanks. After another while Roberto came over to me and asked if he could take me to school. I said yes. So we started to talk inside of the car as we were cruising down the street. We finally got to my school Park View Junior High School. I told him to take me in the parking lot but he took me across the street and he told me that I could at least take one day out with him. I thought about it and it was kind of hard for me to agree but I finally gave in.

He took me to a place that I had never seen before so that means I cut school. He took me to a park and we watched the cars and people pass by. He really wanted to do something that I definitely didn't want to and so he kind of got mad. I started to leave. I turned around and there were his keys so I decided to take them. While he was searching for me I was in the car listening to his music. When he spotted me I was kind of lying down in his car. When he got inside the car it was an hour later he was very mad. He was so mad but he didn't hit me and then I started to love him even more. Then we went to the store and we ate. After we had finished eating he took me to a place that looked like a place that you and your loved one cut school and go to do whatever it is that they do, but we didn't do anything. When we got there I tried to make him run off a cliff. I tried to kill us because I felt bad. He stopped the car in time so I got mad and got out of the car.

The next day my mother got a telephone call from my counselor telling her that I didn't come to school and when I got home everyone got the idea that he had done something to me that shouldn't have been done but I am telling the truth. HE DID NOT DO ANYTHING. Boy when I got home I got the whipping of my life. I learned a lesson. Right today I know not to ever cut and go with someone that I call myself in love with.

In an interview Geya revealed that she would have been uncomfortable sharing this writing with the students in her class but that she was not uncomfortable with the distant British audience. "In a way I didn't want to do it, because I thought everybody [in the class] was gonna read it, and she [Bridget] wanted us to read it out loud. Then I asked her about it, and she said no, you know, it's gonna be, the class not gonna read it" (Interview, April 27, 1988). She then told why she selected this particular rash deed: "And so I had to think about a couple of things I did. And that was just the one thing I, I learned a lesson from . . . It just sticks in my mind. Every time I think about it, I try to wipe it out, it just won't leave. And the bad thing about it, he lived right down the street from my house. My mother don't like him" (Interview, April 27, 1988). Geya wanted to share her experience with the students in England because she "hope[s] they just learn from this . . . It could teach a person a lesson." She was satisfied with the way she wrote about her rash deed because she thought it "has the details" and was graphic. She explained what made this and other pieces of writing vivid for her: "When you read it you can really feel what's happening . . . Like if I read a book or something, you can actually picture yourself in the book. Sometimes I read a book, and I thought I seen a movie, but it was in a book" (Interview, April 27, 1988).

Cool J. wrote about breaking the window of a house with a rock while playing baseball with his cousin, Worm. A couple of weeks after the incident the owner of the house came to his front door and asked his father if Cool J. had broken his window. Cool J. describes his confession: "In about 5 minunts my father called me in the living room. He asked me if I broke the the man's window. I didn't know what to say. I told the man and my father the truth. I told them how it all happened. My father made me say I was sorry and my father paid for the cost of the repairs. I got this long talk and he made me pay him back for the window." In his interview, however, Cool J. admitted that only part of his story is true:

> Just about everything in this story is true. Everything up until the point where, let's see, everything up to the point where we broke the window and we put stuff in my backyard like nothing happened. To this day, the only people that know what happened is my cousin and myself. We never told nobody, and now some new people live in, in the house, and so like, a couple of months had passed, and we went to play back there. And he said, he the man said somebody had broke his window. And I had another friend with me, then it was my cousin, my friend and myself. My friend said, "Well, we didn't break your window." He never knew nothing about it. I said, "No, you know, we didn't break it." He said, "Well, it's a small hole." He said, "It looks like a rock had been through it," and I said, "No, we don't throw rocks, because rocks are dangerous. You can put somebody's eye out." So I said, "A tennis ball probably couldn't have done it." So he said he had to have it fixed and it cost $75 for a small hole this big. Right because it was big glass, and you had to have the whole thing taken out, put it back in. So we play there now, and the new people there, they're, they pretty, they said if a ball goes over there, go ask him and he'll get it for us. (Interview, April 28, 1988)

He invented the ending to make the story better: "The assignment was to do something that you did without thinking, and then got punished for, so I made, you know, I put a little fiction, like any other author would do. Have facts and then stretch the truth to give it a ending" (Interview, April 28, 1988).

Unlike Geya, Cool J. chose not to include certain ideas because his writing was being sent to England. As he explained, "Like, some things is personal that you did without thinking. I don't want people in England reading." He also thought some of his ideas were inappropriate from his teacher's point of view: "Miss Franklin, she wouldn't really want us to send this type of stuff to England . . . when you write to yourself, you can tell any detail. You don't have too much edit this, edit that, fix this up, and fix that up" (Interview, April 28, 1988).

Bridget was worried by the fact that when her students wrote about rash deeds, they often did not seem to think about the connection between their own or their parents' rash deeds and the impetuosity of Romeo and Juliet. Like Geya and Cool J., most of the students made no reference to the play in this writing, although they did write about rash deeds that caused them or their parents to get into trouble, and most suggested a lesson or moral for the reader. Only Easy E. explicitly linked his ideas about himself to *Romeo and Juliet:* "I remember once my best friend and I snuck out of our houses late at night and went swimming. We knew we were going to get in trouble but we didn't care. I guess we acted without thinking just like some of the actors did in the play Romeo and Juliet."

Bridget was pleased that her students had generally become conscious of their British audience, and she noted that even for the Shakespeare papers, "there's a social element with this for the kids. Socially they care about this audience in some way, and they want to connect socially, and that's the motivation. So then the social can bring in some of the academic things" (Interview, February 24, 1988). In her analysis of the exchange, Bridget also noted that the British audience allowed her students a performance opportunity, something that became particularly apparent with the Shakespeare writing (Cone, 1989).

Philippa's students appreciated the "rash deed" papers from the United States. Ream thought they were the best of the U.S. writing because the students wrote directly and got to the point: "They just went straight into it." He elaborated on what he liked: "Sometimes it was funny what things they had done, and they got into trouble, and how they got told by their parents, and how they got told off or beaten or something like that. They're generally very funny" (Interview, May 1988).

In an electronic mail message replete with typos, Philippa told Bridget that her students responded positively to the "rash deed" papers:

These acted as a wonderful stimulus. These pieces are I think far more pwersonal than anything qwe have written eartlier. I think that this is because the kids have begun to very much personalise their audience. I will get my kids to do a RASH DEEDS task over the Easter vacation. I will also send off their ROMEO and JULIET pieces during the holiday. I am sorry that these will be handwritten as we only have linited access to the computer. (April 23, 1988)

In their own e-mail, surrounded by messages on other topics, Philippa's students made comments like the following one by Joshua, Kendall, John, and Ahmed to U.S. students Rose, Tu-tu, and Geya: "We were just reading your 'RASH DEED' assignments and they were GREAT everybody in the form enjoyed them and they kept us captivated and the class has not been so quiet for a long time" (April 23, 1988). Tootsie and Swivel addressed their response to Cool J.:

> We both liked the one which Cool J. wrote. Tootsie reckons that his dad treated him fairly in the punishment that he gave him after he found out about the window. We liked it because it was really funny and entertaining and it made us laugh. We understood why you and your cousin, Worm (is that his real name?) didn't tell anyone. We wouldn't have either!!
>
> We can't think of anything really rash that we have done but Tootsie remembers something that her Mum has done. My older brother, Edward had been winding her up and eventually he got so angry that she chased him into my room. By now he'd managed to get infront of the window so my mum, her being a good thrower, and all that took off her shoe and flung it at him. My brother, ducked just in time and didn't get hit. Lucky for him but not the window. (April 23, 1988)

Unfortunately, Philippa had little support in operating the e-mail. The computer work, including these replics, Philippa said, "frustrated me . . . In the end I felt that I had to cut it [the computer work] off . . . They were all very angry with me because they'd enjoyed it, but I knew that the time I'd allowed for that was far outweighing the time I would have allowed for anything else, and I felt that I had . . . a responsibility to their examinations" (Interview, April 20, 1989). Marisa confirmed the students' reaction when she expressed her frustration at trying to respond to the "rash deed" papers: "I was reviewing their rash deeds. I, I was reviewing it, and then I didn't, um, get to finish it off, and then it was sent off, and then I haven't got a copy of the actual [computer] file. So I can't complete it. Or I don't know what I writ on it, like, cause . . . I didn't get to put that down, anything that was actually on the file . . . Now I don't [know] if I'll finish that one because Miss might have sent it off, and if she gets rid of the disk then that's the end of it" (Interview, May 1988).

At this point in the year, Philippa's students had begun to change their minds about the U.S. group's capabilities. As Philippa recalls, "In the end it was quite clear that there wasn't such a mismatch, was there" (Interview, November 2, 1990). In addition, some of the students felt that the initial monopoly held by the black kids had dissolved. Because the U.S. writing had been directed at all the students, a number of the initially alienated, nonblack students became involved. For example, Andi felt included once she had received a letter from Run: "As soon as I received the letter from Run, I thought, yeah, you know, they really are interested in me and not just sort of the other people in the class . . . not just sort of Titch and that lot, and I thought they're interested in sort of Garney and the people who aren't just black and have something in common with them . . . [Run] made me feel as if he wanted to talk to me" (Interview, May 1988).

Regardless of their level of involvement in the exchange, Philippa and her students felt the growing pressures of the examination. Now that the school year was approaching its end, Philippa worried constantly about getting her students to produce enough work for the examiner audience, and she was particularly worried that those who were involved in the exchange were distracted by it. In Philippa's mind the Shakespeare papers would have to be primarily for the examiner, even though she would send them to the U.S. students as planned.

The Shakespeare papers were part of a two-play unit. As Philippa reported, "I did *Romeo and Juliet* and *Macbeth*. And we saw both the films. And we didn't read the texts as a whole group. Those kids who felt able to and interested enough, they went on and read the texts, and I explained to them that if they really wanted to get a C or above [on their GCSE folder] they would have, need to have read the text" (Interview, April 20, 1989).

Overall, however, Philippa did not feel happy about her students' reactions to the Shakespeare unit or about the quality of their writing: "They did not feel particularly stimulated by the work, and even the real high fliers in the class, and one in particular, Tootsie, even Tootsie, said that she, she felt she'd really had to work at it, um, in order to be rewarded by it, to get enjoyment out of it" (Interview, April 20, 1989). Philippa recalled that her students thought the U.S. students would be bored by their Shakespeare pieces: "They actually wrote letters saying, before the stuff was sent off, because there was a time gap because of the mismatch in the holidays, they actually decided they wanted to write some chatty 'Hi! Are you still there? We're still here. We've got some work coming to you but it's pretty boring.' And I can remember being mortified by that and saying to them, 'But it's not boring.' I mean a lot of what they'd written wasn't boring at all.

And they said, 'Well, if we were those American kids, we would not want to read these things'" (Interview, April 20, 1989).

According to her analysis, Philippa's students were intimidated by writing about Shakespeare. As she concluded, "Something that's frightening equals boring because it's better to say that you're bored with something than that you're scared of it" (Interview, April 20, 1989). She also felt that their judgments about their work were relatively immature. By the next year, they were able to see the virtues of these pieces: "It's interesting when they're putting their [examination] folders together how when they look back at them [the Shakespeare writing], they say, 'Oh yeah, there's all that really good stuff that I did on Shakespeare'" (Interview, April 20, 1989).

The British students' writing exhibited a great deal of variety. Two of the pieces were on *Macbeth,* a play the U.S. class had not read. Of the *Romeo and Juliet* writing, some seemed boring but other pieces were quite interesting. The forms of the writing ranged widely, from Joshua's brief GCSE "Controlled Assignment";[2] to Garney's personal reflections on how the play related to her everyday life, showing the links between *Romeo and Juliet* and Hinduism; to imaginative news reports by Garney and Marisa; to Lionel's character sketches of Tybalt and the Nurse; to Kendall's and Jetty's character sketches of Romeo and Juliet; to Tootsie's twelve-and-a-half pages for five separate pieces ("The Nurses Description of Scene Five"; "The Characters"; "Puns"; "Word Play"; and "Get thee to church," which consisted of seven paragraph-long answers to questions about aspects of the play).

Joshua's "Controlled Assignment," which consists solely of his impressions of the Zeffirelli film, represents the least lively end of the spectrum:

> When I first learned that we were going to be watching Romeo and Juliet, the balcony scene entered my mind instantly.
>
> When we started to watch the film the first scene was set in the town square. The film was filmed on location and the film was filmed in some very authentic places which did improve the quality.

Joshua goes on to comment, but with few specifics, on the acting, the costumes, the fight scene, and the use of language. He concludes his single page:

> Whilst watching the film I was shocked to find that the balcony scence was nothing like I expected it be, infact I found it quite funny.

The use of music in the film was rare and not very effective as it could have been.

Taking another approach to the Shakespeare writing, Jetty opens her character sketch of Juliet with a plot summary and then comments on Juliet's clothes and her personality:

> Juliet daughter of Lady Capulet, first appears in Act 1 Scene 3 where Juliet, Lady Capulet, and the nurse discuss about marridge and about Juliet's age and life. Juliet is only 14 but is already being persuaded to marry. Juliet's clothes are nothing near glamourous and are very dull and boring, as she is not aloud to wear any clothes which will attract other men's attention, so she wears very baggy dresses which does'nt show off her figure. Juliets personality is that if she wants something she goes ahead and does it, she does'nt wait around, also she has a strong relationship with the nurse, who she depends on, to get things done for her. She gets on best with the nurse than anybody else out of her whole family.

Kendall's character sketch of Juliet begins in a similar way but includes more plot summary and less commentary:

> Juliet's father wants Juliet to marry Paris but Juliet couldn't care less. But one night when the capulet's hold a party and Romeo had crashed and they felt something for eachover Juliet less than Romeo. But as they get to know eachover they get very close. But one day Mercutio is killed by tybalt and Romeo kills tybalt. When Romeo is on his own, he thinks he's relationship's at an end. But Juliet is still in love with Romeo, one night Romeo returns to the capulets house but Juliet is still in love with Romeo. That night Juliet let Romeo spend the night with her.

Garney's newspaper article and her piece connecting *Romeo and Juliet* to Hinduism, along with Tootsie's "The Nurses Description of Scene Five," show the other end of the spectrum for this writing. Garney's opening paragraph for her newspaper article, "The Fight Goes On," runs as follows:

> Once more, the peace was disturbed in Verona yesterday, by the family feud between the Montague's and Capulet's. Nobody really knows how the feud started, but it was over somesort of misunderstanding.

The family feud which has been going on for years, is still at its peak! About 8 people were injured during the fight, 2 of which were serious.

The article continues with a full report of the fight.

For her Hinduism piece, Garney veers from Philippa's suggested topic. At the top of the page she writes Philippa's directions, "Write a story based on one of the themes explored in either plays," and continues: "This is'nt a story, its just a piece of writing explaining about the Indian religion! It is based on the play, Romeo and Juliet, and why the 2 teenagers were'nt allowed to see each other." Garney goes on to explain that the teenagers could not get together because the adults were feuding and then says, "Well, its the same with the Hindu religion, and a lot of other Indian religions." She writes for two pages on her favorite topic, arranged marriages, and concludes, "So, all this boils down to the sort of situation Romeo and Juliet went through!"

Tootsie's imaginative plot summary presents one scene in the play from the Nurse's point of view, replete with the Nurse's gossipy voice and with invented punctuation conventions, presumably the Nurse's, since Tootsie did not use them in her other writing:

> Ohhhh! "I really do not know what to think. I was only telling my lady Juliet what I thought would be the most practical thing to do her being in such an unfortunate situation and all." "What situation is that!?" "You mean you don't know?" "But of course you wouldn't, what with you being new and all." "Well you've heard of the feud between the Capulets and the Montogues haven't you?'"

Then the Nurse retells the scene and concludes with her feelings about the events:

> "The good Lord knows that I was only trying to do the right thing by my Lady Juliet,". But it just seems to have driven a wedge between us two thats near enough about to break my heart. "S'pose you can't blame the poor love for reacting in the way she did, Oh I do worry about her so, you know,".
>
> "There you have it, now, you know, whats going on,". "Well we can't stand here in the passageway gossiping all day, we've both got enough work to do and little enough time to do it in,". "So I'll be saying farewell for now."

Bridget's students reacted exactly as the British students predicted they would, with disappointment. However, there were many possible causes, only some of which were connected to the quality or interest level of the British students' writing. In the first place, the U.S. students had waited a long time to hear from their British friends, and many British students sent nothing at all; in fact, only ten of Philippa's twenty-two students sent writing about Shakespeare. Bridget's students had only received two batches of computer mail from England in the second semester, and they expected to hear from everyone in this last major package of writing. Second, given their general disappointment about the few pieces that arrived, Bridget's students had little tolerance for writing they thought was intended more for school or exams than for them. They needed to feel that they could reconnect with the British audience through this writing. Finally, the writing arrived so late in June that Bridget's students had little time to attend to the more interesting pieces—to read them as a group and discuss those that interested them.

As Bridget observed, and as her students remarked in their interviews, they felt such strong personal ties to the British students that they blamed Philippa, not her class, for this writing that they had difficulty connecting with: "My kids decided it was all their teacher's fault. They said, 'Well why did they write such boring things?' I said, 'Don't say that.' And they said, 'It's all their teacher's fault'" (Interview, December 13, 1988). Oblivious to the constraints of the GCSE examination, Easy E. reiterated: "We were wondering if their teacher had anything to do with that . . . Is their teacher, um, you know, making them, you know, like say, 'Well this week I think you should write about this' or something like that?" (Interview, June 10, 1988). Ice T. expressed similar feelings: "Most kids they just said maybe the teacher was holding them back or something" (Interview, June 7, 1988). Geya provided advice to Philippa: "I think the teachers should just let 'em go on, and just write about what they want to write about, not what they want them to write about" (Interview, June 7, 1988).

The Importance of the Peer Culture

Bridget's approach to the writing exchange project provides a model for how to involve traditionally low-achieving students in a range of literacy activities and thereby help them increase their literacy skills. It was particularly heartening to watch the growing enthusiasm and progress of the African American males who populated Bridget's class in disproportionately large numbers, a phenomenon not uncommon in low-tracked classes. Their experiences show that it is possible for educators to harness peer culture in ways that counteract the powerful forces of resistance to schooling that Ogbu (1990) found at work among low socioeconomic status African American teenagers in the United States. As Easy E. explained:

> Once I met all the people [from the British class] or whatever, I started opening up and . . . instead of just doing it, for credit or whatever, I was talking to a friend. And, um, I think, that made my reading, my writing better, because, I wanted to do it, you know, instead of just, ahh! I gotta do this assignment. You know, just writing something down. Yeah, okay, all right Ms. Franklin, I'm finished, you know, or whatever. Give me the grade. You would . . . think about what you're going to write because this is your friend now. You know you got to keep them up to date on what's going on, and so you would really work. You would really, you know, concentrate, and work hard on, um, trying to make it perfect. You know, as best you can. (Interview, June 10, 1988)

By creating a strong classroom community, Bridget was able to satisfy the needs of a variety of students at the same time—both students in different ethnic groups and students within each group. Students as diverse as Geya the loner and the sociable Ice T., Easy E., and Cool J. all found a place in the writing exchange. With a history of being tracked in "remedial" classes, Cool J. admitted, "I did a lot more this year than I've ever wrote" (Interview, June 7, 1988).

Bridget's students talked about how they thought they had improved as writers. For example, Ice T. felt that he had developed his imagination: "At the start of the year I didn't, um, when I wrote, I didn't have any imagination. Now I do" (Interview, June 7, 1988). Cool J. and Easy E. said they had slowed down and become more careful with their work. Instead of just dashing it off, they cared and so they improved.

The students' involvement in developing the curriculum evolved during the year. As Easy E. tells it, at the start of the year the students' writing choices were somewhat restricted, but as the year went on, Bridget began telling him and his classmates, "This is your story now" and you can write about "whatever you want to talk about" (Interview, June 10, 1988).

Although Bridget's group was labeled remedial, students ended the year with many accomplishments. But they still had much to learn. They were just beginning to become sensitive readers of literature and to write about the connections between their reading and their lives in ways that would prepare them to write analyses of what they had read. They were still working on sentence boundaries, sentence structure, spelling, and standard punctuation. They still seemed more comfortable with the social writing in the exchange than with the more academic work, although they were making academic strides, always building from their social base. Easy E. explained how he envisioned the connections between writing for the exchange and his future writing for school: "It's like, you know, I was just writing to some kids, and then . . . they changed the way I felt . . . And instead of just writing to some kids, I never knew or whatever, I was writing to some friends, and so then I cared about what I was writing. And then, you know, that slowed it down, and, you know, I took my time. And, you know, I got it all finished. And that would be, a way I would write to a teacher. I would make sure everything's, you know, best as it could be" (Interview, June 10, 1988).

Complications from the British Exams

The British students' experiences and the U.S. students' responses highlight the restrictions posed by the national examinations, even when they were based on portfolios of writing completed as part of the regular curriculum. Bridget's students all commented that Philippa's students wrote similar things, both from one student to the next and from one piece of writing to the next. As Cool J. remarked, "We tend to write more, freely and open, and about more topics" (Interview, June 7, 1988).

Clearly the British GCSE curriculum demanded that Philippa's students complete varied kinds of writing, including serious analyses of literature of a type Bridget's students had not yet attempted. With mixed-ability classes and an examination curriculum, no students could be tracked into either "remedial" classes or "remedial" subgroups within a class. Thus, no students could be systematically denied the opportunity to do serious academic work, as had happened to both Bridget's and Ann's students before they entered the ninth grade.

Philippa was convinced that the conflicts between the exchange curriculum, which she interpreted as primarily social, and the examination curriculum, which she interpreted as primarily academic, had important consequences for her students' performance on their examination. For Titch, Philippa thought the exchange was helpful: "Titch wouldn't have got a *D* without that exchange. Titch would have got an *F* . . . That exchange fired her. She suddenly realized she could write. She suddenly realized she'd got an audience. She suddenly realized she could do it" (Interview, July 18, 1989). Tootsie, meanwhile, was a strong black student whom Philippa feared received a *B* rather than an *A* on the GCSE because of her involvement in the exchange:

> She [Tootsie] felt that she had to be patient with the [U.S.] class because I had spelt it out for them that this was a low-tracking class and what it meant. Because that class was primarily black and she was a black girl who was very aware with the problems of being a black pupil at school, she was tolerant. She went out of her way to try and be nice, to be understanding, to be supportive. But I'm not so sure it was the time in her life where she really needed that one laid upon her . . . I know there are one or two kids in that class that if I'm absolutely honest that perhaps if it wasn't for this exchange, if it hadn't of been for this exchange, they might have got *A*s, and they said, "Okay, we know you, we know you're right about this. And we'll trust you." And at the end of the day, as I said to you before, Tootsie got a *B* . . . I am concerned as to what extent my own class were guinea pigs. (Interview, July 18, 1989)

When Ellie O'Sullivan asked Philippa if she had any strategies she would use to help students like Tootsie get an *A*, Philippa replied: "No, I'm frightened by it. I'm frightened to sit here and admit it . . . That has worried me for ages" (Interview, July 18, 1989).

In the end, the exchange led to complications for Philippa's examination class, but it allowed Bridget to link the social and the academic lives of her "remedial" student writers. Bridget made sure that the links remained tight, always encouraging her students to get caught up in the social fun but being careful not to let academic opportunities slip away.

Chapter 8

ᔌ Crossing Cultures

This book is above all a study in contrasts—between U.S. and British culture; between U.S. and British educational systems, policies, and institutional structures; and between teachers and students. These contrasts, from the subtle to the dramatic, showcase the differing educational policies and institutional structures that affect how students learn to write and how their teachers teach in U.S. and British classrooms. Clearly, U.S. and British educators can learn a great deal from one another about the teaching and learning of writing by building on successful approaches and avoiding policies that have proven unworkable or detrimental.

The surveys focused on a broad-based national sample in both countries, but the writing exchanges were set up between urban schools serving high percentages of students of color from poor and working-class families and thus have special relevance for teaching and learning in these contexts.

Informing Policy Debates

Differing educational policies and institutional structures revealed contrasts that can inform a number of important educational debates. These debates focus on the desirability of national examinations, on ways schools and curricula might be organized, on the appropriate professional roles and realms of responsibility for teachers, and on the tensions surrounding ability grouping and issues involved in implementing mixed-ability teaching.

National Examinations

Policymakers and educators in the United States are currently contemplating the introduction of a system of high-stakes national examinations and certification at the end of secondary school, and hopes are high that the "right" kind of examinations will lead to improved instruction (see, for example, Simmons and Resnick, 1993). But the British national examinations in language and literature, which at the time of the exchange were precisely the kind of exam writing educators were advocating—assessments based on portfolios of student writing collected as a natural part of classroom instruction—worked against student learning. In the British exam classrooms, writing became an experience charged with pressure. More often than not, the pressure was so strong that the examinations rather than the students' experiences controlled how students approached their writing. In this regard, Philippa Furlong's reflections on what went wrong in her exchange with Bridget Franklin are particularly poignant: "I was geared by an examination. I'd forgotten how frustrating I actually found that . . . because it was a nightmare that . . . I think if they [my students] hadn't have had the restraints of an exam, they would have gone further" (Interview, November 2, 1990). Although the British teachers had lived with national exams for their entire lives and could not imagine a school system without them, the overriding presence of the exams, even in the portfolio format, proved to be deeply frustrating as they worked with their students.

Beyond the sheer pressure of the exams, there were other problems. First, the exams required so many separate pieces of writing that individual pieces were rushed. The writing exchange teachers did not have time to nurture the kind of extended projects that were prevalent in the lower forms.[1] Second, the rules created for managing the exams restricted the kinds of help teachers could offer students on examination pieces and in the end inhibited their ability to teach. Third, the British exams perpetuated a lack of educational equity across social classes, despite efforts to use the exams as social equalizers. In England, the percentage of students with good scores who go on to university remains much higher in the private schools than in state-supported schools serving large numbers of working-class students, and even in the state schools, middle-class students routinely outperform working-class students. Hampden Jones, where Philippa teaches, enrolls a higher percentage of middle-class students than the other three schools involved in the exchange project. As Table 8.1 illustrates, Philippa's class had the highest percentage of students who passed the language examination with a C or better (32 percent as compared to 19 percent for Peter and 18 percent for Gillian).[2]

Indeed, as in the United States, many British students sit attentively at their desks, but the gates to higher education are closed to them.[3] In Gillian Hargrove's class, only three of her seventeen students received high enough scores on the language exam to continue on in school and prepare for university in the A-level course: K. C. received a *B* and De Mille and Deenie each received a *C*. None of Gillian's students received an *A* in English language. Of the others, four received a *D*, two an *E*, four an *F*, and two a *G*; one did not take the examination and another transferred to another school. Only four

Table 8.1 British examinations

| Grade | Language examination results | | |
	Ross (N = 18)	Hargrove (N = 17)	Furlong (N = 14)
A	2 (11%)		
B		1 (6%)	3 (21%)
C	4 (22%)	2 (12%)	4 (29%)
D	4 (22%)	4 (24%)	5 (36%)
E	5 (28%)	2 (12%)	1 (7%)
F	2 (11%)	4 (24%)	
G		2 (12%)	
Number taking language examination	17 (94%)	15 (88%)	13 (93%)
Number taking literature examination	17 (94%)	4 (24%)	5 (36%)

took the English literature examination, and of those, two earned a *D,* one an *E,* and one an *F.*

In Philippa Furlong's class of twenty-two, six did not take either examination or left Hampden Jones. Of the thirteen taking the language examination, only seven earned scores that would make them eligible to continue on in school. Three earned a *B* (Swivel, Tootsie, and Andi) and four a *C* (Garney, Ream, Reg, and Marisa). None of Philippa's students received an *A* either. Five of Philippa's students received *D*s and one an *E.* Only five of Philippa's group took the literature examination, and of those, one received an *A* (Tootsie), two got *B*s (Swivel and Andi), and two *D*s.

In Peter Ross's class, eight of the original group of twenty-six left the school before taking their exams. Of the eighteen who remained, only six earned high enough scores to continue. Dickens and Delbert received an *A,* and Nikita, Drago, Amelio, and Catherine received a *C.* Of the others, four received a *D,* five an *E,* two an *F,* and one did not take the exam. Of Peter's students, all except one who took the language exam also took the literature exam. The literature scores included *B* for Dickens and Delbert; *C* for Nikita, Amelio, Bonet, and Catherine; and five *D*s, four *E*s, and one *F.* Although these scores are not representative of all British schools, they are illustrative of what happens to students in inner-city schools with a large percentage of working-class students, bilingual students, and students from poor families.

Even if these exams had supported the curriculum, the reality is that any examination system, once in place, is subject to shifts in the prevailing political winds. Although at the time of the writing exchanges the British examinations were based on portfolios, that has now changed. The British team reports that the government became uncomfortable with complete reliance on portfolios because students could get help, and officials feared that this would erode national standards. All the exchange teachers felt strongly that the new British portfolio examination represented a pioneering step for the examination system, and all expressed extreme disappointment at the withdrawal of the portfolio-only option in Britain.

Plans for the "right" kind of national examinations in the United States mimic the British system as it was during the year of the writing exchanges in many ways. In 1990, the National Center on Education and the Economy and the University of Pittsburgh's Learning Research and Development Center received a grant from the MacArthur

Foundation to "help launch work on a 'national examination system' that eventually could be used as the basis for high-school diplomas, college admissions, and employment decisions" (Olson, 1990, p. 5). Like the British exams, the U.S. exams would also have high stakes, would be based on a national syllabus, broadly conceptualized, and would include portfolios (as well as performance examinations and projects).

Even with a well-conceptualized examination system, it is sobering to look back at what happened in the British examination classes during the exchange project. The British experience raises important concerns for U.S. educators who support a national exam system. The path to curriculum reform through a system of high-stakes national exams is tempting, but its benefits remain elusive. What the U.S. teachers saw in the classrooms of their British counterparts convinced them that this kind of high-stakes national examination and its associated curriculum would ultimately inhibit their students' thinking and experimenting, confine their imaginations, and limit their writing development.

School and Curricular Organization

While the British experience argues against the wisdom of using national examinations to reform the writing curriculum, the British have instituted a number of educational structures to support the teaching and learning of writing that suggest interesting possibilities for U.S. educators. The U.S. teachers in the writing exchanges were particularly envious of those structures that helped the British teachers get to know their students and build strong intellectual communities. To this end, the British fund community schools; they subdivide large schools into small units; they have policies to ensure small classes; and they arrange for the same teacher to work with the same class of students over several years.

Community Schools

Community schools house community activities, and the school faculty takes community needs into account in designing the regular curriculum insofar as those needs can be assessed. Activities that bring the larger community onto the school grounds and create a responsive curriculum make the school the kind of place where children and their families feel they belong. In community schools, teachers have more opportunities to get to know their students' families, and this ongoing exchange between the school and the community helps teachers better understand the diverse students in their classrooms and encourages parents to support the goals of the school. Only two of the four British schools participating in the writing exchanges were community schools: Garden Hill, where Peter Ross teaches, and Manderley Grove, where Gillian Hargrove teaches. Peter was distressed that the ideal of community collaboration was not always fully achieved at Garden Hill. The other British teachers, Fiona Rodgers and Philippa Furlong, would have liked to have had the resources of a community school, while the U.S. teachers were unaware of the possibilities such support could offer them. Unfortunately, funding for community schools is on the decline in Britain, and in the United States, although there is a great deal of rhetoric about involving local communities in reformed schools, there are few models that create the collaborative school-community exchange of the British community school.

Subdivisions within Schools

Along with community schools, the British also create smaller, more intimate working units within large schools, which aid teachers in their efforts to get to know their students and build a sense of community. Students are first divided into year groups and then, within each year group, into seven or eight tutor groups of approximately twenty-five students each. Some British schools also have "houses" for students across age levels. A teacher is assigned to take charge of and supervise each of these smaller units, and the teacher in charge holds regular meetings with the year and tutor groups. For the first three years of secondary school, the tutor group will remain together for most classes. For these three years, as well as two additional years, the form tutor meets once a week for one period with her tutor group for personal and social education. At this weekly meeting, the group discusses topics such as friendship, teachers, bullying, sex education, careers, and the like.

The tutor groups do more than keep a small cadre of students together. They also function as part of the system of pastoral care, which focuses teachers' attention on students' personal welfare within the school setting. As the *Teacher's Guide* for Fiona Rodgers's Broadbent School explains, from the pastoral point of view, group tutors are "to KNOW and be directly responsible within the school for each individual student within the tutor group." The tutor is also "to be the 'first line of action' in helping each student to cope with her/his difficulties. Sometimes this will demand a disciplinary response, at others the offering of a listening ear or helping hand, at others the sharing of ideas and experiences." The tutor also reports about the students in her or his tutor group to the "Head of Year"; serves as "a 'resource person' to other members of staff"; keeps the students' records up to date; "co-ordinate[s] the subject reports to parents and give[s] a coherent report on the 'whole' student"; "make[s] him/herself known to the family of each student . . . and . . . interpret[s] to the parents the philosophy and practice of Broadbent Community School"; and finally, meets with other tutors of students in the same year and makes "a positive contribution to the development of the Year team and the ethos of the year" (p. 33).

U.S. schools have no formal subdivisions of this sort. The middle and junior high schools from the questionnaires were smaller than the senior high schools. Similarly, in the exchange classes the two middle schools, Webster and Central (grades 6 to 8), had enrollments of 850 and 586, respectively, while the senior high schools, Costa Mesa and Los Padres (grades 9 to 12), had enrollments of about 1,500 each. In the British secondary schools from the questionnaires, which covered the equivalent of grades 6 to 12, the enrollments ranged from 900 to 1,200. The smaller size of the U.S. middle schools was meant to provide an intimate community; however, these schools were not that much smaller than the British secondary schools, and without special programs, such as the GATE program at Webster, a sense of community was not easily achieved. Also, since fewer grade levels were represented in the U.S. schools, the number of students in a given grade was significantly larger than that at the British schools.

Neither did the U.S. schools recognize or formalize that part of the teacher's job having to do with students' social welfare. Guidance counselors were supposed to perform many of what the British call pastoral duties, but they were generally in short supply and relatively isolated from the teaching staff.

Small Classes

The size and organization of the school affected the overall academic community and school ethos as well as the teachers' ability to learn about their students, but class size was also a factor in how well the teachers could get to know their students. And here there was a striking contrast. Except for the Philippa Furlong–Bridget Franklin pair, every British exchange class was smaller than its U.S. counterpart. A total of 113 students were enrolled in the four U.S. classes as compared to 90 students in the British classes, a difference of 23 students across four classes.

In Great Britain, teacher unions have mounted a vigorous campaign for a maximum of 30 students in a class nationwide and a maximum of 25 in London. These targets have generally been achieved. The norms for U.S. schools in the San Francisco area are generally between 30 and 35 students, but class sizes have sometimes gone above 35, as was the case for Carol Mather, who taught 37 students. In fact, in California the average class size is among the largest in the United States. Carol Mather talks about the activities she has had to drop, and Nancy Hughes struggles to meet the needs of all her mixed-ability students. From these teachers' point of view, the impact of the loss of individual contact in large classes is clear.

Maeroff (1991) emphasizes the importance of teachers' perceptions of class size, whatever empirical data on the effects of smaller classes on student achievement seem to show:

> The debate over class size is surely one of the most exasperating controversies in education. Common sense dictates that smaller is better, yet findings from research produce no consistently compelling evidence that this is so . . . Teachers may pay a price for having larger classes even if adding students to a class does not undermine learning. Is it advantageous, in other words, to tolerate large classes if doing so is apt to demoralize teachers and perhaps drive them from the profession, regardless of the effect on student achievement? (p. 56)

The teachers in the exchanges gave us a firsthand view of how conditions that tend to perpetuate large classes contribute to teacher demoralization and keep schools from creating optimal learning environments.

Keeping the Same Students

A final factor that influenced student-teacher interactions and the emergence of strong intellectual communities was the amount of time teachers spent with students. In Britain, teachers routinely keep the same class for two years or more. Fiona Rodgers and Gillian Hargrove had taught the same group of students for two years, Peter Ross and

Philippa Furlong for five. In the United States, however, teachers rarely stay with the same students for longer than one year. Ann Powers's positive experience when she arranged to keep her class almost intact for a second year is an exception to the norm that demonstrates the community-building and writing growth a U.S. teacher can foster when she has the same class for more than one year.

Professional Roles for Teachers

Just as the U.S. teachers were envious of the organizational structures in British schools that seemed to support the teaching and learning of writing, they also found the professional opportunities available to British teachers very appealing. British administrators are always teachers, blurring the distinctions between the two groups. Teachers in England see promotions to academic or administrative leadership positions as natural extensions of their teaching. Even the position that is equivalent to the U.S. school principal is viewed as an instructional leadership role for which only an outstanding teacher is qualified. The British teachers we followed in the exchanges played major roles in running their schools, particularly in designing and revising the academic programs. While remaining in the classroom with only slightly reduced teaching loads, they oversaw first-year teachers in their own departments and throughout the school, coordinated activities with local teacher education institutions to provide instruction and experience to teachers-in-training, coordinated the scoring and administration of the GCSE examinations and the A-level examinations, organized in-service education programs, and coordinated the curriculum, including drama and the teaching of nonnative speakers. In future years they could move to jobs as headteachers, roughly the equivalent of principal in the United States, or become English advisors for Local Education Authorities, roughly the equivalent of school district curriculum specialists. British teachers expect to change schools to accept promotions. Since the time of the exchange, both Philippa Furlong and Fiona Rodgers have assumed higher-level posts at different schools.

In the United States a number of areas of educational practice are impoverished because no one assumes leadership roles. For example, first-year teachers have no trial period in which they receive support from senior mentors, experienced teachers have no well-structured ways to collaborate with universities in teacher credentialing programs, and U.S. department chairs often perform jobs that are more bureaucratic than conceptual. British department chairs by contrast are expected to facilitate departmentwide discussions of ideas, theories, and practices. In the schools that participated in the exchange, they organized regular and often lengthy department meetings, during which the teachers learned from each other and collaborated as a group with a strong sense of purpose. Department heads led the teachers to consult, argue, discuss, and work toward consensus.

The literature on school reform in the United States asserts the importance of the principal as an instructional leader (see, for example, Deal and Peterson, 1990). Yet school culture in the United States does not nurture and then gradually promote able teachers to such positions. Changing the role of the principal will require more than rethinking and redefining the job of principal. It will require restructuring the entire teaching profession so that the most able teachers are prepared, through gradually increased levels of responsibility, to assume the newly defined leadership posts.

Because the U.S. exchange teachers had no opportunities for promotion that would also allow them to remain in the classroom, they found other outlets for their talents. All spent substantial time on consulting jobs that took them away from their schools. Ann Powers, Nancy Hughes, and Bridget Franklin offered workshops through the National Writing Project. Bridget was also involved at other schools in efforts to spread the Promoting Achievement through Collaborative Teaching (PACT) project, which she had initiated as a collaboration with the University of California at Berkeley with the goal of raising teachers' expectations for low-achieving students and raising students' achievement levels. Carol Mather conducted workshops related to her women's studies projects. On the whole, these external efforts were of minimal benefit to the teachers' schools, and contributed mostly to the growth of the teachers themselves. At the same time, administrators often greeted these consulting opportunities with disapproval since the administrators defined the teachers' jobs solely as classroom teaching, and consulting took the teachers away from their regular classroom duties.

Over the years, leadership opportunities in British schools have given British teachers a strong sense of professional identity and provided ongoing ways for them to contribute to critical changes in instructional practice. Teachers have pushed for mixed-ability teaching, for classrooms full of student talk, for extended writing, and for control of curricular decision making, which they share with their students. In the United States, classroom teachers have less voice in movements for educational reform, in large part because they have no way of staying in the classroom and, at the same time, growing into leadership positions that involve transforming the educational system itself. And when U.S. teachers do speak, their voices are too often ignored, to the detriment of U.S. education. Some reformers in the United States are calling for the development of teacher promotion scales modeled on the British system; however, this call has been slow to be heard, and when it has been heeded (for example, in merit pay and teacher mentor programs), it has produced its own problems, since it has too often been designed in ways that patch rather than revamp the profession of teaching.

Mixed-Ability Classes

Many researchers in the United States and Britain have argued against tracking and in favor of mixed-ability teaching (for example, Goodlad, 1984; Jackson, 1964; *Mixed Ability Work in Comprehensive Schools,* 1978; Newbold, 1977; Oakes, 1985; Postlethwaithe and Denton, 1978; Rosenbaum, 1980; and Slavin, 1990). Findings show that students in the higher tracks learn just as much in mixed-ability classes and those in the lower tracks learn significantly more. Further, as Oakes (1985) points out, ability grouping produces social stratification, since the lower tracks are commonly populated with disproportionate numbers of students of color. She argues that tracking policies not only reflect, they also perpetuate institutionalized racism.

What is most perplexing is why tracking has been such a persistent policy in the United States. According to Gardner (1983), it is because U.S. schools have moved away from an "interpersonal" focus, which is part of "the traditional religious model," in favor of an "intrapersonal" or logical and mathematical focus, which he calls "the modern secular pole" (p. 358). British teachers rely on an "interpersonal" focus to make mixed-ability teaching work, while in the United States, this historical trend away from the "interpersonal" makes mixed-ability teaching especially difficult. In addition, because class size in these California schools is often over thirty students, because teachers usually keep the same class for one year or less, and because school organization provides few supports in creating close communities, even in a tracked class it is hard for teachers to create interpersonal interactions or to develop a sense of community, much less meet the varied needs of individual learners. In light of historical trends and the current situation in the schools, many practicing educators seem to be convinced that, regardless of research findings to the contrary, discontinuing tracking will create more problems than it will solve. Goodlad (1984) explains the continuing resistance to research findings against tracking in this way: "Tracking appears to be such a rational, commonsense solution to a vexing problem . . . The more sensible or rational the conventional wisdom appears to be, the more difficult it is for research findings to penetrate. And when following the conventional wisdom promises to make a difficult practical problem more manageable, these findings have a difficult time gaining a hearing" (p. 151).

Little has been written about precisely what is involved in teaching mixed-ability classes effectively. Here, the British experience provides some guidance. In Britain, institutional and classroom organization allows teachers to attend to the needs of diverse groups of learners. Institutionally, British teachers are supported by structures that help them get to know their students (community schools, subdivisions in the school, small class size, and student continuity over multiple years). At the classroom level, they have ways of building a sense of community from a collection of diverse individuals by carefully organizing opportunities for cooperative social interaction among students. The next section explains the British teachers' philosophies, which guide their implementation of mixed-ability teaching.

Rethinking Relationships with Students

The British teachers in the exchange all espoused a consistent philosophy. They believed that for students to learn to write, teachers and students have to exchange responsibilities. In practice this means that students, together with their teachers, share in the responsibility for the curriculum and for the teaching-learning process. The British call this back and forth exchange within the classroom "negotiated teaching" or a "negotiated curriculum." The U.S. teachers in the writing exchange, by contrast, followed varied philosophies about the teaching and learning of writing, so that their classrooms differed from one another as well as, in varying degrees, from the classrooms of their British counterparts.

It is ironic that, despite their differences, both the U.S. and the British teachers engaged in classroom practices that were consistent with Vygotsky's theories, which emphasize the processes by which experience becomes part of the learner's usable knowledge through social interaction. However, the British teachers were united in their emphasis on social interaction as a way of learning about the world and how society works (see Barnes, 1976; Britton, 1970, drawing on Vygotsky, 1962; and Kelly, 1955). To the British, social interactions build on students' social and cultural experiences, both at the micro-level of the classroom and the group, and at the macro-level of the community and the nation. Students are seen not merely as individuals but as members of varied social groups—including the classroom community, which is also part of a school, a town, and a district—all with characteristic interactions between cultural and social processes (Hardcastle, 1985). Students talk and write, formally and informally, about their community and its history; they are encouraged to talk and write not only about personal experiences, families and family occasions, and family problems but also about serious critical issues (see Hardcastle, 1985; and McLeod, 1986). This is not to say that students in British classrooms discuss and write about serious critical issues all the time. The point is that such discussion and writing occur at all.

The British teachers see their main job in the classroom as setting "motivating contexts," that is, promoting activities that capture their students' interest, challenge them, and stimulate their writing. Within the contexts the teachers set students are responsible for motivating themselves or working with the teacher to decide on new contexts and activities that are personally motivating. As time goes on, the British teachers expect students to assume increased levels of responsibility, even to the point of suggesting motivating activities for the entire class. To a British teacher, an important part of a student's writing development is an increasing ability to be personally responsible and make mature choices about what to write and how to proceed. Since British teachers keep the same students for more than one year, they can help students assume increased responsibilities for the curriculum-making process gradually.

The British approach to curriculum making was most successful in the nonexamination classes when the British teachers and students were free from external controls and teachers were in charge of the teaching and learning in their classroom. In the examination classes external mandates from the examination took control away from both the teacher and the students. The examination syllabus and the looming specter of the examiner readers, who would judge the students' writing, left teachers and students feeling that their choices were constricted.

British teachers also hold themselves responsible for seeing that students write in a variety of ways. They do not worry if at a given time a student does not want to do a particular type of writing or even to write at all, even though they think the student needs to practice that particular type of writing. They simply allow the student to focus on a language activity that student is interested in, and they try again to find another motivating context. Teachers monitor the kinds of writing each student completes successfully and try to set contexts to encourage mastery of new types of writing. They exploit the notion of a spiral curriculum: students cycle and recycle through varied types of writing, the level of complexity increasing with each new spiral.

In this approach, activities are based on the interests and experiences particular to a group of students and include input from the group itself. Any plans for the class provide space for individual students to find engaging activities, including writing topics, that really interest them and approaches that they can manage and that challenge them. It is common for some students to choose an activity that differs from the group activity. Teachers do not expect to repeat the same activities with different groups of students because the interests and experiences of each student group will inevitably differ.

The U.S. teachers who participated in the writing exchanges followed what they call "a process approach," which focuses on getting students to go through a process of planning, writing, and revising, learning to solve problems along the way. Descriptions of process approaches vary and are usually quite general. They do not imply a common set of practices. Perhaps for this reason, variety abounds in U.S. classrooms, although one of the U.S. teachers followed something very similar to the British philosophy.

In spite of the fact that both U.S. and British educators organized their classrooms in ways that were consistent with Vygotsky's theories, a number of leaders in the writing process movement in the United States suggest approaches that conflict with the British framework. They propose mainly that teachers need to give children opportunities to interact and learn, allowing them independence and freedom, which will challenge them to grow (for example, see review in Hillocks, 1986). Perhaps for this reason popular pedagogical writers like Nancie Atwell (1987) do not emphasize the potential power of the classroom community, nor do they consider the implications of the students' membership in a variety of social groups. In this regard, Peter Ross identifies several fundamental differences between U.S. and British practice. He objects to what U.S. teachers call a student-centered approach, which he associates with the individualization of the 1960s, and emphasizes how British teachers value the classroom community. He also argues that the British curriculum "has a slightly harder edge" than that in the United States; the "harder edge" refers to the ways British teachers challenge their students to raise difficult questions that take them into worlds where things are not always secure and comfortable.

Contrasting Student Writing

How well students wrote and how much they progressed depended on the amount of choice they had in defining their topics and the type of support they received in making challenging yet engaging choices. Several prominent national trends also influenced students' writing. First, the British students wrote serious fiction as a regular part of their English class throughout their secondary years, while U.S. students wrote mostly expository prose as they moved from the middle school to the high school. Second, the British students were more inclined than the U.S. students to work on extended projects, which resulted in longer pieces of writing; only Carol Mather's "gifted" students engaged in extended projects of the sort that were routine in the British mixed-ability classes. Finally, the U.S. writing was mechanically and grammatically more correct than the British writing because U.S. teachers provided substantial support for their students in mastering the mechanics of the language, while the rules governing the national exams restricted the British teachers from providing such help. At the same time, the U.S. teachers, who generally cared a great deal about mechanics, worried about how their students would be judged if their papers were riddled with mechanical or grammatical errors, while the British teachers worried about how their students would be judged in terms of the prettiness of the presentation and the weight of the paper.

Topics: Degree of Involvement and Challenge

The writing exchanges highlighted two major relationships between the students' writing and those aspects of the curriculum that engaged teacher and students in an open exchange with one another. The first relationship centered on the level of student involvement. Students who selected topics they cared about felt connected to their topic and put their personal voice into what they wrote. The more fully the students discussed their ideas with their teacher, the more likely they were to make meaningful choices and the more evident their personal imprint on what they wrote. In U.S. schools, however, students do not expect to participate in the curriculum-making process, and even when teachers encouraged their participation, many did not recognize the opportunity or know how to take advantage of it.

The second relationship between the curriculum and the students' writing had to do with the kinds of challenges students undertook—in particular, in moving beyond the personal world of the everyday to consider issues that affected their communities and the world at large. Although students in all eight classes began the year by writing about personal topics in their autobiographies, as time went on some students in some classes began to connect with larger social issues. In Bridget Franklin's class, Geya responded to a British piece about abortion by writing about the perils of teenage pregnancy. She selected the topic because it was personal; her mother had been a teenager when Geya was born and had made her fear such a fate. But in addition, Geya saw teenage pregnancy as a problem in her community as well as across the nation, especially for African Americans. In Carol Mather's class, some students, like Elizabeth, felt that they had participated in selecting their topics when they wrote about "women in history" for the NOW contest, but others, like Iggy, did not. As a result, Elizabeth was able to move from the personal to the social in her Winnie Mandela paper, whereas Iggy remained unengaged on either level when he wrote about Mother Teresa. In Britain, Fiona Rodgers felt that she had not pushed her youngsters to progress beyond the personal. Even so, at the end of the year, in their magazines, they sometimes tackled issues with social as well as personal implications, like the upcoming assessments, and Fiona planned to move them further in this direction in the coming year. Peter Ross recognized some examples of such movement in some of his students' stories and their school and community books, particularly when they wrote about issues raised by the Docklands development.

Purposes: Imaginative versus Analytic Writing

According to the national surveys, the British students at the secondary level spent most of their time doing imaginative writing, which included poems, plays, and short stories, as well as writing that conveyed personal experiences. By contrast, the U.S. secondary students spent most of their time doing writing that forced them to think for themselves by focusing on the discovery of ideas and the analysis and synthesis of information. The teachers' reasons for teaching writing supported these different purposes. In Britain the teachers' primary reason for teaching writing was to allow students to use their imaginations, while in the United States it was to force students to think for themselves and to connect what they were learning to their personal experiences.

To a certain extent, these findings are played out in the exchanges. Figures 4.1, 5.1, 6.1, and 7.1 graph the flow of writing between each pair of exchange classes. As the questionnaires would predict, the youngest students in both countries (Figure 4.1) produced a substantial amount of imaginative writing (spooky tales in Carol's class and magazines with their share of fiction, including spooky tales, in Fiona's class). In the Peter Ross–Nancy Hughes exchange (Figure 5.1) both classes wrote stories; however, the British students wrote serious fiction while the U.S. students' stories were minimal. Nancy's students also sent poems, but they were quite formulaic. In the case of the older students (Figures 6.1 and 7.1), the British students were required to include imaginative writing in their examination folders, although they did not send it as part of the exchange. The U.S. curriculum offered scant opportunity for serious imaginative writing. Although Ann Powers provided options for imaginative writing, during the exchange year her students did not take advantage of these options. She reports, however, that in their second year with her, they began to choose to do some imaginative writing. In Bridget Franklin's class, students had the option at the end of the year of writing imaginative fiction—an adventure story or a myth—to contribute to a multiauthored booklet, but only nine of the twenty-two students took the option. The other thirteen chose between writing extensions to their autobiographies and pieces of exposition about how to succeed at Los Padres High School.

The British researcher Peter Medway (1986) argues that the British overemphasize imaginative writing at the expense of analytic writing and suggests that British students have insufficient opportunities to reach beyond their immediate experience and to think and write about ideas. In the United States, where there are more university slots and no sorting mechanism at age sixteen, analytic writing may be stressed because it is often equated with the kinds of writing needed for continued academic success. However, imaginative writing and, more particularly, imaginative thinking may be undervalued in U.S. schools.

Given our observations of daily life in the exchange classes, I would argue that in both countries we wrongly equate critical and imaginative thinking with particular forms of writing. In fact, critical issues can be considered as easily through fiction as through nonfiction, and imaginative thinking is as important a part of the good essay as it is of the good poem. McLeod and I (Freedman and McLeod, 1988; see also McLeod, 1992), citing Raymond Williams (1983), have argued that, regardless of the form, to write really well students need to learn to use their "critical imagination" to give voice to possibilities, to tell what might happen or what might have happened, to offer a different view, and to offer the hope that "it all could be better than this." The critical imagination sometimes achieves its purpose by offering a frightening vision of the future, as in Orwell's *1984,* or, at other times, by proposing a fairer society, as Cool J. and Tootsie do when they discuss Martin Luther King (Freedman, 1994). Although writing that involves the critical imagination takes varied forms, it always connects the writer with the world beyond.

Length and Scope

In comparison to the U.S. students, the British students wrote more well-developed pieces and worked more often on elaborate projects over longer spans of time. Word counts for two relatively parallel pieces from the four focal students in each exchange class show that the British students wrote longer individual pieces than their U.S. counterparts, with the exception of the students in Carol Mather's sixth-grade "gifted" class, who wrote slightly longer pieces than the students in Fiona Rodgers's seventh-grade equivalent mixed-ability class (see Tables 4.1, 5.1, 6.1, and 7.1). Figures 4.1, 5.1, 6.1, and 7.1, which chart the flow of writing for each exchange, show the more frequent occurrence of long-term projects in the British classes, with the exception of Gillian Hargrove's examination class.

It must be remembered that the British students were slightly older than the U.S. students, by one grade level for each of the two youngest exchange pairs. Thus they might be expected to produce more and to write over longer spans of time. In addition, more students in the U.S. sample were labeled low ability: all British classes were labeled mixed, while one U.S. class was labeled gifted, one mixed, and two low. For this reason as well, the British students might be expected to produce more and to sustain their attention on a single piece over a longer time.

More important, however, is the fact that some of the exchanges present models of what can happen when teachers have high expectations for their students. Peter Ross shows what is possible for mixed-ability students at the eighth-grade equivalent level. Given what Peter's mixed-ability students accomplished, it seems reasonable to assume that what Carol Mather expects of her sixth-grade "gifted" students might be quite appropriate for a mixed-ability group. In fact, in the United States we might turn to gifted programs, usually marked by high expectations for all students, for models of what we might expect more generally.

Grammar and Mechanics

Even a cursory look at the student writing shows that students in the United States sent writing to their British counterparts that contained fewer grammatical and mechanical errors than what they received. The contrast was less sharp only when the two U.S. "remedial" classes, in which students had very weak control of mechanics, were paired with mixed-ability British groups.

This observation about mechanics led me and Alex McLeod to consider how mechanical errors are handled in the two countries. To our surprise, we found major conflicts in the value placed on mechanical correctness and in how teachers help students achieve correctness. The British exchange teachers cared about mechanics but not to the extent that their U.S. counterparts and the U.S. students did. For example, they did not think it was necessary to help their students clean up their mechanics before sending their writing abroad, whereas the U.S. teachers worried about how their students would be perceived if their writing was full of mechanical errors. Not surprisingly, the U.S. students were also critical of British writing that contained errors. The U.S. teachers and students were not obsessed with mechanics, but they did feel it was necessary to edit the writing they were sending.

Besides the issue of values, the way mechanics were taught was radically different in the two countries. In the United States the teachers would help their students correct their writing during the final editing stages. At times, they would even do the final editing. But the British teachers were reluctant to take this step. They would point out errors in a sample paragraph and then ask the student to fix other similar errors. Or they might indicate where a word was misspelled but they would not correct the spelling. The teachers of the examination classes faced ethical issues in terms of the amount of help they were allowed to give when students were writing for their examination folders. Most felt that if they pointed out a few errors, their students would, with practice, learn to write correctly. However, Gillian Hargrove, who specialized in working with bilingual and second language students, felt that such policies did these students a disservice. From her point of view, it would have been better teaching practice to tell students how to spell particular words or to do more than model corrections in a single sample paragraph and then expect the students to correct the rest themselves. In her experience, bilingual students often needed more support than the system allowed.

Moving beyond Past Cross-National Comparisons

Recent comparisons of U.S. schools with schools in other parts of the world commonly ask just one question: Whose children are achieving more? In this worldwide horse race, we want to know if students in the United States are winning. We want to assess our standards against those in other countries. When the statistics tell us that our children are not even keeping up, much less winning, the public panics, and educators are expected to try harder to get better results. However, little guidance is forthcoming from these comparisons.

This cross-national comparison was designed to provide some guidance. The goal has been to look beyond whether or not U.S. students are winning in order to discover what we can learn from approaches to education in another country. The data do not consist of test scores but rather of ongoing observations of daily life inside classrooms in both countries. These observations point out where we are doing well and where we might improve.

In the field of English education there have been attempts over the years to compare U.S. and British schools. This book confirms some findings from earlier studies, updates others, and adds new perspectives. The 1966 Anglo-American Conference at Dartmouth College proposed "a new interest in the learner, his development, and the processes of using language to learn" (Dixon, 1975, p. 112). The British students and teachers who participated in the exchanges and who responded to the questionnaires demonstrate that these new interests are firmly in place. In fact, just two years after the Dartmouth conference, in their observational study of U.S. and British schools, Squire and Applebee (1968) showed that this emphasis on the learner and on the learner's development was already evident in Britain. By contrast, U.S. educators have experienced much more difficulty in focusing on the learner and the learner's development. Interest in these issues permeates the professional literature in the United States, but in point of fact, these concerns often receive little attention in U.S. classrooms. A focus on the student learner and on the student's development remains a British orientation that is nourished by the way the British school system is structured.

Squire and Applebee also found that the British placed less emphasis on formal language study and promoted less direct teaching but put more emphasis on fluency and practice and emphasized expressive writing more than U.S. educators. Their findings in British schools more than twenty years ago are evident today. But the portrait Squire and Applebee paint of U.S. schools in the late 1960s does not hold up in the 1990s. At that time they observed a U.S. model of "write-correct-revise," with the corrections done in red ink by the teacher. Today, the process approach, which values in-process response, is much more common. However, as both the questionnaires and the writing exchanges showed, the process approach does not necessarily lead to a focus on the student learner and his or her development.

Elaborating Vygotskian and Bakhtinian Theories

This book attempts to create a bridge between theory and practice. It situates theory in the specifics of everyday life inside classrooms, schools, school systems, communities, and countries. In this way it aims to highlight aspects of theory that need amplification in order to be maximally useful pedagogically. From the outset, teachers were selected to participate in the writing exchanges because they promoted classroom practices consistent with Vygotsky's notion of social interaction, in particular as elaborated by Wertsch to include nonverbal social interactions. They also followed Bakhtin's notion that complex and multivoiced dialogues underlie all social interactions. Throughout the exchange year, we observed that the classrooms all promoted a great deal of verbal and nonverbal social interaction. Further, consistent with Vygotsky's observation that social interaction leads to learning, the teachers attempted to promote activities within the students' "zones of proximal development," encouraging activities that students could accomplish with assistance but not alone. But as earlier chapters have shown, the teachers' practices varied in significant ways from one classroom to the next, and these variations affected what and how students learned.

The concepts of social interaction and of multivoiced dialogues are too general to account fully for the interactions in these classrooms. In their work for the writing exchanges, most students were interacting and learning, but the depth of their involvement in classroom activities varied and thus also the extent of their learning. In everyday practice, social interaction is not a binary feature, a yes/no proposition (either there is interaction or there isn't). Rather, the participants in any social interaction position themselves at some point along a continuum of involvement—from highly involved to relatively uninvolved. In the writing exchanges, learners occupied varied points on the continuum—within classrooms, from one classroom to another, and for the same student at different times.

Although students may shift their position from one activity to the next, and although some students in every classroom are more involved than others, the nature of the social space within the classroom seems to affect the level of student involvement and the teacher's ability to keep track of the involvement of particular students. Some classroom spaces led to highly involved interactions for large numbers of students, while others either promoted or allowed more room for surface interactions. In these classes, the settings that led to the most highly involved interactions were those in which students participated in curriculum making and felt that they were an integral part of a close-knit community. For this reason, the British examination, imposed from above, did not allow as rich a pedagogical space for involved social interaction as was found in classrooms where teachers and their students were in control. Likewise, U.S. classrooms in which students took little responsibility for curricular decision making were characterized by less involvement than those in which students assumed more responsibility. The potential power of social interaction in learning is clearly affected by whether it occurs within Vygotsky's "zone of proximal development," but those variables that promote a depth of involvement seem prerequisite to activating the full academic potential of such interactions.

How the classroom was organized was a determining factor in whether students could participate in ways that were both involving and appropriate to their developmental levels and whether the teacher could track their progress. Whatever their official label—mixed-ability, gifted, or remedial—the students in every classroom presented a mixture of abilities and interests. The teachers who seemed best suited to responding to the needs of diverse individuals were most able to create a sense of community, building on the foundation of the interests of the particular individuals in the class. Within the context of communal activities, students were able to continue both to enlarge and to express their interests and, with the help of their teacher, to shape literacy activities that were developmentally appropriate. In these classrooms, the teachers had structured the community in ways that also allowed them to keep track of and stimulate the involvement of varied individuals.

This elaboration of Vygotsky's theory of social interaction—to explicitly include the notion of a continuum of involvement and to examine the kind of social space necessary to promote high levels of involvement—suggests a need for research in several areas. First, it will be important for future bridging studies to define the principles that encourage students to become highly involved in classroom-based social interactions. This study looks at one such variable, the social space in the classroom, but undoubtedly, there are others. Second, we will need ways of accounting for student involvement. On first impulse, we might think about verbal participation as a possible indicator of involvement. Hearkening back to Wertsch, however, who argues against privileging the verbal, we have found that students can be highly involved in the intellectual life of the classroom, actively listening and interacting with texts, with adults outside the classroom, and with other nonverbal media, while interacting verbally within the classroom very little. At the same time, some students may interact verbally, but their interactions might rest on the surface of the material rather than run more deeply into it. According to Bakhtin, our internal conversations, the dialogues that make up our texts, will inevitably be richer if they occur in sociocultural and cognitive spaces where multiple voices and multiple ways of voicing are welcomed. As educators we must continue to try to understand the nature of the pedagogical spaces that meet these criteria; this study attempts to offer a beginning.

Sustaining Progress

Currently, my British colleagues are extremely discouraged about the turns the educational system in Britain is taking. Whenever I talk to them, I leave the conversation with the overwhelming sense that I am hearing stories of a receding wave of school reform. The community schools, which supported deep exchanges between home and school, were already being dismantled at the time of the writing exchanges, and a continuing lack of funding has only accelerated that process. New teachers (probationers) rarely receive the kind of support during their first years of teaching that used to be standard. Most recently, I have heard that some schools are moving away from mixed-ability grouping and returning to ability-level tracking in order to keep middle-class parents from sending their children to private schools. Finally, the national curriculum and its associated examinations have led many teachers to rebel. These changes in British education are undermining a profession that had been strong and viable.

Although the British are discouraged, some infrastructures vital to the profession of teaching as they know it remain in place. These are not found in U.S. settings. The scale posts for teachers continue to provide promotions that integrate them into the management of the school. Many teachers of English have also continued their strong ties to the Institute of Education and to professional organizations such as the National Association of Teachers of English and the London Association of Teachers of English. These affiliations, along with their initial teacher education programs, allow them to maintain a coherent theoretical framework that explains how students learn to write. They work within a school system that at least in some respects is organized to support their theories explaining how students develop literacy skills across time—the gradual assuming of responsibility by students, the essential role of motivation and making choices that lead students to grapple with complex issues that matter to them and to their society, the coherent social and intellectual community in schools and classrooms that personalizes education and supports student growth.

The goal of this cross-national comparison has been to provide educators with a new lens through which to view learning to write. The writing exchange provided opportunities for an exchange of cultures—between researchers, teachers, and students in England and the United States. As Lisa and Leabow implied in the words that opened this book, the writing exchanges helped them cross the boundaries of their everyday worlds and learn from their experience. Lisa began to "feel what it's like in other parts of the world," and Leabow remarked that she and her classmates are "finding out different things about each other." As educators, we too can make discoveries as we reflect on the kinds of local exchanges we foster—between schools and their communities, between teachers and administrators, between students and teachers, and among students themselves. Ideally, all of these discoveries will help us expand our world views and broaden our vision as we rethink how students in our classrooms learn to write.

Appendixes

Notes

References

Index

⟳ Chapter 2 Tables

Table 2.1 Response rates

	Teachers			Students	
	Nominations requested	Nominations received	Number responding	Number contacted	Number responding
United States	696	644 (92.5%)	560 (87.0%)	820	715 (87.2%)
Great Britain	218	179 (82.1%)	135 (75.4%)	244	187 (76.6%)

Table 2.2 School size

		Percentage of teachers reporting			
Enrollment	US GB	Primary ($N = 188$) ($N = 36$)	Secondary ($N = 354$) ($N = 82$)	All ($N = 542$) ($N = 118$)	Chi-square tests Primary vs. secondary
Under 500	US GB	60.1 88.9	19.2 12.2	33.4 35.6	US: 117.46** (df = 3)
500–999	US GB	33.0 11.1	36.2 45.1	35.1 34.7	GB: 65.04** (df = 2)[a]
1,000–2,499	US GB	6.9 —	42.1 42.7	29.9 29.7	
2,500+	US GB	0 —	2.5 —	1.7 —	
Chi-square tests US vs. GB (df = 3)		16.04*	7.69	7.12	

a. There are only two degrees of freedom because no British schools had over 2,500 enrollment.

*$p < .01$,   **$p < .001$.

Table 2.3 Class size

| | | Medians | | | |
| | | Secondary teachers | | | |
		Elementary teachers	Usual class	Selected class	All teachers	Chi-square tests[a] (df = 1)
Class size	US	26.4 (N = 182)	25.0 (N = 367)	26.5 (N = 361)	25.4 (N = 549)	(a)18.83* (b) 3.51
	GB	29.0 (N = 43)	25.0 (N = 90)	25.0 (N = 90)	26.0 (N = 133)	(c)45.39*
Chi-square tests US vs. GB (df = 1)		1.44		0	.03	(d)19.57*

a. The first median test (a) compares the U.S. elementary class with the usual U.S. secondary class; the second (b) compares the U.S. elementary class with the focal U.S. secondary class at the secondary teacher's school; the third (c) compares the British (GB) primary class with the usual secondary class; the fourth (d) compares the British primary class with the focal British secondary class at the secondary teacher's school. Medians rather than averages are used here because the range of class sizes for the U.S. elementary sample was great; those reporting extremely large class sizes were likely resource teachers.
  *$p < .001$.

Table 2.4 Class load

Normal class load	US GB	Percentage of secondary teachers reporting (N = 279) (N = 63)
4 classes or below	US	5.4
	GB	1.6
5 classes	US	66.7
	GB	23.8
6 classes	US	26.9
	GB	44.4
7 classes or above	US	1.1
	GB	30.2
Chi-square test US vs. GB (df = 9)		160.75*

*$p < .001$.

Table 2.5 Length of time with same teacher

Time with same teacher[a]		All classes (N = 369) (N = 90)	Selected class (N = 367) (N = 84)
		Percentage of secondary teachers reporting	
	US GB		
More than two years	US	—	—
	GB	6.8	10.7
Two years	US	—	—
	GB	43.8	41.7
One year	US	75.6	75.5
	GB	45.6	45.2
One term or less	US	20.3	21.5
	GB	3.5	2.4
Other	US	4.1	3.0
	GB	0.2	0

a. Length of time with the same teacher cannot be compared statistically since the forms for the U.S. and British teachers contained different categories, with two years or more not appearing on the U.S. forms.

Table 2.6 Students' post-secondary plans

		Percentage of students reporting			
		High achieving students	Low achieving students	All students	Chi-square tests High vs. low achieving
School-leaving age					
< 16		0	1.1	0.5	
16		23.4	42.4	32.8	
17		11.7	12.0	11.8	10.29*
					(df = 4)
18		63.8	44.6	54.3	
Don't know		1.1	0	0.5	
		(N = 94)	(N = 92)	(N = 186)	
Plans after leaving school					
4-year college	US	78.8	53.8	66.2	US: 49.79***
	GB	52.1	27.8	40.2	(df = 3)
Job training	US	3.4	5.4	4.4	GB: 11.78**
	GB	9.6	16.7	13.0	(df = 3)
2-year college	US	6.9	15.0	11.0	
	GB	13.8	23.3	18.5	
No plans	US	10.9	25.8	18.4	
	GB	24.5	32.2	28.3	
	US	(N = 349)	(N = 353)	(N = 702)	
	GB	(N = 94)	(N = 90)	(N = 184)	
Chi-square tests US vs. GB (df = 3)		27.29***	25.99***	47.43***	

*p < .05.   **p < .01.   ***p < .001.

Table 2.7 Grades in sampled class

Grade		High achieving students US (N = 355) GB (N = 79)	Low achieving students (N = 354) (N = 79)	All students (N = 709) (N = 158)	Chi-square tests High vs. low achieving (df = 2)
		Percentage of students reporting			
A	US	69.3	10.7	40.1	US: 270.10*
	GB	41.8	8.9	25.3	
B	US	23.9	46.6	35.3	GB: 32.95*
	GB	50.6	53.2	51.9	
C or below	US	6.8	42.7	24.7	
	GB	7.6	38.0	22.8	
Chi-square tests US vs. GB		23.66*	1.14	17.18*	

*p < .001.

Table 2.8 Electives

Class status		All classes US (N = 369) GB (N = 90)	Selected class (N = 364) (N = 86)
		Percentage of teachers reporting	
Required	US	68.0	69.5
	GB	78.8	91.9
Option in required area	US	18.0	17.9
	GB	4.7	4.7
Elective	US	14.0	12.6
	GB	16.3	3.5
Chi-square test US vs. GB (df = 2)			17.97*

*p < .001.

Table 2.9 Keys to achieving success: Free responses

	Percentage of teachers reporting		
	US (N = 135)	GB (N = 135)	Chi-square tests
Role			
Challenger	11.1	22.2	5.23*
Collaborator	25.2	25.2	0
Support-giver	38.5	51.1	3.83*
Traits			
Enthusiastic	23.7	23.0	0
Open to others' feelings and ideas	10.4	18.5	3.00
Love of words/literature	10.4	21.5	5.42*
Capacity for understanding students	16.3	34.1	10.40**
Risk-taker	19.3	7.4	7.21**
Love of children	15.6	10.4	1.18
Pedagogical emphases			
Practices process approach	39.3	25.9	4.87*
Focuses on meaning	17.8	31.9	6.43*
Assigns variety of writing	16.3	38.5	15.66***
Nurtures creativity	8.9	19.3	5.18*
Knows goals	13.3	14.1	0
Shares teacher's writing	24.4	13.3	4.74*
Writes along with students	30.4	19.3	3.89*
Believes in student-centered approach	40.0	52.6	3.81
Resources			
Professional reading	25.2	19.3	1.05
Professional writing	52.6	25.2	20.20***
National Writing Project	25.9	—	37.95***
Other teachers	17.0	14.8	0.11

*p < .05.   **p < .01.   ***p < .001.

Table 2.10 Reasons for asking students to write

Reasons *List 1*		Percentage of teachers rating as one of two "most important" Primary	Secondary	All	Chi-square tests Primary vs. secondary (df = 2)
	US	(*N* = 189)	(*N* = 367)	(*N* = 556)	
	GB	(*N* = 45)	(*N* = 87)	(*N* = 132)	
To help students remember information	US GB	13.8 11.1	14.2 8.0	14.0 9.1	US: .02 GB: .76
Chi-square tests US vs. GB (df = 2)		.77	2.43	2.33	
To correlate personal experience with topic	US GB	44.4 31.1	64.3 51.7	57.6 44.7	US: 20.14*** GB: 5.13
Chi-square tests US vs. GB (df = 2)		5.18	4.81	9.00*	
To test students' learning of content	US GB	3.2 2.2	16.6 9.2	12.1 6.8	US: 21.28*** GB: 5.48
Chi-square tests US vs. GB (df = 2)		3.47	8.39*	11.19**	
To share imaginative experiences	US GB	68.8 84.4	42.2 67.8	51.3 73.5	US: 35.20*** GB: 5.01
Chi-square tests US vs. GB (df = 2)		5.81	20.32***	24.34***	
To summarize material covered in class	US GB	4.8 8.9	7.4 6.9	6.5 7.6	US: 1.65 GB: .74
Chi-square tests US vs. GB (df = 2)		1.35	.43	.75	
To allow students to express feelings	US GB	66.7 62.2	55.3 56.3	59.2 58.3	US: 6.66* GB: .43
Chi-square tests US vs. GB (df = 2)		.62	.43	.15	

Table 2.10 (cont.)

Reasons List 2		Percentage of teachers rating as one of two "most important"			Chi-square tests Primary vs. secondary (df = 2)
		Primary (N = 189) (N = 45)	Secondary (N = 367) (N = 87)	All (N = 556) (N = 132)	
To explore material not covered in class	US GB	12.3 13.3	6.0 7.1	8.1 9.3	US: 6.65* GB: 4.04
Chi-square tests US vs. GB (df = 2)		1.25	.81	.20	
To practice writing mechanics	US GB	20.3 31.1	12.0 25.0	14.8 27.1	US: 7.72* GB: 4.33
Chi-square tests US vs. GB (df = 2)		7.09*	10.06**	11.63**	
To force students to think for themselves	US GB	65.8 46.7	70.1 45.2	68.6 45.7	US: 1.08*** GB: .11
Chi-square tests US vs. GB (df = 2)		6.75*	40.71***	41.36***	
To clarify what has been learned by applying concepts	US GB	44.9 35.6	46.2 29.8	45.8 31.8	US: .08 GB: 2.04
Chi-square tests US vs. GB (df = 2)		2.60	7.85*	8.38*	
To teach proper form for writing	US GB	16.0 28.9	20.7 42.9	19.1 38.0	US: 1.71 GB: 2.51
Chi-square tests US vs. GB (df = 2)		4.78	18.79***	22.68***	
To test students' ability to express themselves clearly	US GB	42.2 42.2	46.7 50.0	45.2 47.3	US: 1.14 GB: 2.39
Chi-square tests US vs. GB (df = 2)		3.07	1.72	4.43	

*$p < .05$.   **$p < .01$.   ***$p < .001$.

Table 2.11 Frequency of types of writing taught: Teachers' views

	Means[a]			Standard deviations		
	Primary US	Secondary US	GB	Primary US	Secondary US	GB
Writing for oneself	2.0	1.9	1.4	0.9	0.9	0.9
Writing to correspond with others	1.9	1.3	1.4	0.7	0.8	0.7
Writing to convey personal experience	2.5	2.2	2.3	0.9	0.9	0.9
Writing for poetic experience	2.3	1.8	2.5	0.8	0.9	0.9
Writing to discover ideas	2.2	2.1	1.8	1.0	0.9	1.0
Writing to present facts	1.7	1.6	1.7	0.8	0.9	0.7
Writing to analyze and synthesize	1.1	2.0	1.6	1.0	1.2	1.1

a. U.S. primary and secondary teachers' means and standard deviations are reported separately because there were important differences in the ways the two groups responded to the questions.

Table 2.12 Frequency of types of writing taught: Students' views

	Means		Standard deviations	
	US	GB	US	GB
Writing for oneself	1.5	1.0	1.2	1.1
Writing to correspond with others	1.6	1.1	1.3	1.1
Writing to convey personal experience	2.0	1.5	1.2	1.0
Writing for poetic experience	2.1	2.4	1.3	1.2
Writing to discover ideas	1.9	1.4	1.2	1.2
Writing to present facts	1.8	1.5	1.2	1.0
Writing to analyze and synthesize	2.3	2.2	1.2	1.1

Appendix 2

∽ Value Orientations in Teaching Writing

List 1
Transmit information:
  help students remember information
  test students' learning of content
  summarize material covered in class
Understand personal experience:
  correlate personal experience with topic studied
  share imaginative experiences
  allow students to express feelings

List 2
Understand content:
  explore material not covered in class
  force students to think for themselves
  clarify what has been learned by applying concepts to new
    situations
Develop skills:
  practice in writing mechanics
  teach proper form for types of writing
  test students' ability to express themselves clearly

The lists identified four value orientations. The first list contrasted teaching writing to help writers *transmit information* with teaching writing to help writers *understand their personal experiences*; the second list contrasted teaching writing to help writers *understand concepts* with teaching to help them *develop skills*. These lists were first used by Applebee (1981), who elaborated on the work of Barnes and Shemilt (1974) in England. Barnes and Shemilt identified two opposing views of writing among British teachers—the *transmission* view, in which writing was a vehicle for acquiring or recording information, and the *interpretation* view, in which writing was for helping writers learn and explore ideas through the act of writing.

Barnes (1976) provides a detailed account of the two views. The teacher with a transmission view "saw the purpose of writing primarily as the *acquisition or recording* of information . . . thought mainly of the *product* . . . and of whether the *task* he set was appropriate and clear to the pupils. He saw marking primarily in terms of *assessment,* and either handed back written work to pupils with *no follow up* or used it as a basis for the *correction* of errors" (p. 140).

The teacher with an interpretation view "saw the purpose of writing either in terms of *cognitive development* or more generally as aiding the writer's *personal development* . . . was concerned with *pupils' attitudes* to the task being attempted, and was aware of aspects of the *context* in which the writing was done, such as the audience to be addressed, the range of choices available and the availability of resources. He saw marking primarily in terms of making *replies and comments,* and was concerned to *publish* his pupils' work by various means, and to use it as the basis of his *future teaching*" (pp. 140–141).

When the lists were prepared for the questionnaires, the value orientations were not labeled, and the order of the items on each list was randomized.

Appendix 3

↪ Data Collection and Analysis
for the Exchange

Theoretical Considerations

A number of theoretical considerations drove the plans for data collection and analysis. First, as Wertsch (1991) explains, "Any setting obviously has cultural *and* historical *and* institutional aspects. What these three terms refer to are *dimensions,* or *ways of looking* at settings associated with disciplines, not some kind of fundamental essence of the settings themselves" (p. 121). Thus, one goal of the data collection and analysis was to examine the relationship between individual action, in this case student writing, and the cultural, historical, and institutional contexts in which individuals carry out such action.

According to Bakhtin (1986), we engage in dialogues with others from our varied cultural, historical, and institutional contexts, and these dialogues enter into whatever we communicate, be it oral or written. They include literal conversations with others, but they also include imagined conversations and our interactions with what we read. Understanding the student writing for the exchanges required analyzing the dialogues, broadly conceived, that entered that writing. Thus, the analysis considers the dialogues that came from within the classrooms in which the writing was produced as writers interacted with one another, with their teacher, and with other texts, including the student writing from abroad. And the analysis also considers other dialogues that entered from policies inherent to the institutional structures surrounding the classrooms and schools, such as national testing policies, classroom tracking practices, and community communication practices such as raps and graffiti art.

Collecting the Data

To uncover the dialogues that entered into student writing, from the points of view of the teachers and the student writers as well as the researchers, and thereby to examine the dynamics of learning to write in the United States and Britain, research teams on both sides of the Atlantic collected a variety of kinds of data. There were 5 tape-recorded interviews with each of the four teachers in the United States and 3 with each of the four teachers in Britain, for a total of 32 teacher interviews; 3 tape-recorded interviews with each of the seventeen focal students in the United States and 2 with each of the seventeen focal students in Britain, for a total of 85 student interviews (all 117 interviews were transcribed); six to seven tape-recorded observations of class meetings in each classroom, evenly spaced across the year and timed to coincide with the sending or receiving of writing for the exchange, along with field notes from these visits, which also included descriptions of the schools and the communities surrounding the schools; all student writing for the exchange; and, in the United States, teachers' and focal students' journals.

Three of the interviews with the U.S. teachers were spread across the second half of the exchange year, and the last two occurred during the following year. In Britain one interview occurred during the exchange year and two were conducted the following year. In the first school-year interview in the United States, teachers described their students and their interactions with the exchange to help select focal students; in the second, they described the focal students' participation in one exchange activity; in the third, they described the progress of the focal students across the year. In Britain, the first interview was done informally and the second interview was omitted; in the single school-year interview the teachers assessed the progress of the focal students. One of the two interviews following the exchange year was conducted in both countries by Ellie O'Sullivan. She interviewed all teachers to ascertain how they thought "going public" had affected their teaching. The second post-exchange interview was conducted by me in the United States and by Alex McLeod and me in England. In both countries, after reading about the preliminary findings from their classrooms we asked all the teachers to add to the findings and reflect back on their exchange experience and on differences across the two countries.

In their first interview, the focal students in both countries discussed their thoughts about the foreign audience, their process for writing two of their pieces, their assessment of their writing, and their assessment of the exchange. In the second interview (which was not conducted in England), students recounted the details of writing one of their pieces. In their final interview in both countries, students commented on the cross-national differences they had observed and evaluated a portfolio of their writing.

Since the interviews did not begin until midyear, the journals provided an important way of collecting the U.S. teachers' and students' thoughts, especially during the early parts of the exchange. Although the journals took various forms and contained a varied number of entries, all focused on recording observations about learning to write in the home classroom and in the classroom of the partner class.

As secondary data, we collected minutes and audiotaped teacher meetings (nine in the United States and seven in Britain). At these meetings, teachers and researchers generated and shared ideas and worked together to solve problems. Minutes were distributed to teachers and research teams in both countries after each meeting. Other secondary data included various interchanges between the teachers and researchers in the form of notes, casual conversations, and telephone calls; between the teacher pairs in the form of letters and an occasional telephone call, and in some cases computer mail; and between the research teams in the form of computer mail and occasional letters and telephone calls; written reports by three of the teachers (Chapman, 1989; Cone, 1989; Reed, 1989); and demographic data and official documents about the schools and school districts.

Analyzing the Data

After the data had been collected, case study descriptions were compiled for all eight exchange pairs, and these formed the basis for Chapters 3 to 7 (Freedman and McLeod, 1991). Following Wertsch (1991), Chapter 3 focuses first on the cultural, historical, and institutional aspects of the setting, and Chapters 4 to 7 on the flow of activity across the year in each classroom, showing the participation of individual students, from the points of view of the teacher, the students themselves, and the research team. For the analysis, all data sources were combed for themes related to each research question. Whenever a data source contained any information relevant to the theme, that aspect of the data was coded. To explicate each theme, all relevant data were brought together and synthesized and sub-themes were identified.

Chapter 3 addresses the first research question—the institutional supports and constraints surrounding learning to write—for the four exchange classes in the San Francisco Bay area and the four exchange classes in the London area. Three aspects of the exchanges became central to this analysis. The first involved the histories of the teachers, including the kinds of training they had had and the professional opportunities that were available to them; the second was the structure of the schools where the teachers taught; and the third was the place of the exchange class within the school. We used field notes from visits to the schools and the communities, teacher interviews, and demographic data and documents collected in the schools and school districts to put together a picture of the teachers, their schools, and their classrooms. These data sources were supplemented with information from students' writing, which occasionally provided descriptions of the school setting. When I had written a draft of Chapter 3, all eight of the participating teachers reviewed the sections about themselves and their classrooms for accuracy.

The second phase of data analysis involved answering the second two research questions. Chapters 4 to 7 move from the institutional level to examine individual students as they were involved in everyday classroom activities. These chapters follow both classroom activities and student writers within the classroom across the course of the exchange year. For each pair of classrooms, where possible, I focused on three exchanges. These were chosen to span the year (one toward the beginning of the year, another toward the middle, and another toward the end) and to demonstrate parallel writing in the two countries. For the Powers-Hargrove exchange in Chapter 6, there is no end-of-year writing for Hargrove's students. However, I include the examination folders of a class in a later year, since folders for the exchange class had been shredded by the examining board (see Chapter 6, notes 3 and 5). I made this choice because at this point in the year the only serious writing Hargrove's students were doing was for the examination, and I wanted to present samples of examination writing that would be much like what the exchange students produced.

For Chapters 4 to 7, teacher and student interviews as well as classroom visits and student writing provided the most important data sources. These were supplemented with letters and notes between the teachers, and with student and teacher journals. Again, for each exchange pair, key points of contrast and commonality emerged from the data, and all data sources were coded to indicate evidence of these points. Generally, the data included many examples that could have been selected to make the various points. Whenever any data source offered contrasting evidence or added to the complexity of a point, I included it; otherwise, I chose those examples that were clearest or most poignant to illustrate my points.

For the student writing, I counted the number of words in two pieces of parallel exchange writing for each of four focal students in each class, one piece toward the start of the year and one toward the end of the year. When one of the four focal students did not send a piece of writing, the writing of another similar student was substituted (as indicated on Tables 4.1, 5.1, 6.1, and 7.1). These counts show differences in the length of particular pieces and provide a sense of how expectations in the two countries differed in terms of the amount and depth of students' writing. In addition, linguistic analyses were performed on selected pieces of student writing when such analyses revealed how the students' written language functioned.

Given that a major aim of this project was to compare students and classrooms in two countries, it is crucial to point out that each country, each city or county, each community, and thus each school contained a range and diversity of cultures, histories, and social practices. All of these became part of the dialogues that underlie and support learning to write. Schools and classrooms are one of the places where various versions of life and living meet. The writing exchanges were based in specific classrooms, which could not fully represent the complexity and social diversity of the two countries. The exchange data from each country thus reflect only some of the diversity within that society and provide only one view of what classrooms in that society shared when compared to classrooms in another.

↜ Notes

1. Borders Are Not Boundaries

1. All students, schools, and teachers are identified by pseudonyms. Students selected their own pseudonyms.
2. At the time of the writing exchanges, British Form 1 was equivalent to U.S. grade 6, and so on through Form 5, which was equivalent to U.S. grade 10. Lower Sixth Form was equivalent to U.S. grade 11 and Upper Sixth Form to U.S. grade 12. In 1991 the British revised the labeling and adopted a system of year levels. Under the new system, Year 1 is equivalent to U.S. kindergarten, and so on through Year 13, which is equivalent to U.S. grade 12. I refer to forms in this book since that is how levels were designated at the time of this project.
3. Ninth grade overlaps the junior and senior high sample because of the varying organization of U.S. schools. It can be part of either junior high/middle school or senior high school.
4. In one U.S. classroom (Franklin's) and in one British classroom (Ross's) we included a fifth focal student. One of the focal students in Franklin's class worked so closely with another student in the class that it was necessary to study the two as a pair, and the British researchers felt that the students in Ross's class were too diverse to be well represented by only four students.

2. Learning about Policy and Curriculum: The National Surveys

1. For most items on the questionnaires, Chi-square or t-tests were used to make the comparisons.
2. According to Babbie (1973), 50 percent is an adequate return for mail surveys, 60 percent is good, and 70 percent or over is very good (p. 165). In his survey of U.S. secondary teachers, Applebee (1981) reported an overall

return of 68 percent, with a higher rate of 75 percent from English teachers (p. 20). For more detail on response rates, see Table 2.1 in Appendix 1.

3. In 1991 a new system of naming school classes was adopted throughout Britain, from Year 1 (U.S. kindergarten) to Year 13 (U.S. grade 12). As indicated in note 2 of Chapter 1, I use the British year designations that were in use at the time of the project.

4. Table 2.2 in Appendix 1 compares differences in school size across the two countries and shows statistically significant differences.

5. See Table 2.3 in Appendix 1.

6. See Table 2.4 in Appendix 1.

7. See Table 2.5 in Appendix 1. The primary teachers were not asked how long they kept the same class. For the U.S. primary teachers, we assumed that there would be too little variation for the question to be meaningful, because teachers generally keep the same group for one year; since we had no comparative data, we did not ask the question to British teachers. Queries about current practices in Britain reveal that primary teachers most usually keep their class for only one year (Lazim, personal correspondence, 1992; Stainton, personal correspondence, 1992).

8. At the time of the survey, there was another examination for older students called the CEE or Certificate of Extended Education. Along with the other old examinations, the CEE has now lost favor. This examination was offered to secondary students whose CSE grade was good but not good enough to count as equivalent to an O level, or who wanted only one year after this exam, or who remained in school after age sixteen but believed (or whose teacher believed) that they could not pass an A level. Only 5.9 percent of the sample reported that they were planning to take the CEE.

9. See Table 2.6 in Appendix 1.

10. Also, see Table 2.6 in Appendix 1.

11. The student mean for U.S. grades was 3.6 on a four-point scale, with a standard deviation of .8; the student mean for British grades was 3.3, with a standard deviation of 1.1. This difference was significant at the .002 level ($t = 3.14$, $df = 243$). The British teachers' mean frequency for grades on final versions was 2.3, with a standard deviation of 1.3; the U.S. teachers' mean frequency for grades on final versions was 2.8, with a standard deviation of 1.1.

12. Table 2.7 in Appendix 1 gives a comparison of grade distributions in the two countries.

13. See Table 2.8 in Appendix 1 for reports on distributions of elective versus required classes in the two countries.

14. The frequency of mentions across countries was compared with Chi-square tests.

15. See Table 2.9 in Appendix 1 for comparisons of how often the teachers in the two countries mentioned varied topics.

16. The U.S. mean for helpfulness of response after writing was 3.4, and the standard deviation was .82; the British mean was 3.4, with a standard

deviation of .76 as compared to lower means for response during writing (U.S. mean = 3.3, standard deviation = .96; British mean = 3.0, standard deviation = .76), with a significant difference at the .001 level in both countries (U.S. $t = -3.23$, $df = 711$; British $t = -5.25$, $df = 135$).

17. Table 2.10 in Appendix 1 provides a summary of how often the different items were checked as well as statistical tests for significant differences across countries and across levels of schooling.

18. Besides these frequently selected categories, Table 2.10 also reveals that, unlike their British counterparts, the U.S. teachers did not always agree about other less frequently selected reasons for having students write: secondary teachers were significantly more interested in testing the learning of content than were elementary teachers, and elementary teachers were somewhat more concerned about having students write to explore material not covered in class and to practice writing mechanics than were secondary teachers.

19. Poetic writing is defined by Britton et al. (1975) as writing that is "a special kind of self-presentation: not so much the embodiment of local or particular feelings as a glimpse into a 'lifetime of feeling', to use Susanne Langer's phrase." Such writing is "the verbal object as work of art"; Britton and his colleagues contrast poetic writing with "transactional" writing, which "meets the demands of some kind of participation in the world's affairs" (p. 83).

20. Table 2.11 in Appendix 1 gives the mean frequency for all types of writing the teachers say they taught.

21. Table 2.12 in Appendix 1 gives the mean frequency for all types of writing the students say they experienced.

22. The U.S. teachers in Applebee's (1981) study did not emphasize having students write to share imaginative experiences either.

23. Since the sample consisted largely of English teachers, it is likely that they were less interested in writing as a vehicle for learning than a cross-curricular sample would be.

3. Comparing Local Contexts: Exchanges among Teachers, Schools, and Classrooms

1. Appendix 3 provides detail on data collection and analysis techniques.

2. In Britain the normal college course is three years, and students focus their studies on their major from the start.

3. There is no word in American English equivalent to "seconded," likely because there is no equivalent concept. In England, when teachers are seconded they are released from their regular duties while receiving their full salary in order to obtain training or experience that will help them perform their job better or qualify them for higher-level posts.

4. For an explanation of the British examination system and the accompanying two-year course for the GCSE (equivalent to grades 9 and 10) and for the A levels (equivalent to grades 11 and 12), see Chapter 2.

5. The department-based supervisor serves as an official advisor to the new teachers, routinely visiting their classes and supervising their teaching. Two of the other British exchange teachers, Fiona Rodgers and Gillian Hargrove, supervised probationers in their departments during the exchange year.

6. In 1992, the British probation system was abolished because of lack of funds, in spite of protests by the teachers' union.

7. Aspects of the current reform movement in U.S. education have begun to involve teachers in local reforms. Both Nancy's and Bridget's schools were part of one such effort, the School University Partnership for Educational Renewal (SUPER) program with the University of California at Berkeley's School of Education. The SUPER program, although temporary and experimental, hoped to change the reward structures for teachers and to provide incentives for them, along with university faculty, to participate in improving their schools. Nancy was the SUPER liaison for schools in the Central district. Along with staff from Berkeley, she planned and helped organize Saturday workshops, called SUPER Saturdays, for Central teachers, led meetings, and worked on a writing evaluation project in her district that culminated in the publication of the District Writing Book, a collection of student writing. Nancy's work with SUPER was relatively well integrated with her school's needs, since it directly involved the teachers in her school and in immediately surrounding schools.

In a somewhat different league was Bridget's highly focused collaboration through SUPER with Rhona Weinstein, a Berkeley professor, and other faculty and administrators at Los Padres High School. As initiated by Bridget, the project's goal was to use the SUPER collaboration to bring about major reform that could yield significant shifts in the achievement of those students most at risk for school failure. During the exchange year Bridget was deeply involved in this project, called Promoting Achievement through Collaborative Teaching (PACT). PACT aimed to raise teacher and administrator expectations for lower-tracked students and then trace changes in student behavior and achievement. The PACT program proved highly successful in reducing dropout rates, improving achievement patterns, reducing referrals for disciplinary action, and generally providing new opportunities for many formerly low-achieving students at Los Padres (Cone, 1992; Weinstein et al., 1991).

As part of PACT, Bridget and her colleagues continue to organize and lead weekly teachers' meetings at Los Padres. Together she and the PACT teachers have spread their ideas to other schools in the district and the county, giving informational workshops and sometimes working intensively with interested schools. The PACT team received some supplementary support through the County Office of Education and the school district.

As a tribute to the extraordinary nature of such teacher involvement in school-site change, PACT received three awards, one to Weinstein from the California Association of Teachers of English for her collaborative work with the teachers, one program of excellence award from the California Association of School Superintendents, and another program of excellence award from the National Council of Teachers of English. Members of the PACT team have given papers at meetings of the American Educational Research Association, the National Council of Teachers of English, and state teachers' organizations. Bridget has also written articles for national journals, and her teaching was featured in an article in a national magazine for teachers in 1989. In addition, after the exchange year, Bridget received two local "Teacher of the Year" awards.

Bridget pushed to create new institutional frameworks that would support a schoolwide collaboration aimed at school improvement. Although not part of the original organization of Los Padres, Bridget placed the PACT program at the center of the workplace she and her colleagues shared. Bridget got credit for her efforts within her school and at the state and national levels, but because PACT depended on a very new and fragile institutional framework and because the district office considered itself, rather than local schools and teachers, to be in charge of directing the change process, even Bridget and her colleagues often felt that they did not get the credit or recognition they deserved. At the district office there was little sense of how to handle or support school-site activism even when it was part of an official school-university partnership. Bridget's situation shows how inhospitable educational structures can be to those implementing reform and the extraordinary efforts required to get it started. In the end, the successes at Los Padres illustrate the benefits of teacher empowerment and school-university collaboration.

8. Students are designated as gifted if they fall in the top 2 percent of the students in the school district for their age. This designation is determined by scores on an IQ test, scores on the California Test of Basic Skills (over 90 percent in at least three subjects for at least three years), or teacher recommendation. Criteria are shifted to include additional members from ethnic groups that traditionally score below the group norms on standardized tests.

9. For a detailed report of Garden Hill policies and practices with respect to diversity, see Hickman and Kimberly (1988).

4. Sharing Responsibility, Releasing Control: Carol Mather, Fiona Rodgers

1. For a complete narration of the ebb and flow of writing across the year for all exchange pairs, see Freedman and McLeod, 1991.

2. For detail on the methods of analysis, see Appendix 3.

3. Fiona and Carol first began working together during 1986–87, the year before the exchanges reported here. During that year the research team worked with five pairs of teachers to try out the concept of the exchange; some of those teachers moved on to other things but some stayed on to participate during the 1987–88 exchange year. Carol and Fiona were the only intact pair from the 1986–87 year. During those two years, Carol and Fiona wrote frequently and sometimes sent audiotapes instead of letters, they asked the research team to transmit messages through e-mail, and they met in

person when Carol visited London on two occasions and when Fiona stayed with Carol for a month-long summer holiday in San Francisco.

4. Chapter 3 explains Carol's institutional difficulties in some detail.

5. In Table 4.1, when one of the four focal students did not send a piece on the selected topic, the name of the substituted student is indicated.

6. Elizabeth is a pseudonym, but the references in her name paper are to her real name, which is unusual, with a pronunciation that is not clear from the spelling.

7. Another problem arose because Fiona's students wrote their "women in history" papers on the school computers and sent them via e-mail. Fiona feels that, for several reasons, this first experiment with the computers negatively affected the students' writing. First of all, her students did not have enough time on the computers to write extended pieces, and some struggled with typing. In addition, the technical support for using the computers was inadequate, and she found her time taken up with the logistics of computer mail, leaving her less time than usual to support her students in their writing.

8. When the section labels are not self-evident, descriptions of the content of the section are included in brackets. The numbers to the left of the section labels indicate the page number of the section.

5. Managing Mixed-Ability Teaching, Raising Standards: Nancy Hughes, Peter Ross

1. Of the other eleven, six (20 percent) made no mention of the relative quality of their writing and the British writing, two felt that the writing of students in the two countries was equivalent, and three (10 percent) felt that the British students were better writers than they were.

2. Four students decided to send "another assignment . . . about . . . what they thought a typical day in their life would be like in twenty years from now," a piece the students had written as part of a "science fiction unit" (Nancy Hughes, Interview, May 25, 1988).

3. See Figure 3.1 for a picture of Peter's classroom seating arrangement.

4. Three students were absent for the walks because of a Moslem holiday, Eid. They wrote about the holiday and included their pieces with the London walk papers.

5. Within the four types, ten separate pieces were required.

6. Creating Opportunity, Implementing National Examinations: Ann Powers, Gillian Hargrove

1. To Gillian's disappointment, in 1992 the British government changed the examination system back to a more conservative format. Students were once again tracked into multiple examination courses, making mixed-ability examination courses impossible. In addition, the government eliminated the 100 percent coursework option. The language exam now consists of 20 percent coursework, 60 percent "terminal examination," and 20 percent oral

examinations. The literature exam consists of 30 percent coursework and 70 percent "terminal examination." For each "terminal examination" students write two papers. The first paper topic is provided two to three months prior to the exam date, and the second is assigned during the examination.

The British government argued that a more traditional examination format was necessary because it feared that the 1987 changes eroded standards, since teachers could help their students prepare their folders.

2. The teachers' union called the strike because the borough had proposed cuts in educational spending, which would have reduced staffing levels and meant that many of the borough's teachers would face dismissal. At first only a few schools in the borough were brought out on strike and for three days a week only—Tuesday, Wednesday, and Thursday—so that teachers' salaries would not be so seriously reduced. Manderley Grove was one of the schools selected. Unfortunately, the exchange class met only on Tuesday and Thursday. In Britain, teachers' strikes often do not involve a complete work stoppage but rather a work slow-down. When British teachers strike in this way, they commonly refuse to do extracurricular work or they may not teach on some days of the week, as was the case here. The strike ended, however, only after it had been expanded to include all schools in the borough and had continued for a full week. During this week, Broadbent, the other exchange school in this borough, where Fiona Rodgers taught, was also on strike.

3. As described in Appendix 3, it was not possible to collect examination folders from students in Gillian's exchange class because at that time, the folders were not returned to the school but were shredded after they were graded. That policy changed the next year, and Gillian was able to provide us with a range of examination folders from a subsequent examination class, which she considered similar to those the students in this exchange class produced.

4. Each school was a member of one of the five national examining boards. The boards all adhered to existing national requirements, but within those requirements they varied slightly in how they formulated and administered the examination. Schools chose the board with philosophies most compatible with their own. Gillian's school subscribed to the Northern Examining Association.

5. Although the examples from the 1991 examination folders come from a different group of students, they are relatively parallel to those in Gillian's exchange class. She did her best to replace the 1989 examination folders from the exchange class with similar writing. (See also note 3.)

6. The literature that formed the basis for the 1991 portfolios included: *The Basketball Game* by Julius Lester; "The Coll Doll" by Walter Macken; "The End of an Old Song" and "One Wednesday Afternoon" by Stan Borstow; "The Choosing" by Liz Lockhead; "School Master" by Yevgeny Yevtushenko; "Dulce et Decorum Est" by Wilfred Owen; "The Happy Warrior" by Herbert Read; "All the Hills and Vales Along" by Charles Hamilton Sorley; "In Mortal Danger" by John Kay; and "The Driving Test."

7. Elevating Expectations, Facing Constraints: Bridget Franklin, Philippa Furlong

1. I would like to thank Ruth Forman for identifying the connection between the framing of Ice T.'s autobiography and the NWA record.
2. For this controlled assignment Philippa's students had to complete their writing in three seventy-minute periods.

8. Crossing Cultures

1. The year after the exchanges the number of required examination pieces was reduced, lessening but not completely alleviating this problem.
2. Results for Fiona Rodgers's students are not included in Table 8.1 since they moved on to new teachers when Fiona left for another school. Grades of *A, B,* or *C* are considered high enough for a student to be eligible to enter the A-level course required for university entrance; grades below *C* generally are not. The cut-off for A levels and therefore university eligibility is not always clear-cut. Students generally need at least a *C*, but schools and teachers have considerable discretion. In the end, however, students who would be considered very good and who would certainly go on to a university in the United States routinely do not receive high enough scores on the GCSE examinations to continue their education beyond the normal British school-leaving age of sixteen. The percentage passing with a *C* or better in Table 8.1 may actually be slightly higher than shown because some of the students who left the exchange school may have gone to another school, taken the exam, and received a *C* or better.
3. Examination results at this GCSE level and then again after another two-year course determine eligibility for the limited slots available for higher education in Britain. Only about 20 percent of British secondary students go on to higher education immediately after secondary school as compared to 56.5 percent of U.S. students (*The Condition of Education*, 1990). A cross-national comparison of 1988 enrollees in higher education indicates an even greater disparity: 44.6 percent full-time equivalent enrolled in the United States versus 8.7 percent in Britain, with 41.3 percent enrolled part time and 24 percent full time in the United States, and 10.3 percent enrolled part time and 3.6 percent full time in Britain (Salganik et al., 1993).

↪ References

America 2000: An education strategy. 1991. Washington, D.C.: U.S. Department of Education.

Applebee, A. N. 1981. *Writing in the secondary school: English and the content areas* (NCTE Research Report No. 21). Urbana, Ill.: National Council of Teachers of English.

Applebee, A. N., J. Langer, and I. Mullis. 1986a. *The writing report card: Writing achievement in American schools.* Princeton, N.J.: National Assessment of Educational Progress, Educational Testing Service.

——— 1986b. *Writing: Trends across the decade, 1974–1984.* Princeton, N.J.: National Assessment of Educational Progress, Educational Testing Service.

——— 1987. *Grammar, punctuation, and spelling: Controlling the conventions of written English at ages 9, 13, and 17.* Princeton, N.J.: National Assessment of Educational Progress, Educational Testing Service.

Applebee, A. N., J. A. Langer, I. Mullis, L. Jenkins, and M. Foertsch. 1990a. *Learning to write in our nation's schools: Instruction and achievement in 1988 at grades 4, 8, and 12.* Princeton, N.J.: National Assessment of Educational Progress, Educational Testing Service.

——— 1990b. *The writing report card, 1984–1988.* Princeton, N.J.: National Assessment of Educational Progress, Educational Testing Service.

Atwell, N. 1987. *In the middle: Writing, reading and learning with adolescents.* Portsmouth, N.H.: Boynton/Cook—Heinemann.

Babbie, E. 1973. *Survey research methods.* Belmont, Calif.: Wadsworth Publishing.

Bakhtin, M. 1986. *Speech genres and other late essays,* ed. C. Emerson and M. Holquist; trans. V. W. McGee. Austin: University of Texas Press.

Barnes, D. 1976. *From communication to curriculum.* Harmondsworth, Middlesex, Eng.: Penguin Books.

Barnes, D., J. Britton, and H. Rosen. 1969. *Language, the learner, and the school.* Harmondsworth, Middlesex, Eng.: Penguin Books.

Barnes, D., and D. Shemilt. 1974. *From communication to curriculum.* Harmondsworth, Middlesex, Eng.: Penguin Books.

Bereiter, C., and M. Scardamalia. 1987. *The psychology of written composition.* Hillsdale, N.J.: Erlbaum.

Bobbitt, S. A., E. Faupel, and S. Burns. 1991. *Characteristics of stayers, movers, and leavers: Results from the teacher followup survey, 1988–89.* E.D. TABS. Washington, D.C.: National Center for Educational Statistics, U.S. Department of Education, Office of Educational Research and Improvement.

Boyer, E. L. 1983. *High school: A report on secondary education in America.* New York: Harper and Row.

Britton, J. 1970. *Language and learning.* Harmondsworth, Middlesex, Eng.: Penguin Books.

Britton, J., T. Burgess, N. Martin, A. McLeod, and H. Rosen. 1975. *The development of writing abilities: 11–18.* London: Macmillan Education.

Bullock, A. 1975. *Report of the committee of enquiry appointed by the Secretary of State for Education and Science: A language for life.* London: Her Majesty's Stationery Office.

Calfee, R., and P. Perfumo. 1993. Student portfolios: Opportunities for a revolution in assessment. *Journal of Reading,* 36(7): 532–537.

California Education Code, Article 4. California Mentor Teacher Program, 44490, 44496. a.

Calkins, L. M. 1986. *The art of teaching writing.* Portsmouth, N.H.: Heinemann Educational Books.

Caplan, R., and C. Keech. 1980. *Showing writing.* Classroom Research Study No. 2. Berkeley, Calif.: Bay Area Writing Project.

Carnegie Forum on Education and the Economy. 1986. *A nation prepared: Teachers for the 21st century.* The report of the task force on teaching as a profession, Carnegie Forum on Education. Washington, D.C.: The Forum.

Cazden, C., P. Cordeiro, and M. E. Giacobbe. 1985. Spontaneous and scientific concepts: Young children's learning of punctuation. In G. Wells and J. Nicholls, eds., *Language and learning: An interactional perspective* (pp. 107–124). London: The Falmer Press.

Chapman, K. 1989. The response factor. *The Quarterly of the National Writing Project and the Center for the Study of Writing,* 11(3): 7–9.

Cheney, L. 1991. *National tests: What other countries expect their students to know.* Washington, D.C.: National Endowment for the Humanities.

The Condition of Education, 1990. 1990. Vol. 2, Postsecondary Education. Washington, D.C.: U.S. Department of Education, National Center for Educational Statistics.

Cone, J. 1989. Real voices for real audiences. *The Quarterly of the National Writing Project and the Center for the Study of Writing,* 11(3): 3–5.

———— 1992. Untracking Advanced Placement English—Creating opportunity is not enough. *Phi Delta Kappan,* 73(9): 712–717.

Deal, T., and K. Peterson. 1990. *The principal's role in shaping school culture.* Washington, D.C.: U.S. Department of Education, Office of Educational Research and Improvement.

Degenhart, R. E., ed. 1987. *Assessment of student writing in an international context.* Institute for Educational Research, Publication Series B, Theory into Practice 9, University of Jyvaskyla, Jyvaskyla, Finland: Kasvatustieteiden Tutkimuslaitos.

Delpit, L. 1986. Skills and other dilemmas of a progressive black educator. *Harvard Educational Review,* 56: 379–385.

——— 1988. The silenced dialogue: Power and pedagogy in educating other people's children. *Harvard Educational Review,* 58: 280–298.

Department of Education and Science. 1988a. *English for ages 5 to 11.* Proposals of the Secretary of State for Education and Science and the Secretary of State for Wales. London and Cardiff: Department of Education and Science and the Welsh Office.

——— 1988b. *Report of the committee of inquiry into the teaching of English.* Appointed by the Secretary of State under the chairmanship of Sir John Kingman, FRS. London: Her Majesty's Stationery Office.

Dixon, J. 1967. *Growth through English,* 1st ed. London: Oxford University Press.

——— 1975. *Growth through English,* 3rd ed. London: Oxford University Press.

Dyson, A. H., and S. W. Freedman. 1991. Writing. In J. Flood, J. Jensen, D. Lapp, and J. Squire, eds. *Handbook of research on teaching the English language arts.* New York: Macmillan.

Emig, J. 1971. *The composing processes of twelfth graders.* Urbana, Ill.: National Council of Teachers of English.

Flower, L., ed. 1989. *Reading-to-write: Exploring a cognitive and social process.* New York: Oxford University Press.

Freedman, S. W. 1987. *Response to student writing.* Urbana, Ill.: National Council of Teachers of English.

——— 1994. *What's involved? Setting up a writing exchange* (Occasional Paper No. 37). Berkeley, Calif.: National Center for the Study of Writing. (Also forthcoming in *Language Arts.*)

Freedman, S. W., and A. McLeod. 1987. *Surveys of successful teachers of writing and their students: The United Kingdom and the United States* (Final Report for Project 5, Study 2). Berkeley, Calif.: National Center for the Study of Writing.

——— 1988. *National surveys of successful teachers of writing and their students: The United States and the United Kingdom* (Technical Report No. 14). Berkeley, Calif.: National Center for the Study of Writing. (Also *Resources in Education,* ED 294 244, May 1988.)

——— 1991. *Comparing the teaching and learning of writing in the United States and the United Kingdom: Audience exchanges* (Final Report for Project 5). Berkeley, Calif.: National Center for the Study of Writing.

Gardner, H. 1983. *Frames of mind: The theory of multiple intelligences.* New York: Basic Books.

Goodlad, J. I. 1984. *A place called school.* New York: McGraw-Hill.

Gorman, T., A. Purves, and R. E. Degenhart, eds. 1988. *The IEA study of written* composition I: The international writing tasks and scoring scales. Vol. 5. Oxford: Pergamon Press.

Graves, D. H. 1978. Balance the basics: Let them write. New York: Ford Foundation.

———— 1983. Writing: Teachers and children at work. Portsmouth, N.H.: Heinemann Educational Books.

Greenleaf, C. 1990. Computers in context: An ethnographic view of changing writing practices in a low-tracked, ninth-grade English class. Ph.D. diss., University of California, Berkeley.

———— 1994. Technological indeterminacy: The role of classroom writing practices and pedagogy in shaping student use of the computer. Written Communication, 11(1): 85–130.

Gubb, J., T. Gorman, and E. Price. 1987. The study of written composition in England and Wales. Windsor, Eng.: NFER-NELSON.

Hardcastle, J. 1985. Classrooms as sites for cultural making. English in Education, 19: 8–22.

Hickman, J., and K. Kimberly. 1988. Teachers, language and learning. New York: Routledge and Kegan Paul/Methuen.

Hillocks, G., Jr. 1986. Research on written composition: New directions for teaching. Urbana, Ill.: ERIC Clearinghouse on Reading and Communication Skills.

Holmes Group. 1986. Tomorrow's teachers: A report of the Holmes Group. East Lansing, Mich.: Holmes Group.

Jackson, B. 1964. Streaming: An educational system in miniature. London: Routledge and Kegan Paul.

Jaggar, A., and T. Smith-Burke, eds. 1985. Observing the language learner. Urbana, Ill.: National Council of Teachers of English.

Kelly, G. 1955. The psychology of personal constructs. New York: Norton.

Langer, J., and A. N. Applebee. 1987. How writing shapes thinking: A study of teaching and learning. Urbana, Ill.: National Council of Teachers of English.

Lazim, Ann, Librarian, Centre for Language in Primary Education. Personal correspondence to James Lobdell, January 15, 1992.

Lloyd-Jones, R., and A. Lundsford, eds. 1989. The English Coalition Conference: Democracy through language. New York and Urbana, Ill.: Modern Language Association and the National Council of Teachers of English.

Logan, J. 1993. Teaching stories. St. Paul, Minn.: Minnesota Inclusiveness Program.

Loofbourrow, P. T. 1992. Composition in the context of CAP: A case study of the interplay between assessment and school life (Technical Report No. 58). Berkeley, Calif.: National Center for the Study of Writing.

Maeroff, G. 1991, January 9. Class size as an empowerment issue. Education Week, 56.

McKay, S., and S. W. Freedman. 1990. Language minority education in Great Britain: A challenge to current U.S. policy. TESOL Quarterly, 24(3): 385–405.

McLeod, A. 1969. This is what came out. English in Education, 3(3): 86–120. Reprinted in Daigon and Laconte, eds. 1971. Challenge and change in the *teaching of English.* Boston: Allyn and Bacon; and in M. Torbe and R. Protherough, eds. 1976. *Classroom encounters.* London: Ward Lock.

———— 1986. Critical literacy: Taking control of our own lives. *Language Arts,* 63(1): 37–50.

———— 1992. Critical literacy and critical imagination: Writing that works for a change. In K. Kimberly, M. Meek, and J. Miller, eds., *New readings: Contributions to an understanding of literacy* (pp. 101–118). London: A and C Black.

Medway, P. 1986. What gets written about. In A. Wilkinson, ed., *The writing of writing.* London: Open University Press.

Mixed ability work in comprehensive schools. 1978. London: Department of Education and Science.

Moffett, J. 1973. *A student-centered language arts curriculum, grades K–13: A handbook for teachers.* Boston: Houghton Mifflin.

Moffett, J., and B. J. Wagner. 1992. *Student-centered language arts, K–12,* 4th ed. Portsmouth, N.H.: Boynton/Cook.

Morson, G. S. 1986. Dialogue, monologue, and the social: A reply to Ken Hierchkop. In G. S. Morson, ed., *Bakhtin: Essays and dialogues on his work* (pp. 73–88). Chicago: University of Chicago Press.

Muller, H. 1967. *Uses of English.* New York: Holt, Rinehart, and Winston.

Nelson, J. 1990. This was an easy assignment: Examining how students interpret academic writing tasks. *Research in the Teaching of English,* 24(4): 362–396.

Nelson, J., and J. R. Hayes. 1988. *How the writing context shapes college students' strategies for writing from sources* (Technical Report No. 16). Berkeley, Calif.: National Center for the Study of Writing.

Newbold, D. 1977. *Ability grouping: The Banbury enquiry.* London: Routledge and Kegan Paul.

Northern Examinations and Assessment Board. *English literature: Syllabus for the GCSE 1994 Examination.* (12 Harter Street, Manchester, M1 6HL, England.)

Northern Examining Association, *English literature syllabus B: Syllabus for the 1989 Examination.* (12 Harter Street, Manchester, M1 6HL, England).

Northumberland Park Teachers' Guide. 1986. London: Northumberland Park School.

Oakes, J. 1985. *Keeping track: How schools structure inequality.* New Haven, Conn.: Yale University Press.

Ogbu, J. 1990. Minority status and literacy in comparative perspective. *Daedalus,* 119(2): 141–168.

Olson, L. 1990, December 12. MacArthur awards $1.3 million for national exams. *Education Week,* 10(15): 5.

Our overcrowded classrooms: Findings of the National Union of Teachers National Class Size Census. 1991, September 30. London: National Union of Teachers.

Postlethwaithe, K., and C. Denton. 1978. *Streams for the future? The longterm* effect of early streaming and nonstreaming—the final report of the Banbury enquiry. London: Pubansco.

Purves, A., ed. 1992a. The IEA study of written composition II: Education and performance in fourteen countries. International studies in educational achievement. Vol. 6. Oxford: Pergamon Press.

————— 1992b. Reflections on research and assessment in written composition. Research in the Teaching of English, 26(1): 108–122.

Reed, S. 1989. London calling. The Quarterly of the National Writing Project and the Center for the Study of Writing, 11(3): 5–7.

————— 1992. Packing their own suitcases. Teacher's Journal, 5, 34–42.

Richmond Unified School District. 1991, September 20. Personnel Office Memo, "The Mentor Teacher Program and Application for Mentor Teachers."

————— 1991, September 20. Mentor Teacher Announcement.

————— 1991, October 7. Memo from Debbie A. LaSalle, Administrative Assistant, Educational Services to Elementary Site Principals and Site Mentors.

Rosenbaum, J. E. 1980. Social implications of educational grouping. Review of Research in Education, 8: 361–401.

Salganik, L., R. Phelps, L. Bianchi, D. Nohara, and T. Smith. 1993. Education in states and nations: Indicators comparing U.S. states with the OECD countries in 1988. Washington, D.C.: National Center for Education Statistics, U.S. Department of Education, Office of Educational Research and Improvement (NCES 93–237).

SFUSD Mentor Teacher Handbook. 1991. San Francisco: San Francisco Unified School District.

Shakespeare, W. 1942. Romeo and Juliet. In W. A. Neilson and C. T. Hill, eds. The complete plays and poems of William Shakespeare. Cambridge, Mass.: Riverside Press, Houghton Mifflin.

Simmons, W., and L. Resnick. 1993. Assessment as the catalyst of school reform. Educational Leadership, 50(5): 11–15.

Sizer, T. R. 1984. Horace's compromise: The dilemma of the American high school. Boston: Houghton Mifflin.

————— 1992. Horace's school: Redesigning the American high school. Boston: Houghton Mifflin.

Slavin, R. E. 1990. Achievement effects of ability grouping in secondary schools: A best-evidence synthesis. Madison, Wis.: National Center for Effective Secondary Schools.

Squire, J., and R. Applebee. 1966. A study of English programs in selected high schools which consistently educate outstanding students in English (Cooperative Research Report No. 1994). Urbana, Ill.: University of Illinois.

————— 1968a. High school English instruction today: The national study of high school English programs. New York: Appleton-Century Crofts.

————— 1968b. A study of the teaching of English in selected British secondary schools (Contract No. OEC 3–7–001849–0469). Washington, D.C.: U.S. Department of Health, Education, and Welfare.

Squire, J., and J. Britton. 1975. Foreword. In J. Dixon. *Growth through English,* 3rd ed. London: Oxford University Press.

Stainton, Richard, Principal Officer (Primary/Middle Schools), National Union of Teachers, personal correspondence to James Lobdell, January 8, 1992.

Statistics of schools, January 1988. 1989. London: Department of Education and Science.

The supply of teachers for the 1990s. 1990. London: Department of Education and Science.

Tucker, M. 1992. Toward national standards: Measuring up. *America's Agenda,* 21–22.

Vygotsky, L. S. 1962. *Thought and language.* Trans. E. Hanfmann and G. Vakar. Cambridge: MIT Press.

———— 1978. *Mind in society: The development of higher psychological processes,* ed. M. Cole, V. John-Steiner, S. Scribner, and E. Souberman. Cambridge, Mass.: Harvard University Press.

Weinstein, R., C. Soulé, F. Collins, J. Cone, M. Mehlhorn, and K. Simontacchi. 1991. Expectations and high school change: Teacher-researcher collaboration to prevent school failure. *American Journal of Community Psychology,* 19(3): 333–403.

Wertsch, J. 1991. *Voices of the mind.* Cambridge, Mass.: Harvard University Press.

Williams, R. 1983. *Writing in society.* London: Verso.

Writing assessment handbook: Grade 8/California Assessment Program. 1986. Prepared under the direction of Francie Alexander. Sacramento, Calif.: California State Department of Education.

~ Index